BAe/McDonnell Douglas Harrier

BAe/McDonnell Douglas Harrier

Andy Evans

The Crowood Press

First published in 1998 by
The Crowood Press Ltd
Ramsbury, Marlborough
Wiltshire SN8 2HR

© Andy Evans 1998

British Library Cataloguing-in-Publication Data
A catalogue record for this book is available from
the British Library.

ISBN 1 86126 105 5

Typefaces used: Goudy (*text*),
Cheltenham (*headings*)

Typeset and designed by
D&N Publishing
Membury Business Park, Lambourn Woodlands
Hungerford, Berkshire.

Printed and bound by Butler & Tanner, Frome.

Acknowledgements

A book of this nature would not have been possible without the support and enthusiasm of a veritable army of willing helpers, almost too numerous to mention. However, I would like to make specific reference to four people: Phil Cater from the Harrier Special Interest Group (part of IPMS UK) for his verve and unselfish help; Gordon Bartley at British Aerospace for his considerable patience and support in dealing with requests for help and numerous searches through the archives; my good friend Rick Llinares from Dash 2 Photography; and Nils Mathisrud for his excellent illustrations.

Grateful thanks are also due to the following: Gary Parsons of the f4 Aviation Photobank, Tony Thornborough, Denis J. Calvert, Salvador Mafe Huretas, Alan Warnes, Paul J. Perron, Peter Russell from MPL, Neil 'Joe' Mercer, Dave Philips from McDonnell Douglas and John Oliver at Rolls-Royce.

On military matters I thank the following: Capt Mike Richardson, Capt David Sousa, Maj Don Kappell, Capt John Scott Walsh and Capt Steve Blint of the US Marine Corps, Capt Dan Carlson, USAF, Chris Shepherd and Dale Donovan at RAF Strike Command PR; Flt Lt Bob Chalmers, Flt Lt Gary Waterfall, Sqn Ldr Gerry Humphries, Wg Cdr Glenn Edge, Flt Lt Simon Jessett, Sqn Ldr Alex Muskett and Gp Capt Clive Loader from the RAF, Michael Hill, CPRO Fleet, Lt Cdr David Baddams of the Royal Navy, and Capt Jorge Flethes of the Spanish Navy.

CONTENTS

Introduction

Thirty years ago it was seen as a novelty, it was treated with scepticism and viewed with disbelief. It was said that it would never be able to carry anything more useful than a 'matchbox over a football field', and could never expect to be taken seriously as a warplane. Yet here we are, three decades later, looking in depth at what has become one of the most viable, flexible, potent and combat-proven fighting machines of the twenti-

eth and soon to be of the twenty-first century. It needs no description, no acronym or résumé, its name is synonymous with its capabilities and its style.

From the deserts of Iraq to the skies over Bosnia; from rough, unprepared strips to rolling carrier decks, the unique attributes of the world's first 'jump-jet' are legendary. As with other things, it has had its fair share of trials and tribulations; it has had its emu-

lators and its detractors, yet it has met them all with the same alacrity, and has emerged as the only creditable vertical take-off and landing aircraft in the world, and the only one to bear the name 'Harrier'.

A Harrier GR.7 from No. 20(R) Squadron, armed with SNEB rocket pods. BAe

CHAPTER ONE

Development

Specification – P.1127	
ENGINE	One 11,000lb (5,000kg) BS.53/3 Pegasus 2 turbofan.
WEIGHTS	Empty 10,200lb (4,600kg); loaded 15,500lb (7,000kg).
DIMENSIONS	(excluding nose probe) Span 24ft 4in (7.40m); length 41ft 2in (18.70m). (XP984 span 22ft 10in (6.92m); length 42ft 0in (12.73m).
PERFORMANCE	Max level speed: 625kt (1,150km/h); initial rate of climb: 21,900ft (6,600m) per minute; ceiling: 49,800ft (15,100m).
ARMAMENT	none

The first P.1127 XP831 captured at Dunsfold before receiving any marking and just before its first tethered flight. Despite the carbon fibre technology of the Harrier II, little has changed since the original design. Rolls Royce

'From Little Acorns': an Overview of the Beginnings of VSTOL and the Hawker P.1127

The background to the P.1127 project may be traced to a Frenchman Michel Wibault, who designed a revolutionary 'ground-attack gyrocopter' with a Bristol BE-25 engine driving four centrifugal blowers. Bristol Aero Engines themselves took on the design and further developed the idea into the Bristol BE-53 engine. The exhaust was designed not be at the rear of the aircraft, as in convetional designs, but ejected through four rotating elbow nozzles, with the fan stage discharging through the front pair and the hot gases through the rear pair. This then allowed the engine's thrust to be 'vectored' down as required, while bleed air could be ducted from the fan stage and sent to 'reaction control' valves in the nose, tail and wings, which would control the aircraft in VSTOL mode when the normal flying surfaces become ineffective.

The BE-53 'Orpheus' engine became part of the Hawker Aircraft Company's 'four-poster lift' test bed or 'flying bedstead', in the popular phrase, and was used as a basis for further studies into VSTOL flight, although a suitable airframe still had to be designed actually to achieve the original concept of a VSTOL aircraft. Hawker Aircraft's Ralph Hooper came up with a design for a 'high-speed helicopter' using a rotatable engine nozzle, by which method light short take-off and vertical landings would be possible. Hooper's design was called the P.1127, which had evolved by late 1958 into a

configuration that was very much a 'Harrier' based around the BE-53 engine, as a single-seat strike aircraft carrying an external load of 2,000lb.

Manufacture of a prototype began as a private venture, and construction of a suitable BE-53 engine began in the summer of 1958, with the Ministry of Supply eventually funding further prototypes in late 1959. It was always Hawkers' intention not to just build an experimental aircraft, but to see it as a development to a military machine with

---

Trials and Tribulations - the Search for VSTOL Success

There were many 'wierd and wonderful' designs that came about in the 1950s and 1960s in the search for the elusive prize of an operational VSTOL aircraft. The designers in the USA never ceased to amaze with their ideas, and France and Germany also made a supreme effort to be the first to have such an aircraft in their military inventory. Presented here is a listing of those worthy of note.

Aircraft	Date	Notes
Bachem Ba.349 *Natter*	18.12.44	In an effort to counter allied bombing. The *Natter* (Viper) was a rocket-powered interceptor launched vertically from rails. Most of the aircraft and the pilot were recovered by parachute after an attack was made. The aircraft would be armed with twenty-four Hs 127 *Fhon* rockets fired in salvo.
Lockheed XFV-1 Salmon	16.6.54	One of two research aircraft built using the massive Allison YT40-A-14 turboprop driving contra-rotating propellors. More or less a 'conventional' aircraft, it sat on a cruciform tail with small castors, and transition to vertical flight was made in the air. The project was cancelled in 1955.
Convair XFY-1 Pogo	1.8.54	Rivalling the Salmon, the Pogo was more successful, and used the same Allison powerplant. It made its first vertical flight in June 1954, and was called by many 'The Impossible Plane'.
Ryan X-13 Vertijet	10.12.55	The X-13 originally flew with undercarriage, but operated from a 'hook and trapeze' vertical launcher. It was the first jet to take off vertically and transition to forward flight and then back to the hover in April 1957.
SNECMA C.450.01 Coleoptre	1958	The rather beer barrel appearance of the Coleoptre was in fact a serious contender for a French fighter. Despite being a remarkable machine it was abandonded as a non-starter.
Bell X-14	19.2.57	A small aircraft using a simple diverted thrust system from its twin Armstrong-Siddeley Viper turbojets in the nose. It used puffer jets in the nose and tail drawing bleed air from the engines. The X-14 transited from a VTO in May 1959.
Ryan XV-5a Vertifan	25.5.64	Looking like a small conventional jet, the XV-5 used jet-driven fans in its wings to achieve VTOL, by using the exhaust from its twin GE J85 turbojets. Two were built for the US Army to evaluate.
Lockheed XV-4 Hummingbird	7.7.62	Used a 'mixing chamber' concept, with two conventional engines on the fuselage sides, the XV-4 used giant doors above and below the fuselage through which air was diverted creating lift to push the aircraft up or down. Cancelled in 1969 after an accident.
Short SC.1	12.4.57	A small tailess delta with four lift engines pointing downward and one pointing backwards Two were built achieving forward flight in 1960.
Dassault Balzac	12.10.62	Based on a Mirage III airframe, the Balzac was powered by a single Bristol Siddeley Orpheus engine for forward flight and four RB.108 lift engines for vertical work. A crash in 1963 killed the pilot, and following a second rebuild, the same fate occured a second time. A larger more powerful Mirage IIIV was built using eight lift engines and a single SNECMA TF306 and the first flight of the first aircraft was 12.2.65.
Yakovlev Yak-36 'Freehand'	1962–3	Not intended to be an operational aircraft. Powered by two vectored thrust turbofans, provided data for the MiG YE-23, SU-15 and Yak-38.
EWR SuD VJ101C	10.4.63	An attempt to build a Mach 2 VTOL using six RB145 engines, four in swivelling nacelles on the wing tips (similar to the V-22 Osprey) and two more as extra lift in the forward fuselage. The first prototype went supersonic a number of times in spite of a crash. Cancelled in 1965.
Dornier Do 31E	10.2.67	Two successful prototypes built using two Pegasus vectored thrust engines in underwing nacelles, and four RB162 lift engines in wingtip pods.
VAKI91B	10.9.71	Designed as a VSTOL strike/reconaissance aircraft powered by a RB. 193, which was a smaller version of the Pegasus, and augmented by two RB162 lift jets. Cancelled 1972 despite three successful prototypes.
Rockwell XFV-12	1977	Underwent tethered trials at NASA's Langley facilty in the summer of 1977. It was due to make its first flight in 1980, but the project was abandoned.

The curious bell-mouth shape of XP831's intake is evident here. Note also that the undercarriage doors have been removed and the nose probe will also be taken off before its first tethered hover flight.
Rolls Royce

(Below) A delightful threesome of P.1127s: XP831, XP976 and XP980; note the intake lips and photo-reference marks applied to XP831. Rolls Royce

the ability to carry weapons and make a sound contribution to the British defence industry. The BE-53 was at this stage being seriously redefined by the engineering teams, who eventually produced the BE-53/2, later to be called Pegasus 1, which formed the basis of the P.1127 prototype. This aircraft was to be a high-wing monoplane, the wings so set to avoid the four fuselage-located jets, and allow them to be of one-piece construction. The undercarriage was of a 'bicycle' type to accommodate the unique engine arrangement and similar in design to that of the B-52 Bomber, with outrigger wheels fitted to the wing-tips.

On 15 July 1960 the first prototype P.1127, XP831, arrived at Dunsfold from Kingston, and the refined engine, the Pegasus 2, came in September. The first tethered hover of XP831 took place on 21 October and untethered hovering took place during mid November. The first 'conventional' take-off is recorded as being on 13 March 1961. The second P.1127 prototype, XP836, flew on 7 July 1961, with Bill Bedford making the first transitions from the hover with XP831 on 12 September, using the reaction control 'puffers' in the nose, tail and wings. The first short take-off came in October 1961 and, although the flight trials showed much promise, the aircraft was still underpowered and the originally designed, cropped delta wing was not the ideal. Less happily, Bedford ejected from XP836 near Yeovilton in December 1961 after the left-hand cold nozzle fell off, and perhaps more memorable and embarrassing was the heavy landing of XP831 at Le Bourget in June 1963 during a flight demonstration. In all six prototype or Development Batch (DB) aircraft were built, a further four being funded by the Ministry of Supply, which also helped to fund the Pegasus engine. Each airframe represented a distinct modification standard, with a number of intake configurations being tested, including some highly improbable, inflatable rubber ones. The experience gained with the first two aircraft led to revisions on the third. Problems were occurring too often for the Bristol engine team; they managed to aquire the use of the first production Valiant Bomber, WP199, and fitted a Kestrel-like fuselage with a Pegasus 3 powerplant into its bomb bay. The first flight in this configuration took place on 11 March 1963.

The final aircraft XP984 was retrofitted with the re-engineered Pegasus 5. This particular aircraft served as a trials instal-lation for the Kestrel programme and included dropped tailplanes, up and down 'firing' puffer jets, and a 9in fuselage extension. XP831 made a visit to HMS *Ark Royal* on 8 February 1963, with no particular problems reported in taking VSTOL to sea.

Demonstrating the Technology: Kestrel

The Kestrel is an often forgotten, yet crucial part of the Harrier story. While the P.1127 was purely an experimental machine, and today would be called a 'Technology Demonstrator', the Kestrel pioneered the operational use of VSTOL. Much of the groundwork was performed on it – and that may be taken quite literally, as the Kestrel was more used to operating from grass strips and semi-prepared sites than even today's multi-role Harrier IIs would normally be. To quote Fred Towern, a member of the original evaluation team, 'People have written the "rule book" for the Harrier since the Kestrel, but the essential purpose of the machine was to explore in depth the possibilities, and to define the procedures for, the safe use of VSTOL in a military environment.'

The idea to form an international operational trials squadron based on the development potential of the P.1127 was first

Specification – Kestrel	
ENGINE	One 15,500lb (7,000kg) Rolls-Royce Pegasus 5 turbofan.
WEIGHTS	Empty 11,000lb (5,000kg); loaded 13,000lb (5,900kg)
DIMENSIONS	Span 26ft (7.88m); length 12.73m)
PERFORMANCE	Max level speed: 620kt (1,140km/h); initial rate of climb: 30,000ft (9,100m) per minute; service ceiling: 55,000ft (16,700m).
ARMAMENT	Experimental

Kestrel XS689/9 makes a rolling vertical landing at West Raynham in a haze of heat from the Pegasus engine; quite noticeable are the cropped wingtips and the large mainwheel door, which also served as an airbrake. Rolls-Royce

enthusiastically proposed by the American aviation businessman Larry Levy, who was then working for the Mutual Weapons Development Program in Paris. This body was partly responsible for the funding of the P.1127, and Levy was keen to show a more tangible result from this investment. At this stage, however, the RAF's operational requirement for the P.1127 had been withdrawn and all efforts were being directed towards the far more ambitious P.1154, so any British involvement would be on the premise that the lessons learned from the proposed squadron could be fed to the P.1154 team. With hindsight, it was indeed fortuitous that the RAF retained an interest in the P.1127 test programme, as it kept the subsonic aircraft alive during the time they pursued, and subsequently were denied the more sophisticated P.1154.

It was in May 1962 that the governments of Britain, the USA and West Germany agreed to fund an improved P.1127 and an agreement was signed in 1963. The 'Tripartite Kestrel Evaluation Squadron' or TES was therefore formed on 15 October 1964 at RAF West Raynham in Norfolk under the command of Wg Cdr David Scrimgeour, and operational flying began on 1 April 1965. In all nine aircraft and eighteen Pegasus 5 engines were provided, and the TES was funded and flown by the RAF, the Luftwaffe the US Navy, the US Air Force and the US Army, who also provided a Bell Iroquois helicopter to aid deployments, with the RAF attaching two Hawker Hunter T.7s to act as chase planes.

The Kestrel FGA.1 differed from the original P.1127 concept (although by the end of the P.1127 programme all the aircraft were much improved from the basic starting form) in having a new swept wing, rather than the P.1127's cropped delta (first tested aboard XP984, the last Development P.1127 which was used as a trials aircraft for many of the systems to be installed on the TES Kestrel, and also introduced the up and down puffer ducts and the increased 9in length) and also featured a longer span tailplane with a kinked leading edge, elongated fuselage and redesigned all-metal intakes. It had no dedicated armament positions, but did have two wing hardpoints stressed for 100-gallon tanks. Also included were a simple gunsight and a nose-mounted, forward F.95 oblique camera hidden by 'eyelids' in the nose. The first Kestrel, XS695, made its first flight on 7 March 1964, and the last, XS696, on 5 March 1965.

Four of the Tripartite Squadron Kestrels make an impressive fly-past over West Raynham. Rolls-Royce

(Below) **Although it started life as a P.1127, XP984, the last of the DB aircraft was essentially a 'Kestrel'; it was used as a trials aircraft and had the Pegasus 5 engine and the new wing; in typical 'Harrier' style XP984 makes a vertical exit from a prepared pad in a woodland clearing.** Rolls-Royce

Looking more than a little sorry for itself is Kestrel XS696, rescued from a rather ignominious fate by the RAF Museum's restoration centre at Cardington. Its previous 'owners', the Royal Navy, were perhaps unaware of the importance of the aircraft and it seems to have received more than its fair share of rough treatment over the past two decades, when it was employed as a maintenance trainer. You see it in its 'before' state, as it now figures in a major restoration project by the Museum.

A general view of the current state of XS696, still in its 'Navy' uniform.

Note the early P.1127-style leg design and the hydraulic drum.

The ultimate sacrilege – a Sea Harrier RWR bolted on to the tailboom: Philistines!

XS695

All photographs: Harrier SIG via Phil Cater

Although the US contingent included flyers from the Army and the Air Force, there was no one from the Marine Corps – who, ironically, became the world's largest Harrier operators. The US Army insisted on representation as a result of an on-going interservice battle over the control of tactical air assets, and any development of the Kestrel was seen as an obvious candidate for the Army's fixed-wing use; thus its participation was used to promote its own claims, a dispute which was finally settled on Capitol Hill. The Army did not help its ambitions with a serious accident on the first day of operational flying, when Lt Col Lou Solt left the 'handbrake on' while attempting to take off in XS696/6, the newest of the Kestrel fleet. The aircraft slewed on to its left outrigger as the engine speed built up, bursting the mainwheel tyres, followed by the aircraft's cartwheeling along the runway edge, eventually breaking into two with its engine still running. Solt's ejector seat had shifted on its mountings and was likely to 'go' at any moment; however, three members of the Squadron pulled him out of the wrecked aircraft, for which they later received Queen's Commendations. XS696 never flew again and neither did Solt, but the remaining aircraft were modified with a throttle 'fix' that prevented its use with the brakes still applied.

The West Germans' participation was directly related to their own VSTOL projects, including the VAK.191. Their involvement provided the TES with an above-average Luftwaffe Colonel, Gerhard Barkhorn, who had amassed a not inconsiderable 301 wartime kills, ranking him as the second highest scoring ace in the German Air Force in World War II. On one occasion the very experienced flyer cut the throttle a little early on descent, and his Kestrel dropped like a stone, wrecking the undercarriage. Col Barkhorn kicked the aircraft as he walked away, disgusted with himself and trying to hide his embarrassment. He exclaimed to a fellow pilot that this was now the 302nd Allied aircraft he had destroyed!

Not to be outdone, the RAF pilots had their own frightening incident when a Pegasus engine disintegrated during a transition to a vertical landing. Rather than ejecting the pilot, Flt Lt 'Porky' Munro had the presence of mind to pull back the nozzle lever to obtain a degree of conventional flight and then make a hasty, dead-stick landing. This coolness earned him the Air Force Cross.

On less eventful days the TES concentrated on the exploration of flight operating procedures, comparing the various types of take-off and landing, air handling, dispersed operations and the use of varying levels of support, and also dabbled with night flying and instrument landings. Trials were conducted using artificial surfaces as landing pads, and thence came one of the more unusual experiments, inspired by the ever resourceful Americans. A helicopter was tasked with dropping a bag full of polyester 'gunge', which splatted 'cow-pat' fashion on the intended landing site. This then hardened in a couple of hours to provide a heatproof, reinforced pad. The very unmilitary colour of bright pink, plus the practical aspects of depositing the pad, not to mention the expense, led to this particular avenue remaining unexplored. The TES was wound up in November 1965 having flown 1,367 sorties and some 600 flying hours.

The conclusions drawn from the TES trials in the official reports stressed that regular squadron pilots should be well able to operate the aircraft, that dispersed operations were possible, and that no force could really be without a VSTOL capability. During the time of the trials the British government had decided to cancel the P.1154 and proceed with a development of the Kestrel to be provisionally named P.1127(RAF), but later inherited the name 'Harrier' from the aborted P.1154 project. It must be said, however, that for once the British actually got their money's worth with the Kestrel, feeding as it did valuable information into the operational planning for the Harrier to come. Further enthusiastic reports were sent back to both the USA and West Germany, but these fell on stony ground. The West German government viewed the report with great optimism, but the military were more conservative, as a result, no doubt, of their continuing poor experiences with the Starfighter, and any radical new designs were viewed with more than a little scepticism. The British retained their two Kestrels XS693 and XS695, whereas the Americans took the Kestrels that had been allocated to them at the close of the programme, plus another three allocated and now unwanted – sold to them by the West Germans – and shipped them home to continue flying trials as redesignated XV-6As.

Markings

The Kestrels all flew in natural metal finish with black codes and a single digit ID number on the nose. Tail fin markings were vertically striped (front to rear): black, red, yellow, red, white, blue, red, white and blue, reflecting the individual countries' colours contained in a single 'flash'. On the wings was a single roundel broken into 'thirds' with the markings of the RAF, the USAF and the Luftwaffe.

XS688 was the prototype Kestrel, and although in service with the TES, it dif-

---

An American Trial: XV-6A

With their arrival on US soil following their Atlantic crossing by ship, the now designated XV-6As were to take part in a series of the Tri-Service Trials, which began shortly after the six aircraft were unloaded. They were first transferred to the US Army's Fort Campbell base and undertook a number of ground-support tests that lasted until April 1966 to complete. Five aircraft were then sent to the Naval Air Test Center at Patuxent River where they underwent sea trials on several Navy ships, and 64-18267 suffered landing-gear damage during a heavy 'bounce'. This programme lasted only six days, from whence the four remaining airworthy aircraft were ferried to Norfolk NAS, Virginia. There they were taken on board the USS Independence for carrier suitability trials, which also included their operating from the Marines' LPD, USS Raleigh.

Following the Navy's trials they were once again returned to Fort Campbell, and then on to the Air Proving Grounds at Eglin AFB. This lasted from 15 to 31 July, and once completed the aircraft were turned over to two agencies: 64-18262 , 18265, 18266 and 64-18264 went to the Edwards AFB and 64-18263 went to NASA at Langley AFB along with 64-18267. At Edwards 64-18264 was mounted on a rig for acoustic tests.

The NASA aircraft were give the following registrations: 64-18263-NASA 521 and 64-18267-NASA 520, and eventually they were joined by 64-18265 and 64-18266 for spares recovery. The aircraft were used for a wide range of exploration tasks, including VIFF tests which began in January 1970 with NASA 521.

XV-6A Colours

All XV-6As retained their Kestrel natural metal finish, with all markings being in black, with full-colour national insignia. Once with NASA the national insignia were removed, and NASA 521 was fitted with an undernose camera bulge, and red and white striped nose boom. For the Tri-Service Trials each aircraft received a white tail band edged top and bottom with red containing the wording 'TRI-SERVICE'.

XS688, which, although its nose claims it to be P.1127, is in fact the first Kestrel FGA.1, and carries the TES tail markings; XS688 was allocated to the Luftwaffe but was taken over by the Americans and became XV6A 64-18262, ending its days at the USAF Museum at Wright-Patterson AFB, Ohio. Rolls-Royce

fered from the other aircraft by being fitted with rubber intake lips (later replaced by metal), had no dogtooth on the wing nor any vortex generators, the mesh behind the canopy frame was replaced on the other Kestrels by the 'Harrier style' cut-outs, plus it had the smaller stabilators. The wing roundels were 'handed', a feature not repeated on the other aircraft, and the Hawker Siddeley P.1127 logo was replaced by the code number '8'.

Nearly There ... P.1127(RAF)

With the cancellation of the P.1154 in January 1965, the Ministry of Defence softened the blow by announcing that the Kestrel was to be developed further into a fully operational aircraft for the RAF. Work got under way at Kingston in a low-keyed manner following the loss of such an important contract as the P.1154. However, enthusiasm soon returned as the Ministry issued a requirement for six DB aircraft, which were officially ordered in

February 1965 under the designation P.1127(RAF). It was stated that the Kestrel needed a 50 per cent redesign over the original P.1127 and, if that were so, then the P.1127(RAF) represented more than a 90 per cent redesign over the Kestrel!

Critical to the success of the P.1127 (RAF) was the new Pegasus 6 engine, later to be called the Mk.101, which was rated at 19,500lb, compared with the Kestrel's Pegasus 5 rated at 15,500lb. To better meet the engine's mass flow the intakes were redesigned and six 'blow-in doors' (later increased to eight) were added to each side, set back behind the lip. The wing was also redesigned, with vortex generators, and the wingtips themselves were extended making the outrigger wheels an 'inboard' item. An integral, ventral airbrake was also fashioned, and provision was made to incorporate an in-flight refuelling (IFR) probe, mounted on the upper portion of the port intake, together with a rounded-off tail cone. The pitot tube was also relocated on to the tip of the nose, rather than the leading edge of the fin as

on the Kestrel. A further change came with the discarding of the Kestrel's Martin Baker Mk.6HA ejector seat in favour of the 'zero-zero' Mk.9. The P.1127(RAF) also featured a new undercarriage to improve rough field work, and a Marconi Autostabilization system was also fitted.

The aircraft was also to benefit from the enormous amount of work that had gone into the P.1154, and one of the major items it received from that project was the Ferranti FE.541 INAS, a real 'state of the art' piece of equipment. At its core was the inertial platform which forms the heart of the IMS (inertial measuring system) which works in concert with a present-position computer in the avionics bay. This fed a revolutionary NDC (navigational display computer), whose information was displayed on to a cockpit moving map utilizing 35mm colour-film images and situated in front of the pilot's 'stick'. The aircraft's current position was shown at the centre, and the pilot could select way points or offsets with a controller at the rear of the throttle quadrant. Weapon

Having just made a vertical assent, P.1127(RAF) XV279 tucks in its undercarriage for transition to forward flight; now looking more like the Harrier it was soon to become; the aircraft is now at RAF Wittering; *see* 'The Plastic Pig' in the text. RAF Wittering

The Pegasus 6 made the P.1127(RAF) a much more formidable aircraft than any of its predecessors, and XV277, seen here, was able to carry extra fuel tanks, SNEB rocket pods and a centreline reconnaissance pod; also visible are the vortex generators and the extended wing tips. Rolls Royce

Harrier Power - The Pegasus Engine

There can be little doubt that without the unique design and power of the Pegasus engine there would have been no Harrier. The efforts of the early VSTOL pioneers pay testament to that. And even today, the Harrier stands alone in its engine design. Only the former Soviet Union have produced a VSTOL aircraft, and even then it uses the 'lift engine' technique, not vectored thrust. Put simply, there has been nothing to match the original British concept, which powers a family of aircraft, whose abilities are unsurpassed.

Type	Year	Thrust	Description	Aircraft
BE.53/2 Pegasus I	1957	9,000lb (4,100kg)	Two-stage overhung fan. Single stage compressor-4 nozzles	
BE.53/3 Pegasus 2	1960	11,000lb (5,000kg)	Orpheus 6 HP spool, later rated at 12,000lb	P1127
Pegasus 3	1961	14,000lb (6,400kg)	Improved compressor blades, 8 stage HP spool and turbine.	P1127
Pegasus 5	1962	18,000lb (8,200kg)	New 3-stage fan as part of major redesign programme	Kestrel
Pegasus 6 - Mk.101	1965	19,000lb (8,600kg)	Titanium fan, water injection, air-cooled 2nd stage	P1127(RAF) Harrier GR.1 Harrier T.2 Harrier T.2A
Pegasus 10. Mk.102 USMC F402-RR-400	1969 T.2A	20,500lb (9,300kg)	Increased water flow, Mk 802 export version	GR.IA
Pegasus 11 - Mk.103 F402-RR-4016402	1969	21,500lb (9,800kg)	Increased airflow, better fuel and water Injection	GR.3 AV8A AV8C TAV-8A T.4A T.4N T Mk.52
Pegasus 11 Mk.150	1969	21,500lb (9,800kg)		AV-8S TAV-8S
Pegasus 11 Mk.I5I	1969	21,500lb (9,800kg)		T.Mk.60
Pegasus 104 F402-RR-404/404A	1976	21,500lb (9,800kg)	Aluminium cased fan, better gearbox, anti-corrosion	FRS.1 FRS.51 F/A-2 T.8N
Pegasus 105 11-21 F402-RR-404/404A	1984	21,750lbs (9,900kg)	Uprated gearbox. DECS in 404A.	YAV-8A GR.5/5A GR.7 T.10
Pegasus 11-21 Mk.152		21,450lb (9,800kg)		EAV-8B
Pegasus 106 11-21 F402-RR-406/406A	1985	21,450lb (9,800kg)	Single crystal blades, more powerful HP turbine	AV8B TAV-8B
Pegasus 11-61 F402-RR-408	1987	23,800lb (11,000kg)	New front fan. New combustor.	AV8B(NA) Harrier II Plus TAV-8B

Harrier Power - The Pegasus Engine

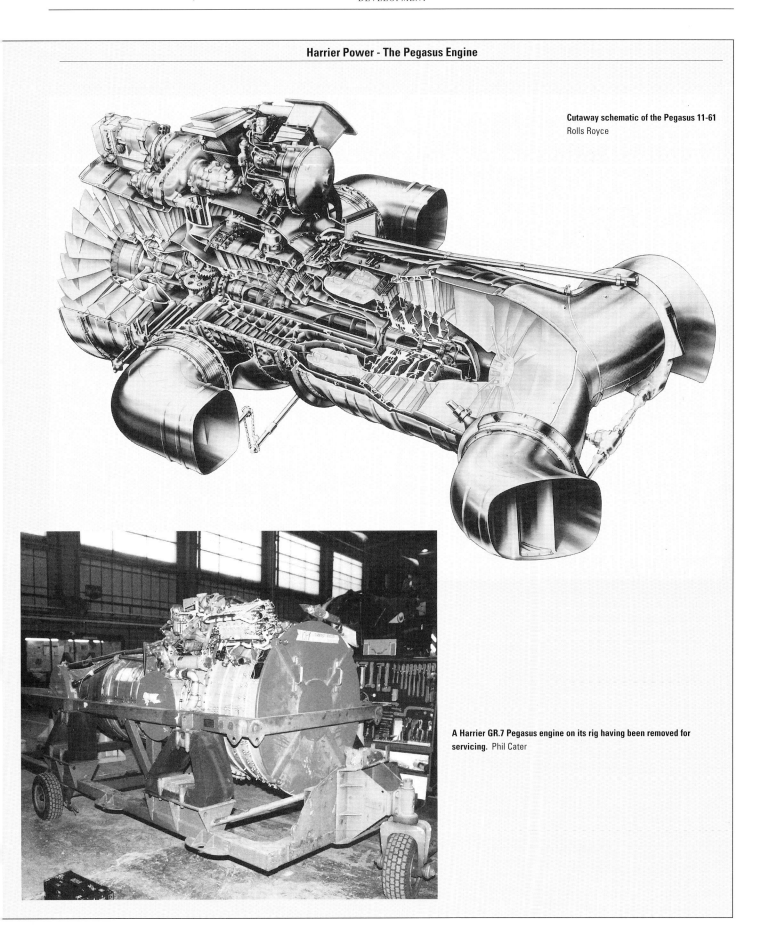

Cutaway schematic of the Pegasus 11-61
Rolls Royce

A Harrier GR.7 Pegasus engine on its rig having been removed for servicing. Phil Cater

aiming, primary flight data and navigational cues were to be projected in front of the pilot's eyes by the use of a Smiths Industries HUD, allowing for safe, low-level flight. Other avionics included a TACAN, Sperry compass, UHF and VHF radios and a homing IFF.

The internal fuel capacity was raised to 632 imp. gallons, and provision was made for five weapons pylons and two 130-rounds Aden gun pods under the fuselage. A lateral F.95 oblique camera was added to the port side of the nose, and a reconnaissance pod developed for use on the aircraft's centreline, carrying five 'wet film' cameras. The first of the DB aircraft to fly was XV276 in August 1966, and the final one was XV281 in July 1967, with XV279 and XV280 being used to develop the aircraft's nav-attack system. One of the aircraft, XV276, was lost on 10 April 1973 when it crashed near Dunsfold. After only a few months of operations with the DB Harriers, the government committed itself to the production of the aircraft as an operational type: the Harrier GR.1.

Called by many the 'First Harrier', P.1127(RAF) XV276 started its service in all-over natural metal, with full-colour roundels and tail flash. The following aircraft received the more familiar grey/green, light grey finish, receiving the name 'Harrier' on their noses in a smart shade of yellow.

Fate of the P.1127(RAF) Aircraft
XV276: crashed, 10 April 1973 near Dunsfold
XV277: privately owned at Ipswich
XV278: Luftwaffenmuseum Berlin/Gatow
XV279: RAF Wittering, restored as 'Gate Guard' for 20(R) Squadron
XV280: RNAS Yeovilton Fire Section
XV281: BAe Warton, ground instruction

G-VTOL: Harrier Ambassador

In early 1970, and as a direct result of a decision by Hawker Siddeley Aviation's (HSA) management to promote the Harrier aggressively in the world's export markets, a privately funded company demonstrator G-VTOL, the only non-military owned 'twin stick' Harrier, was produced to serve as a 'flying showroom' to aid the sales efforts. It also had the distinction of being the only T.Mk.52 designation created, and was based on the RAF's T.2 trainer, fitted initially with the Pegasus Mk.102 engine,

then later with the Mk.103. G-VTOL was produced on an 'embodiment' loan basis, with items supplied by all the aircraft's major systems builders. As a civil registered aircraft, G-VTOL was granted a 'special category airworthiness certificate', and differed from the run of the mill 'T Birds' in that it was fitted with a comprehensive airliner-standard nav suite, including ADF (with fuselage spine-mounted aerial array) and ILS, thus aiding its immediate deployment to any site in support of the company's sales efforts. The second seat was intended as a potent sales tool, enabling the non-flying 'purse-string' holders to experience the Harrier for themselves.

Assembled at Dunsfold by the export department of HSA, G-VTOL was first flown on 16 December 1971, after being unveiled wearing a somewhat garish decor of overall gloss middle blue, BS.381C:109, bright red, ICI Spec. F407/711 and white, with markings in light aircraft grey, BS.381C:627, a scheme which lasted only a couple of weeks. The reason that the colourful design was so short lived was that the pride and joy of HSA was extensively damaged in an unfortunate mishap when its pilot ran out of available runway at Dunsfold. Anonymous, hand-written notes recently unearthed by the author add a little insight on the incident:

> [The aircraft] expired into pit at west end of runway after aborting an 'end speed' check when piloted by A.J. 'Tony' Hawkes with Mike Craddock in back seat at 15.30 hrs, 6 Oct 71 (at great speed!). Had carried out VL at Thorney Island prior to this. Aircraft dug out and removed by crane from RAE 8 Oct 71. First flown after rebuild 24 May 72.

Apparently 150 tons of aggregate had to be laid to allow access for the crane to get to G-VTOL from among the mud and thickets, thus totally ruining its vibrant colour scheme.

The Harrier was subsequently repainted during its rebuild and gained a smart, three-tone desert scheme of disruptive RAF dark earth and RAF light stone upper surfaces and RAF azure blue undersides, a design that reflected the main sales hopes of the HSA export team – the Middle East. A tour was organized and display flights were arranged, first in Iran, where the aircraft arrived in June 1972, and as a result an order of Sea Harriers was expected at some point (but the Shah's subsequent overthrow ended such hopes). Kuwait was

the second stop-off sales point, and the final stop of the tour was Abu Dhabi. What happened next is well documented, but another extract from the same handwritten notes reveals that G-VTOL and the same unfortunate pilot were once more involved in an 'accident': 'G-VTOL was then screwed into the desert by Tony Hawkes whilst on a demonstration tour in the Middle East.'

The Harrier was successfully hovered in front of the Abu Dhabi ruler's residence with good effect. Hawkes however, became suddenly disorientated when hovering backwards, and fell prey to his own Pegasus 102-generated 'sandstorm'; resulting in a landing that was rather on the heavy side. The damage was a snapped starboard outrigger and a severely bent nose, and along with the broken bits of Harrier went the pilot's pride and HSA's Middle East export hopes.

G-VTOL was ignominiously flown back to Dunsfold as air freight and patched up yet again. In July 1972, now in the hands of the Harrier's Chief Test Pilot John Farley (who had successfully demonstrated another Harrier to the Spanish), G-VTOL was sent out to Bombay and demonstrated intensively to the Indian Navy in extreme tropical weather, which led to a number of early system failures in the aircraft from the monsoon conditions. A number of demonstration flights were undertaken from on board INS *Vikrant*, and this successful display schedule resulted in the sale of twenty-eight Sea Harriers (albeit seven years later and following much juggling of limited budgets) thus ultimately proving that G-VTOL had been a worthwhile investment, not only for Hawker Siddeley but for all of the suppliers who contributed to the original embodiment loan. Another sales tour took G-VTOL to Brazil and the Sao Paulo International Airshow in 1973, but again with no trade success.

John Farley also saved the plane from oblivion during a demonstration flight with a Swiss pilot in the front seat. Following the failure of the automated fuel feed at 200ft following take-off, G-VTOL sank to 'just above the trees' before Farley took over and recovered the aircraft with a manual fuel-feed override system which had been installed following earlier Harrier losses through fuel starvation.

During the mid 1970s G-VTOL's career continued as a promotional vehicle, generating great interest wherever she went, but did nothing to garner any further sales

Taken at the 1978 SBAC Show at Farnborough, G-VTOL in its desert garb; note the 'Navy' title in white on the tailfin. Harrier SIG via Phil Cater

(Right) **Still in desert camouflage, but now sporting the ZA250 code; note the positioning of the roundel in the middle of the rear fuselage.**
Harrier SIG via Phil Cater

interest in the Harrier, although it may be presumed that its first visit to Italy helped in the eventual decision to place a TAV.8B/Harrier II Plus order. The sales work of G-VTOL was combined with operations as a 'chase plane' and it further served as a training vehicle for Indian Navy pilots, who 'borrowed' the aircraft during their work-up period at RNAS Yeovilton. The aircraft also participated in trials work on VIFF-ing (described later) and ski-jumping at RAE Bedford. G-VTOL acquired a 'dual' military and civil identity just before the 1978 Farnborough Air Show, where the serial ZA250 was added, along with 18in roundels on the

rear fuselage. Daily demonstrations of the visually exciting ski-jump spectacle were run for the benefit of the show audiences.

A Chinese delegation visited Dunsfold in December 1978, as part of a serious sales drive directed at selling in excess of 200 Sea Harrier derivatives to China. This resulted in a Mr Mah, the No.2 in the Fighter Command of the Chinese People's Liberation Army, getting a 'trip' in G-VTOL and undertaking some of the main demonstration manoeuvres. As Mr Mah spoke no English and John Farley spoke no Chinese the flight was to be something of a challenge. Farley found that the ideal solution to the language

barrier was to write down all the essential commands, which were validated separately by three interpreters and then had simple Chinese versions for the commands written alongside in morse code; a set of hand signals were similarly devised so he could get the messages across in flight. It must have worked, as G-VTOL returned in one piece.

Some time after this, G-VTOL had a major make-over and emerged from the paint shop in a new look of gloss grey with white undersides. The demonstration work and air show flying continued, sometimes alongside another well-known company plane G-HAWK.

(Above) **Seen here in its final grey/white colour scheme, in the Brooklands Air Museum;. still looking 'factory fresh' in its 'Skyhook' markings.** Harrier SIG via Phil Cater

Skyhook

Her last major use was on the 'Skyhook' trials, hovering rock steady under a large crane, to test the feasibility of 'grabbing' Harriers from the hover when deployed from small ships with limited deck space. The Harrier would hover into a 'landing position' beside the ship, and the specially designed 'grabber' on the crane and the capture fairings on the Harrier would be connected and the aircraft would be swung on to the deck. This could be achieved in a 'launch situation' as well, by reversing the operation. By this time, the ZA250 serial had been removed, while photo-calibration markings were added above the wing, a 'Skyhook' logo was applied to the nose and a cartoon drawn by test pilot Heinz Frick on the tailfin.

G-VTOL was finally retired and placed in storage at Dunsfold during February 1986, having undertaken an amazing total of 1,389 flights amassing 721 hrs 33 min in the air. G-VTOL, the sole Harrier T.Mk. 52 is now on long-term loan to the Brooklands Museum in Weybridge, Surrey.

Heinz Frick's cartoon tailmarking. Harrier SIG via Phil Cater

CHAPTER TWO

UK First Generation

First of the VSTOL Warriors: Harrier GR.1

From the outset, the RAF's new Harrier GR.1 – for 'Ground attack and Reconnaissance' was an out-and-out strike aircraft, this being underlined by the accommodation of five stores pylons and two 30mm Aden gun pods, with the inner stations also being plumbed for jettisonable 100 or 330 gallon fuel tanks. The FE.541 Smiths HUD and the moving map display gave the aircraft an excellent degree in precision and accuracy, especially in a first- pass attack scenario. The internally mounted F.95 oblique camera conferred an integral reconnaissance capability, which could be

Specification – Harrier GR.1 (P.1127(RAF) similar)	
ENGINE	One 19,000lb (8,600kg) Rolls-Royce Pegasus 6 turbofan.
WEIGHTS	Empty; 12,300lb (5,600kg) loaded 25,000lb (11,400kg).
DIMENSIONS	Span 25ft 3in (7.65m) (with ferry tips 29ft 8in (9m)); length 45ft 8in (13.84m).
PERFORMANCE	Max level speed at sea level: 638kts (1,180km/h); climb to 40,000ft (12,000m); 2min 23 sec; combat radius, STO with 3,000lb of stores; 250nm (460km); ceiling: 51,000ft (15,500m).
ARMAMENT	2x30mm Aden cannon, bombs, SNEB rockets.

further enhanced with a centreline recce pod. The GR.1's abilities to operate from difficult sites gave the RAF a unique tactical capability, and from the earliest P.1127 and Kestrel days, the Harrier had finally become a true fighting machine.

The inheritance from the P.1127 and the Kestrel was still apparent in the GR.1, and one RAF Officer commented that the aircraft 'looked like someone had sat on it'. Enlarged engine intakes were added to cater for the more powerful Pegasus engine, this being one of the more obvious external signs of change in the GR.1, and the original number of six 'blow-in' doors was increased to eight. An order for 60 Harrier GR.1s (increased to 61 after the crash of XV743

The first 'official GR.1, XV738, which had a natural metal fuselage and a grey/green camouflaged tail. Note the increased number of 'blow-in doors'; XV738 was subsequently converted to GR.1 and then GR.3 , also being used as the test bed for the Pegasus 10 engine. Rolls-Royce

The Boys pictured on the day that the first Harrier GR.1 arrived at No.1(F) Squadron, RAF Wittering.
RAF Wittering

before delivery) was made by the Defence Ministry, with XV738 being the first true production Harrier, which made its maiden flight on 28 December 1967. With the development work on the six DB Harriers continuing apace, added to the swift delivery schedule, a Harrier Conversion Team was gathered at RAF Wittering (chosen to be the UK-based Harriers' home) in January 1969. The Harrier Conversion Unit (HCU) was then officially formed on 1 April 1969, receiving its first aircraft XV746 on the 18th. The plan was to convert experienced Hunter FGA.9 pilots to VSTOL and to make No.1(F) Squadron, then based at West Raynham, the first operational Harrier Unit, moving it to Wittering.

The first conversion course started in July 1969, but was somewhat pre-empted by the *Daily Mail* Transatlantic Air Race in May, which captured the imagination of the public and firmly announced that

Britain had a credible and flexible jet aircraft entering service. The conversion of the 'new' No.1(F) Squadron pilots began in July, and early trips were in fact flown from West Raynham using the former Tri-Partite Kestrel facilities, as Wittering was not yet ready. No.1 Squadron officially formed on the Harrier on 1 April 1969 under the leadership of Wg Cdr Ken Hayr. After a brief UK work-up it deployed to Cyprus to benefit from the good weather and to build up the crews' confidence in the new aircraft, before returning to Wittering to prepare for the first 'off-base' deployment into 'the woods' during the summer of 1970. The first major, dispersed exercise was 'Snowy Falcon 72' when the GR.1s operated from dispersed sites at Miltown near Kinloss. After operating the Harrier in all conditions for fourteen months, No.1 Squadron was declared operational as the first VSTOL jet fighter unit in the world.

In October 1969 the Harrier Operational Conversion Unit was formed from the roots of the HCU, and was designated No.233 OCU, initially wearing a grasshopper motif on the noses of their aircraft but soon adopting the units more traditional 'Welsh wildcat' emblem, applying these markings to the noses of their Harriers. With the Harrier Force expanding and a number of now experienced pilots available, a second front-line unit was established, this being No.4(AC) Squadron, which was to be based at Wildenrath in Germany. This new unit began its work-up in March 1970, moving to Germany in June and receiving its first GR.1, XV799 in August. A second, and short-lived, unit was also formed at Wittering in October 1970, this being No.20(F) Squadron which moved to Germany in December and began to receive its aircraft later that month, the first being XV801. This was

XW922/49 in the markings of 233 OCU; this aircraft was later converted to a GR.3 and finally allocated to Laarbruch as a BDR Trainer. Denis J. Calvert

followed in 1972 by the formation of the third and final Harrier unit, No.3(F) Squadron, which formed with the Pegasus 6-powered GR.1A, also at Wildenrath By the end of the following year each unit had a complement of twelve aircraft and all were declared combat ready.

When the Harrier Force in Germany moved its operational centre closer to the East German border at RAF Gütersloh, there was less accommodation for three full squadrons and so No.20 was disbanded on 28 February 1977, its twelve aircraft being divided between Nos.3 and IV Squadrons, bringing their complement up to eighteen each. No.20 reformed as a Jaguar unit at Bruggen, but was once again back with the Harrier Force in 1992 when

the Harrier OCU was given the title of No.20(Reserve) Squadron.

GR.1 Operations

No.1 Squadron was originally part of the ACE Mobile Force, tasked with reinforcing NATO's Northern or Southern Flank (see the section on the Arctic Harriers)

The clean lines of GR.1 XV758 in its original, high gloss scheme, as yet unmarked but destined for
No.1(F) Squadron; converted to GR.3, it is currently a gate guard at Decimonmannu in Sardinia.
BAe

and as such was given a 'go anywhere' detail and was required to be ready to deploy as required. This policy was readily practised, with regular deployments being made in support of Allied Ground Forces. No.3 and IV Squadrons formed part of the 2nd Allied Tactical Air Force (2ATAF) tasked with high turnaround CAS and BAI, flying from bare base sites close to the front-line. The Harrier units regularly practised these rudimentary site operations, using camouflage netted 'hides' to cover both the aircraft and the operations centres, and utilizing 75ft square MEXE planking sites as VTO or landing strips. Typical of this was 'Flying Site Ebhardt' which was within the Sennelager Training Area in the former West Germany. This site used a short relief road as a taxiway through the forest where the aircraft's hides were situated, and joined on to a country road from where the aircraft could

use a rolling take-off. These operations were also practised on the German autobahns; this type of operational scenario was undertaken at least three times a year.

Camouflage and Markings

The GR.1s were universally painted in gloss dark green, BS.381C:641, with gloss dark sea grey, BS.381C:638 disruptive upper surfaces and gloss light aircraft grey, BS.381C:627 undersides. A flat matt finish was introduced in 1970; initially the aircraft were oversprayed with matt varnish, with a polyurethane coating being added later. During the early days of the GR.1 the aircraft sported three-colour 'Type D' roundels, but these were found to be too highly visible, especially in dispersed operations, and were replaced by the two-colour 'Type B'. Toward the latter stages of the GR.1 series some aircraft

received a 'wrap around' scheme of grey and green; an example was XW630/U of No.20 Squadron, noted in February 1977 (see the section on Harriers in Belize).

Squadron Histories and Markings

No.1(F) Squadron: formed 13 May 1912 with balloons at Farnborough, saw action in France with reconnaissance tasks and stationed at Tangmere at the end of the War. During World War II it was in action in France, later taking part in the Battle of Britain and also undertaking night-fighter duties. Its role turned to ground attack during the closing months of the war, flying the Hawker Typhoon. Transferring to West Raynham it converted to the Hunter, before becoming the world's first operational VSTOL unit. Emblem: Winged '1' on a white disc, flanked by white diamonds edged in red

The Transatlantic Air Race

The Daily Mail Transatlantic Air Race of 1969 seemed the ideal way to announce the arrival of the unique Harrier on the world's stage. The idea was to obtain the fastest time between the Post Office Tower in London and the Empire State Building in New York, both eastbound and westbound. There were many contestants, including No.892 Phantom Team from the Royal Navy. The RAF entered two Harriers, XV741 and XV744, with the pilots Sqn Ldrs Thomas Lecky-Stewart and Graham Williams. Harrier XV741, flown by Lecky-Stewart, took the overall honours, making a flight from a disused yard near St. Pancras railway station – whipping up a storm of coal dust from his vertical take-off – and landing at a waterfront site in Manhattan 6 hrs 11 min 57 sec later. His total point-to-point time was clocked at roughly 7 hrs 6 min.

XV741 under the control of Sqn Ldr Lecky-Stewart lifts off from a disused coal yard near St. Pancras station at the start of his transatlantic run. BAe

(Below) **Celebrating 20 years of the Air Race, XV741, then a GR.3, was suitably marked for the occasion; the aircraft is now with the Royal Navy.** Denis J. Calvert

No.3(F) Squadron: established at Larkhill in May 1912, No.3 has traditionally been a fighter unit since World War I when it flew the Sopwith Camel. It saw extensive service in World War II, operating from both the UK and France. During the post-war years it flew Vampires, Sabres, Hunters, Javelins, Canberras, and latterly Harriers. Emblem: Squadron cockatrice in a white disc flanked by green rectangles edged in yellow

No.4(AC) Squadron: created in September 1912 at Farnborough as a reconnaissance squadron. It operated the Lysander in France in the early stages of World War II, to be replaced by the Mosquito and the Spitfire. Based in Germany since the war it has flown the Vampire, Sabre and Hunter. Emblem: red '4' divided by yellow lightning flash flanked by red/black rectangles divided diagonally by yellow lightning flashes.

No.20(F) Squadron: commissioned at Netheravon in 1915. Stationed in India during World War II, the squadron took part in the Burma campaign with the Hurricane, moving to Germany after the war to fly the Sabre and Hunter. It had a brief interlude with the Harrier in the early 1970s before re-equipping with the Jaguar in 1976. Following another re-equipping programme with Tornado, the unit saw its front-line status decommissioned in consequence of the defence White Paper *Options for Change*, and its 'numberplate' quite fittingly passed to No.223 OCU, the Harrier training squadron, which later became No.20(Reserve) Squadron. Emblem: eagle motif on a white disc flanked by blue, red, white, green and blue bars

HTU and No.233 OCU: formed at Wittering in 1970 through redesignation as the Harrier Training Unit. Previously it had been the Hunter Training Unit at Pembury. HTU emblem: grasshopper motif; 233 OCU emblem: Welsh wildcat on a white disc flanked by red/blue, yellow/black rectangles.

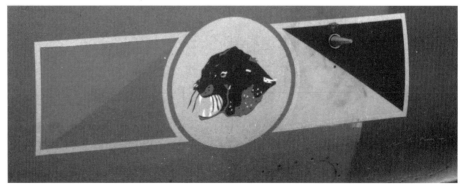

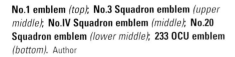
No.1 emblem *(top)*; **No.3 Squadron emblem** *(upper middle)*; **No.IV Squadron emblem** *(middle)*; **No.20 Squadron emblem** *(lower middle)*; **233 OCU emblem** *(bottom)*. Author

Training for the First Generation': Harrier T.2 and T.4

When the Harrier GR.1 first entered service during 1970, there was no two-seater to aid conversion to type, and all new pilots had to undergo 'very extensive' briefings before making vertical sorties and flew the Harrier solo with only radio contact with an instructor on the ground for guidance. For conventional flying training, the instructor would be flying 'chase' in a Hunter, again giving instruction by radio. The idea of a two-seater P.1127 had originally been explored, but production and design efforts were concentrated on what was eventually to become the Harrier.

The RAF soon accepted that a two-seat trainer was badly needed, and issued a requirement primarily for the aircraft to be not only a conversion trainer but also capable of fulfilling a war role and be able, fur-

thermore, to fly operational missions alongside the single-seat GR.1s. A development contract was issued to Hawker Siddeley in 1967, and the challenge facing the design team was the layout. Bearing in mind that the centre of gravity still had to match the thrust, there was no real possibility of adopting side-by-side seating, as in the Hunter T.7, because of the Harrier's somewhat unconventional layout. To attempt to put a widened cockpit between the intakes would have caused a huge design headache, so the designers opted for an extended nose and a tandem seat arrangement, slicing off the front cockpit and inserting a plug that contained a second seat immediately behind it and separated by an integral windshield. Various pieces of avionics had to be moved to accommodate the second seat, including the air-conditioning system and

the F.95 camera and inertial platform. As the rear station was located over the nosewheel bay, it had the effect of raising the cockpit by 18in, giving the occupant an excellent view ahead; and because of its

Specification – Harrier T.2/TAV-8A	
ENGINE	One 19,000lb (8,600kg) Rolls-Royce Pegasus 6 turbofan.
WEIGHTS	Empty with ballast 13,300lb (6,000kg)
DIMENSIONS	Span 25ft 3in (7.65m); length 55ft 10in (16.92m).
PERFORMANCE	Max level speed at sea level: 600kts (1,100km/h); ceiling: 51,000ft (15,500m).
ARMAMENT	2x30mm Aden cannon, bombs, SNEB rockets.

An early Harrier T.2 displaying the grasshopper markings of the Harrier Training Unit. Rolls-Royce

size, the canopy was of a sideways-hinging, two-piece construction. The destabilizing effect of the new front end resulted in the repositioning of the tailfin 33.3in further back and the fitting of an underfin. To further maintain stability, the fin was also enlarged by 11in, and the tailboom was extended and ballasted, with the pitch and yaw 'puffers' being moved accordingly. The result was the Harrier T.Mk.2; the first prototype XW174 flew on 24 April 1969.

The T.2 was some 1400lb heavier than the GR.1, and could be flown with a single pilot from the front cockpit without the reballasting of the tail. Both the front and the rear cockpit duplicate the instrumentation and layout of the single seater, without

the moving map. The aircraft was powered by the faithful Pegasus engine. The early flight testing of the T.2 did not go without incident and XW174 crashed on 4 June 1969 at Larkhill following fuel problems, as did another production T.2, XW264, with the same type of fault. The fin height was also looked at and increased by 6 then 8 and finally 23in, before 18in was settled on as the best stability solution. This fit was tested on XW175; however, the first twelve production aircraft in service all had differing sizes of fin until they were retrofitted with the 'standard' height. No.233 OCU at Wittering introduced the T.2 into service in August 1970, and by 1971 all three front-line squadrons had a 'T-Bird' on strength.

From the T.2 came the T.2A fitted with the Pegasus 102 engine, and with the arrival of the Pegasus 103 the RAF also took the opportunity to bring some two-seaters into line with GR.3 operations. Added to the nose was the LRMTS (Laser Ranging and Marked Target Seeker) and the PWR (Passive Warning Radar) antennas of the GR.3 were added to the tailfin and tailcone; this new version was designated T.4. The addition of the PWR recontoured the tailfin tip, increasing its height by 5in; this increased stabilization and as a result all T.4s with PWR were refitted with the original GR.1 fin. The final version of the T.4 was the T.4A, which covered a small number of the aircraft used solely for

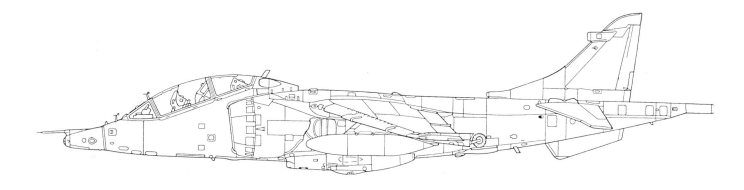

(Top) **Harrier T.4.** Nils Mathisrud
(Bottom) **XW265/W, a short-nosed T.4A used by 233 OCU for pilot conversion.** Author

A short-nosed T.4A shares the Wittering ramp with the 'Snoopy Nosed' T.4 on a dismal February morning. Author

Surrounded by ground-support equipment, ZB600/Z of 233 OCU awaits its next crew. Author

A ground crewman removes a rear access panel to check the T.4's equipment bay. Author

As the T.4 and T.4A shared the 233 OCU ramp, so did the Harrier T.10 and T.4. Author

This viewpoint gives an idea of the two-seat arrangement of the training Harriers; note the 'second cockpit' separated by the 'interior windshield';. also note the canopy restraining bars hooked on to the top of each of the frames. Author

conversion training and which therefore did not require LRMTS or PWR, resulting in a lightweight fit, increasing the aircraft's endurance and performance, and retaining the original nose.

With the introduction of the GR.5 and then the GR.7, the Harrier OCU, where T.4 had continued to serve as the a valuable training and chase aircraft, was the last to relinquish the mark, in 1996. A number of retired T.4s were transferred to the Royal Navy for conversion to T.8 Standard. In all twenty-seven T-Birds were produced for the RAF, including the two development aircraft.

'Snoopy Nose': Harrier GR.3

In the light of the operational experience gained with the GR.1, a number of changes were made to the RAF's Harrier

fleet during the mid 1970s. The addition of a new version of the Pegasus engine, the Mk.103, gave the aircraft an extra 1000lb of thrust, and the jets fitted with this new powerplant were designated as Harrier GR.Mk.3. With the new Pegasus successfully installed, the RAF also decided to take the opportunity to add some other fresh items to the Harrier's inventory.

The most noticeable modification was the fitting of a LRMTS tied into the FE.541 INS/AS (Inertial Navigation System/Attack System) in an extended so-called 'Snoopy' style nose, together with a PWR on the fin and rear fuselage. The LRMTS was a Ferranti type 106, similar in design to that used in the RAF's 'chisel nosed' Jaguar GR.1, but featuring 'eyelids' capable of being closed rather than just a glass panel. The LRMTS was initially trialled in a Ferranti Canberra, and the first aircraft to receive the new nose was

XZ128. Inside the restyled nose was an active laser receiver, with the primary function of supplying a laser pulse from which the range to a ground target could be derived, either boresighted or in conjunction with the FE.154 INS. The result-

Specification – Harrier GR.3	
ENGINE	One 21,500lb (9,800kg) Rolls-Royce Pegasus 103 turbofan.
WEIGHTS	Empty 12,600lb (5,700kg); loaded 26,000lb (11,800kg).
DIMENSIONS	Span 25ft 3in (7.65m); length 46ft 10in (14.2m).
PERFORMANCE	Max level speed at sea level: 638kts (1,180km/h); range: 200nm (370km); ceiling: 51,000ft (15,500m).
ARMAMENT	2x30mm Aden cannon, bombs, SNEB rockets, CBUs.

XV783/N of 233 OCU in the hover at Wittering. BAe

XZ129/29, an IFR probe-equipped example from No.1 Squadron. Graham Causer

ing information was then projected into the pilot's HUD, with the slant range, closure and attack angles also being fed into the ballistics computer. When switched to marked target mode it could detect reflected infra-red energy from a ground- or air-based laser designator, it would then lock-on to the energy and present the range and position to the HUD. The employment of this piece of equipment was quoted by senior officers as 'having a drastic effect on target acquisition and bomb delivery accuracy – especially in a first-pass laydown scenario'.

Weapon aiming relied on the Ferranti weapons-aiming computer, which also made use of information from the LRMTS and data input from the navigation equipment, such as wind speed and direction. A 'ballistics box' mounted on the cockpit had slots for four 'slide-in' plugs, one for the Aden cannons, and three for other types of ordinance. Each plug fed ballistic information for each individual type of weapon, and the pilot therefore needed to ensure that he had the correct plug in place for the weapons he was carrying and the correct pylons selected. The computer then auto-

matically released the stores, having taken into account the distance to the target, the wind speed and the weapons-trajectory characteristics. The FE.541 INS/AS included a moving map display which could be updated from the aircraft's Sperry compass as well as from visual 'fix' input by the pilot. with essential navigational data projected on to his HUD.

The second and perhaps most vital upgrade in terms of the aircraft's survivability was the Marconi ARI.18223 RWR (Radar Warning Receiver). Two passive aerials were fitted, one to the near top of the fin covering the forward aspect and one on the tip of the tailboom covering the rearward aspect. Both gave a sweep of 180°, and this passed a visual warning on to a new cockpit display and an audible alarm to the pilot's head set if a hostile radar emission were detected. A new Lucas 12kVA alternator to replace the original twin 4kVA sets was also fitted, and the F.95 camera gained a new 'teardrop' shaped aperture in the side of the nose. The pitot tube, mounted on the front of the GR.1's nose, was moved to a point above the LRMTS fairing.

The Pegasus Mk.103 was in essence the same engine as that installed in the USMC AV-8A and it was also specified to be fitted to the twelve attrition replacement aircraft which were ordered by the RAF in 1974. The Mk.103 had a rebladed fan, which increased the mass airflow, and was first trialled in 1971 aboard XV738. The first service aircraft fitted with the new engine was XZ128, which flew on 9 January 1976. As well as the new-build aircraft, earlier GR.1s and GR.1As were retrofitted with the new engine when they went in for major servicing. A total of sixty-two GR.1/1As are believed to have been modified to the GR.3 standard.

The GR.3s of No.4(AC) Squadron were the RAF's dedicated Harrier Reconnaissance operators; having 40 per cent of their commitment to reconnaissance and the remaining 60 per cent to the delivery of the BL.755 cluster bomb unit (CBU). Complementing the F.95 oblique camera, carried by all the Harriers, No.4(AC) also carried a centreline mounted BAe sensor pod, containing a fan of five optical cameras, four being of 70 and one of 127mm focal length. Exposed camera magazines were rushed to

RAF Germany: GR.3 Harrier Dispersed Operations

With the UK-based No.1 Squadron, assigned primarily to support the ACE Mobile Force, the UK Mobile Force and to deploy to reinforce the northern flank, three other Harrier units, Nos.3, IV and 20 Squadrons, were initially assigned to RAF Germany during 1970–71 to be based at Wildenrath, close to the Dutch border. In February 1977, however, No.20 Squadron was disbanded, with the other two units absorbing its aircraft. Because of its close air support, battlefield air interdiction and reconnaissance missions assisting 1st British Corps on the Central Front, the Harrier Force was moved closer to the East German border at Gütersloh, the only RAF combat airfield east of the Rhine.

The Harriers' strength of operating from 'anywhere' was demonstrated, with the aircraft operating autonomously in 'field sites', camouflaged under netted hides with PSP (pierced steel planking) flooring and personnel living in tents. The aircraft regularly practised take-offs from the dispersed sites or used any nearby autobahn. In war-time these sites would be some 30 to 50 miles back from the border in order that the aircraft could make rapid flights into the battle area and possibly up to six or eight sorties per aircraft per day. Fuel was fed to the aircraft from rubberized bladders, while groundcrew rearmed the aircraft and re-stocked the 'expendables'. It is likely that the missions over the battle zone would be of only some 30 min duration, and once back at the dispersal point the pilot would remain in the cockpit for a fast OTR (operational turn round)

on at least three occasions, receiving his next set of instructions via a telescramble line from the OP's tent or room, which in turn would be in contact with command by a secure line to the Forward Operations Centre. Because of the threat of chemical weapons attack, pilots and groundcrew could be required to use full NBC kit, and even engine changes in the field were required to be carried out in the cumbersome protective suits.

Despite being described as VTOL (vertical take off and landing), in order to carry a useful warload the Harrier's use STOVL (short take off/vertical landing), which requires a brief take-off run, was practised with the use of a 200yd strip of aluminium planking from which the aircraft 'leapt' into the air. With the weapons released and the fuel lower, a vertical landing could be accomplished, however FOD (foreign object damage) was a constant worry with the huge intakes of the Pegasus 103. Up to 5,000lb of weaponry could be hung on the GR.3's seven weapons points. The two outer 'belly' stations almost always carried the Aden cannons, and perhaps a 1,000lb bomb could be carried on the centreline. The inboard wing pylons were stressed to 1,200lb and could carry bombs or 100-gallon fuel tanks. Outer pylons could carry up to 650lb of ordinance, such as BL.755 CBUs or Matra SNEB rockets. In the battlefield environment height and speed are the Harrier's keys to survival: they would run in at about 550kts and 100ft for maximum accuracy.

Operating from wooded clearings or from autobahns the GR.3 was always at home. Denis J. Calvert

Making a STO launch is a No.4 Squadron aircraft with high visibility tail marking, designed originally to celebrate the Squadron's seventy-fifth anniversary, but also serving as an anti-collision measure. BAe

Pictured just before its retirement at Wittering, the 'front end' of a GR.3 armed with SNEB rockets, used with such devastating effect in the Falklands campaign; it should be noted that armed aircraft may be photographed only from the side or rear, one is never allowed to walk in front of them, and all armed aircraft point to the open countryside.
Author

What becomes of the broken Harrier? XZ969 languishes in Marham's dump. f4 Aviation Photobank

Typical of the wrap-around green/grey scheme, is this example from No.1(F) Squadron, complete with bolt-on IFR probe and SNEB rocket pods. Graham Causer

the Squadron's RICs (Reconnaissance Interpretation Centres) where the films were swiftly processed, with the pilot adding a verbal and written report on the reconnaissance trip, before submission of the results to higher authorities.

The primary weapons for the Harrier GR.3 were the 277kg Hunting BL.755 CBU and 68mm-calibre SNEB rockets housed in 19-round Matra 155 launchers. Alternatively, standard 1,000lb iron bombs could be carried, and laser guidance kits were also added to these weapons during and after the Falklands conflict of 1982. Also available were Mk.117 parachute-retarding tails, developed by Hunting for the 1,000lb bombs, to allow the aircraft to exit safely after releasing its weapons from a low level. Under the fuselage could be

found the standard Aden cannons and the inboard pylons were usually occupied by 455-litre drop tanks. Post-Falklands Harriers were fitted with two Tracor ALE-40 Chaff and Flare dispensers mounted under the fuselage behind the airbrake, and some GR.3s retained the wiring looms for the carrying of Sidewinder AAMs.

By the middle of the 1980s plans were forming for the re-equipping of the Harrier Force with the GR.5; however continuing delays in the Harrier II programme kept the GR.3s operating for longer than had been planned. They still made a full contribution to the exercises in which participated, but by 1988 the writing was firmly on the wall and the run-down began. To mark the twentieth anniversary of the Harriers' entry into service, the decision-makers had

been persuaded to allow enough GR.3s to be left to form a weather-ravaged fly-past at Wittering on 20 May 1994. The last flight of the GR.3s took place on 29 June 1994 when ZD670/3A and ZD668/3E from No.20(R) Squadron made their final bow.

Camouflage

The Harrier GR.3s were universally painted in the standard RAF disruptive wrap-around camouflage of dark sea grey and dark green, introduced to all of the RAF Harriers by mid 1978 in order to make them less visible to fighters when banking away at low level. The individual squadrons' insignia and codes were applied in the usual places, as were the aircrafts' warning and access panel markings. As the

---

The Matchcote Schemes

During the mid 1980s experiments were carried out with two aircraft to test differing types of camouflage paintwork on the GR.3. The 'Matchcote Trials' of 1984 involved first XV738 from No.4 Squadron in Germany, which in February received a two-tone grey finish comprising dark sea grey upper surfaces, underfin and fuselage sides, and medium sea grey tailfin, lower fuselage sides and undersides. Squadron markings were in low-visibility light grey and black, and the single tail letter 'B' was also light grey. Full-colour warning and access markings were carried, as were full-colour roundels of reduced size. The scheme looked similar in appearance to the current Harrier GR.7 greys. This might have been the original colour scheme for the GR.5's service entry had

it not been for the all-over olive green applied to XV809 of No.3 Squadron, which proved more acceptable and as being more suited to the Harrier operations in Europe. This would be made more effective when applied with a lighter shade of green for the undersides. This colour scheme was applied in February 1984 and, following evaluation, was preferred to the greys. XV809 carried full-colour squadron markings with a yellow, two-letter tail code 'AF'; however, the roundels on the intakes and wings were reduced in size. It may be noted that XV809 at one point carried a standard dark grey rudder. Both aircraft were returned to their original colour schemes soon afterwards.

One of the two aircraft involved in the 'Matchcote Trials' was XV738/B, seen here at the Finningley Airshow in 1984, looking similar in style to the pattern eventually chosen for the GR.7; the grey gives the GR.3 the same aesthetic appeal.
Graham Causer

Navy GR.3s

At the end of their working careers six ex-RAF GR.3s were transferred to the EFT School of Aircraft Handling (SOAH) at RNAS Culdrose in Cornwall. The aircraft came from No.4 Squadron and the Harrier OCU and among their number was XV741, famous for the transatlantic air race of 1969. They are now used to train Navy deck-handlers in the fine art of hauling a Harrier around a flightdeck, of which they have a copy painted on the

Culdrose concrete. The GR.3s still 'run' although with their wheels on the ground and are 'piloted' by appropriately trained instructors. Some are even painted in Navy colours, which for a GR.3 trying to emulate a FRS.1 or F/A.2 is quite bizarre. The EFT SOAH also had on their books at one time P.1127 XP980 and Kestrel XS695.

Painted in pseudo-899 Squadron markings, one of the Culdrose EFT GR.3s, XZ129, formerly with 233 OCU.
f4 Aviation Photobank

final operators of the GR.3, No.20(R) Squadron, with the former 233 OCU's aircraft, carried tail number/letter combinations to distinguish their individual numbering system from the GR.5s' that were also on strength, for example, ZD670/3A.

P.1127(RAF) XV279: the 'Plastic Pig'

It seems that in most cases, due to whatever pressures, historic or interesting airframes may often be disposed of or 'forgotten' and a

rich part of aviation history lost forever, save for a few old photographs or perhaps a panel or two hung on a mess-room wall. Such might have been the fate of P.1127(RAF) XV279 had it not been for a chance remark from Cpl Ian Stokes, of No.20(R) Squadron at RAF Wittering, whose suggestion it was to take the unwanted airframe out of storage and turn it into a display piece.

Cpl Stokes takes up the story:

XV279 had been kicking around Wittering since March 1976 when it returned from the Earls Court show. It was used then for towing practice, OTRs and winching, all of which led to less than

careful consideration for the aircraft. In 1983 it was modified using copious amounts of fibreglass to emulate a Falklands aircraft, again returning for an Earls Court show – thereafter being referred to by all as the 'Plastic Pig'.

It was placed in No.5 Shed, forgotten about and left to the mercies of a flaking and crumbling asbestos roof. Having made the suggestion to the Station hierarchy and receiving approval, despite the daunting task, XV279 was extracted from the shed (having first established that the aircraft was still where it was supposed to have been left), washed and left 'downwind' for a few days to blow away the remainder of the 'toxic fallout'. Beneath the paintwork it was still in

So as not to cause confusion with the numbering system of the co-located 233 OCU GR.5s and GR.3s at Wittering, both types had a numeric and alphabetic tailcode to represent each version; here we see **XV753/3F** and **XZ921/3A**. Author

remarkable condition – considering that it had no nose, fin or tailplane; and the wings and engine doors were 'tacked' to the airframe with 6in nails! A massive search was instituted for spares, many of which were salvaged from several sections at Wittering who had 'forgotten' that they still had spares from the GR.3s

XV279 belongs to No.20(R) Squadron as its 'gate guardian', although its longer-term future is less clear. One thing is certain: a dedicated group have saved a vital part of the Harriers' heritage from being scrapped, for which they should be justly proud.

emblem. He even finished off the zap with a neat line of tears running from the eyes of one of the birds. This was all done with the tacit approval of the hosts, who even supplied the paint – the 'unwritten' rule of zapping being that you use washable paint, preferably supplied by your victim.

Seen at the Harriers' anniversary 'bash' at Wittering. f4 Aviation Photobank

brought back from Belize. A 'network' was established, and parts came in from various sources, including a nose cone from RAF Stafford. After many months of hard work, and a few threats from the Station Commander to either 'move it or lose it', the aircraft was given a project deadline – to be ready for the 1994 Officers' Mess ball in the summer, or if possible for the Harriers' Anniversary Bash a few weeks earlier. Bearing in mind that much of this effort was 'spare-time' work, the aircraft was rebuilt with the spares we were given and a few 'home-made' items and, as a result of blood, sweat, tears and the use of a railway sleeper to encourage the first-stage fan into position, XV279 was painted up, badged up and ready for the twentieth anniversary of the Harrier – with literally hours to spare.

Think Pink: 'Le Zapped T.2'

In November 1976, a party from No.1(F) Squadron at Wittering visited Dijon airbase in central France for a squadron exchange with Escadre de Chasse 1/2 Cigones; taking with them four Harrier GR.1s and a single T.2, plus a ground-support party. Once established with their French hosts, the artistic skills of one of the ground party, Cpl John Adams, were called upon, and let loose to apply an imaginative 'zap' to the tail of a Mirage IIIE belonging to the host unit. The Harrier 'cartoon' was based on a design Adams used to draw on letters home to his children, but on this occasion the caricature was engaged in a strictly adult, and probably illegal, activity with the Cigones tail

It was all apparently taken in good humour, and the Squadron's French hosts laid on a superb reception that night and the wine flowed freely. The next morning, slightly the worse for wear, the RAF crew were taken in the shuttle bus back to their Harriers by a more scenic route through the station than they had taken on the evening before. As they approached the apron, they saw a light-coloured 'T Bird' and their first thought was to wonder why G-VTOL or some other Harrier had turned up. Then reality dawned. While their hosts had kept them occupied at the bar, a painting party had been at work overnight on a grand scale. The two-seater XW936/06 had had its camouflage replaced by pink and white paint, one coat sprayed and two applied

Ooh la la! **John Adams's Harrier cartoon performs a 'rolling vertical landing' at maximum thrust!**
Colin Watson via IPMS Harrier SIG

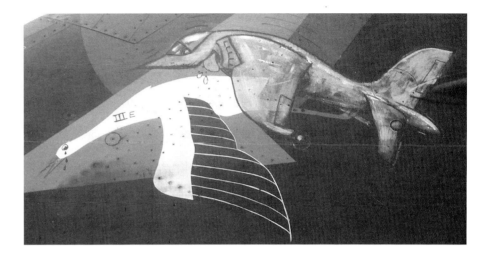

with a roller. The No.1(F) Squadron badge, resembling an eye, had curly red eyelashes painted above, and the drop tanks were painted white, with wobbly hand-crafted red spirals on the front sections. The tip of the nose was also painted red and the green weapons pylons had broken out in white blotches. As the RAF team got over the shock, they soon entered into the spirit of the occasion. The pilots were all extremely keen to be seen 'in the pink', and as a finale to the exchange they flew a rather fast and low vic formation over Dijon, the pink T.2 leading the way flanked by two GR.1s on either side, before breaking and turning for home. The word

had by now filtered back to Wittering, describing the impending arrival *Le Pink 'arrier*. The same exuberant formation flew over Wittering, meeting a *garde d'honneur* which had been hastily pulled together for the reception. This involved a small contingent of officers and groundcrew with their RAF berets worn back to front, thus imitating French berets, and 'presenting arms' with French bread sticks instead of rifles. The Squadron Commander also witnessed the events, but, as the T.2 was parked up, he experienced a serious sense of humour failure. Driving hastily away he left a fairly explicit order: 'That aircraft is to be returned to RAF service colours

before anyone from the exchange party goes home for the weekend.' The groundcrew from France rolled up a few hours later, and it was from this point that the *esprit de corps* deteriorated somewhat. From squadron leaders to LACs, all were required to form a working party and clean the Harrier. However, those 'playful' Frenchies had used emulsion-based paint (so much for the first rule of zapping). Such fun was had in the hangar that weekend – it took ages! But despite the best efforts of all concerned, there was still pink and white paint engrained in the aircraft's panel lines and it eventually had to be totally resprayed in its original camouflage.

The 'zapped' T.2 in all its glory: pink wings and forward fuselage, with white fuselage and tail.
Colin Watson via IPMS Harrier SIG

Specialist Trials Bird: Harrier XW175

About six weeks after its initial handling and assessment flights, the second prototype Harrier two-seater XW175 began its long life as an airborne research and development vehicle. Early testing centred on the different aspects of the two-seater as compared with the single-seater, culminating with the fitting of the now familiar 'tall-fin', synonymous with the Harrier trainers until 1971. The aircraft was then retained by Hawker Siddeley for a variety of trials on RAE ranges, and on 29 June 1976 flew it for the first time from its new base at RAE Bedford. Work in support of the Sea Harrier dominated XW175's workload for the next few years, preparing for sea trials aboard HMS *Hermes* in 1977. XW175 was fitted with either a programmable HUD or MADGE, however it suffered problems from the ship's radar emissions.

On its return from sea it was soon to become involved in ski-jump testing, with the first launch from the equipment constructed by the RAE taking place on 5 August 1977 by the single-seat XV281, followed by XW175 on 23 August. By

October 1978 over a hundred launches had been made from varying degrees of ramp. In late 1978 XW175 returned to *Hermes* for a more successful series of sea trials, and from 1978 to 1983 work was carried out on developing measures to reduce the pilot's workload by testing systems such as auto-stab, low-speed autopilot and auto-deceleration to hover. Toward the end of 1983 the aircraft was involved in 'Nightbird' FLIR trials before it moved to the Cranfield Institute of Technology for a major refit toward a total change of direction in its research career.

XW175 then became RAE Bedford's prime mover in the VAAC (Vectored thrust Aircraft – Advanced flight Control) programme, designed to investigate concepts involved in STOVL. In this the craft was fitted with an experimental active control system which had full authority over the tailplane, nozzle and flap angles, engine thrust, reaction control, roll and auto-stab, thus allowing these to be handled from the rear seat, while a 'safety pilot' in the front seat monitored the systems and could take over if neccessary. Externally the major change was the replacement of the 'tall fin' by a standard T.4A fit; internally the rear cockpit was

rebuilt, thus making this the first fly-by-wire VSTOL aircraft.

During the late 1980s and early 1990s the system had been enhanced and now revolved around a programmable, digital flight-control computer, whereby the Harrier's control systems are digitally copied and fed to the 'pilot' who used two 'sticks' – one controlling speed, and the other direction. These functions were eventually combined into one 'stick', allowing the other 'hand'-free to operate other systems such as radar or armament.

Currently the VAAC Harrier continues its trials into digital flight integration, and it is the only T.4 still serving in its original RAF colours of dark green and dark grey disruptive topsides and light grey undersides. Several logos have adorned the aircraft at different stages; the early days saw it carrying the 'Flight Systems Bedford' name on the forward fuselage sides, later with reference marks painted on its tail. With its 'digital' commitment, large curving white 'VAAC' lettering was applied to the tailfin, with the words 'Active Control Technology' beneath the cockpit sides. Underneath XW175's fuselage may be found rounded 'pods' in place of the gun packs; these can be filled with a variety of trial instrumentation.

XW175 in its VAAC Harrier guise. BAe

CHAPTER THREE

USA First Generation

Marines' Manoeuvre Machines: Harrier AV-8A

The US Marine Corps had taken a keen interest in the British Harrier programme almost from its inception since they themselves had a firm requirement for organic air cover for their amphibious operations. Rotary-winged aircraft had proved inadequate for their needs, but VTOL or STOVL would be high on their 'wants list'. It is somewhat surprising, therefore, that the Marine Corps played no part in the Tri-Partite Kestrel Evaluation Programme, although the US Army had dismissed the Harrier as not being suitable for the roles they envisaged. When the Tri-Partite Harrier trials had ended six Kestrels were shipped to the USA for further trials work and were redesignated as the XV-6A. In 1966 an XV-6A operated from the USS *Raleigh*, a vessel that was clearly too small to handle conventional fixed-wing aircraft but showed how the Harrier (as it would become) could perform. The Kestrel, not being a combat aircraft, was seen as a 'good concept' but not one that could actually carry a useful warload, and it was not until the emergence of the far superior Harrier that the US Marines again took notice. There were many schemes proposed by American manufacturers to provide an indigenous VTO-capable craft, but in 1968 the only substantial programme on the table was the Harrier.

Despite the positive praise given to the Harrier, there was clear opposition to the USA's purchasing a 'foreign' aircraft at the expense of its own aerospace industry, and the popular criticism seemed to be that 'the Harrier couldn't carry a matchbox over a football field.' Against this background of hostility, Gen G. McCutheon of the USMC sent a team to the 1966 Farnborough Airshow, and their number included two test pilots Col Tom Miller, and Lt Col Bud Baker. On finding the Hawker Siddeley chalet they asked if they could be permitted to test fly the Harrier;

Specification – AV-8A Harrier I/EAV-8S	
ENGINE	One 20,500lb (9,300kg) Rolls-Royce Pegasus 10 Mk102 turbofan; later F402-RR-402 Mk 103.
WEIGHTS	Empty 12,300lb (5,600kg); loaded 17,000lb (7,700kg).
DIMENSIONS	Span 25ft 3in (7.65m); length 45ft 8in (13.74m).
PERFORMANCE	Max level speed at sea level: 638kts (1,180km/h); climb to 40,00ft (12,000m): 2min 23sec; combat radius, STO with 3,000lb of stores: 250nm (460km); ceiling: 51,00ft (15,500m).
ARMAMENT	2x30mm Aden cannon, Sidewinder AAMs, bombs, CBUs.

the rest is history. Their reports on the potential of the aircraft gained support from the Commandant of the Marine Corps who lobbied heavily on Capitol Hill until he eventually gained Congressional and Presidential approval for a first purchase of twelve Harriers, sacrificing seventeen new F-4J Phantoms in the process. To facilitate the move, a deal was struck between Hawker Siddeley and McDonnell Douglas to manufacture and maintain the Harrier. To get the feel for operational efforts test pilot Maj 'Bud' Iles and maintenance officer Capt 'Speedy' Gonzales were sent to the UK to learn from No.1 Squadron which already operated the Harrier GR.1, to which the American aircraft would be closely allied.

The US Marine Corps orders between 1970 and 1975 totalled 110 single-seaters and 8 two-seaters, under the designation AV-8A, (HS Harrier Mk.50) the A denoting 'Attack' and the V denoting 'VSTOL'. To minimize the costs, the AV-8As were to be as near to the specifications of the Harrier GR.1 as possible, the main differences arising from the need to carry US weapons. From the outset the AV-8As were wired to carry the AIM-9 Sidewinder missile on its outer wing pylons, reflecting the Corps'

requirement for a secondary air-defence role, and the aircraft also retained the 30mm Aden cannons. The initial examples were outfitted with the standard RAF FE.541 nav/attack system, but this was replaced and retrofitted by a much simpler Smiths I/WAC (Interface/Weapons Aiming Computer), which undertook all the necessary aiming calculations with selectable modes such as CCIP and displayed the information in the HUD, under the Phase 1 modification programme. This also included another retrofit, in replacing the Martin-Baker Mk 9D ejector seat with the US-built Stencel SEU-3A and later with the SIII-3S, which married with the US Navy's types and used the same style of torso harness.

In a similar manner to the Hawker Siddeley/McDonnell Douglas arrangement, Rolls-Royce and Pratt and Whitney collaborated on the Harrier's Pegasus powerplant. The first ten AV-8As were fitted with the Pegasus 10 (Mk.802 export specification), which lacked an emergency fuel control; subsequent aircraft had the uprated Pegasus 11, which under its US designation became the F.402-RR-400 and was then retrofitted to the first Harriers.

Revised IFF gear was installed, and the ram air turbine was eventually 'uninstalled' from all the fleet as an unnecessary item. This simpler fit became known as 'Baseline'. American standard Magnavox radios were also fitted and the Harrier gained a large canted UHF/VHF aerial on its spine, as used by the Sylvania VHF/Tactical UHF, and also the provision to carry MERs (multiple ejection racks) on its wing pylons.

Following the delivery of the first AV-8A (built by BAe Kingston and assembled at Dunsfold) by USAF C-133 transport, 'wings off', from RAF Mildenhall on 20 November 1970, BIS (Board of Inspection) acceptance trials were undertaken at Patuxent River. The aircraft was soon joined by a further three and undertook sea trials aboard USS *Guadalcanal* and USS *Coronado*. Mid 1971 saw the *Project*

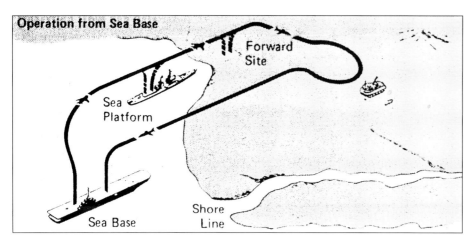

Operation from Sea Base

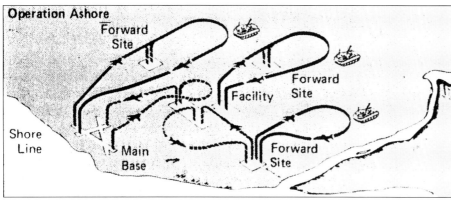

Operation Ashore

Flexible operations. McDonnell Douglas

Two AV-8As recovering on to LHA-4, with a further five arranged on deck; the AV-8A proved to be just what the Marines had wanted from a close-support aircraft: the ability to go anywhere.
USMC via Tony Thornborough

Battle Cry programme, where the Harriers underwent tactical evaluation in terms of off-base deployment, and the writing of the aircraft's tactical manual. The project encompassed weapons delivery, defensive fighter tactics, shipboard compatibility and forward basing.

Operationally the Marine Corps created three squadrons. The first to form with the initial ten Harriers was VMA-513 at Beaufort, North Carolina, in April 1971. By 1976 VMA-542 and VMA-231 were also up and running at Beaufort, with VMAT-203, the Harrier training establishment, also up to strength. All combat units undertook the regular overseas deployment to Misawa AFB, Okinawa. The key to Harrier doctrine was of flexibility: being able to position the aircraft close to the battle area and to provide a unique form of manoeuvre warfare, adding close support to the troops, operating from LPH (Landing Platform Helicopter) or LHA (Landing Helicopter Assault) ships, or from swiftly established shore sites.

By 1976 the Marines had their complete single-seat Harrier force and had undertaken several deployments aboard both Marine Corps and Naval carriers. In 1975 the first six-month cruise was undertaken aboard USS *Guam*, and in 1977 the first squadron-size deployment took place aboard the USS *Franklin D. Roosevelt*, alongside F-4s, A-7s and E-IB helicopter units, where, for the first time, the Harrier was integrated into the hectic, cyclic operations of a large carrier air group.

What had seemed at the outset to be a barely survivable novelty had turned into a first-rate fighter, and close air support aircraft that suited the Marines' manoeuvre warfare concepts completely, and the potential for further improvements led to the AV-8C, covered separately here, and the more powerful AV-8B.

Over the bow and away, as a 'Flying Tiger' departs for another sortie. USMC via Tony Thornborough

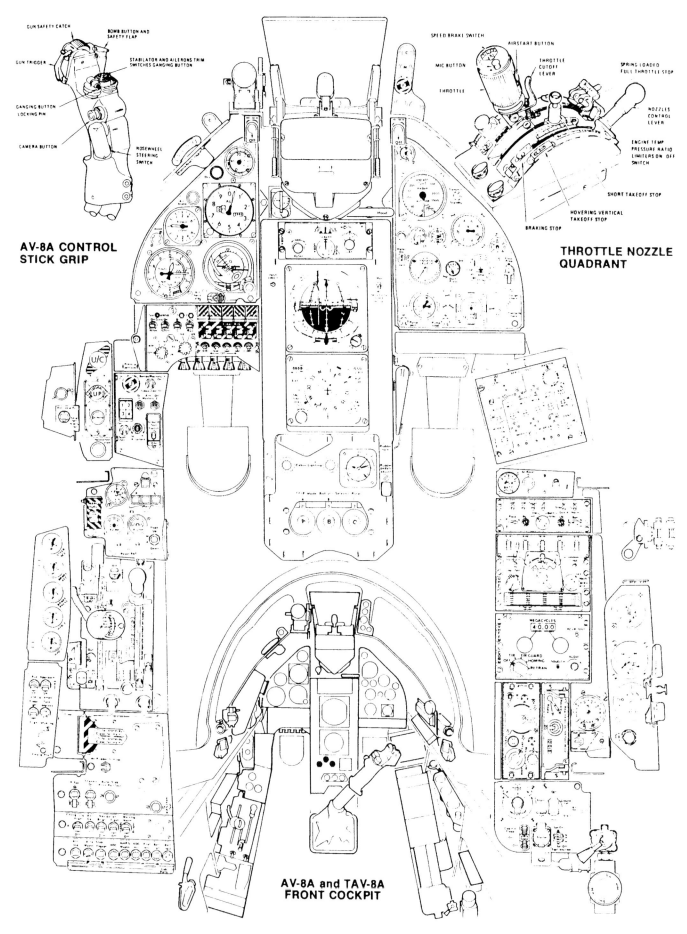

AV-8A CONTROL STICK GRIP

GUN SAFETY CATCH

BOMB BUTTON AND SAFETY FLAP

GUN TRIGGER

STABILATOR AND AILERONS TRIM SWITCHES GANGING BUTTON

GANGING BUTTON LOCKING PIN

CAMERA BUTTON

NOSEWHEEL STEERING SWITCH

THROTTLE NOZZLE QUADRANT

SPEED BRAKE SWITCH

AIRSTART BUTTON

MIC BUTTON

THROTTLE CUTOFF LEVER

SPRING LOADED FULL THROTTLE STOP

THROTTLE

NOZZLES CONTROL LEVER

ENGINE TEMP PRESSURE RATIO LIMITERS ON OFF SWITCH

SHORT TAKEOFF STOP

HOVERING VERTICAL TAKEOFF STOP

BRAKING STOP

U/C

UP

MEGACYCLES 40.00

AV-8A and TAV-8A FRONT COCKPIT

AV-8A cockpit. McDonnell Douglas

A deck officer marshals an AV-8A into position. Of note are the wing tanks, not often seen on the US aircraft as their doctrine dictates that they be positioned close to the battle area.
USMC via Tony Thornborough

Snapped visiting Atlanta in 1979 is AV-8A 159256 from the 'Ace of Spades'. f4 Aviation Photobank

Against a windswept ramp 159373 from VMAT-203, 'The Hawks'; later converted to a 'C', it is now in store at Davis-Monthan. Author

A pair of 'Hawks' transit through Keesler AFB during May 1981; nearer the camera, 159371 is now in store at Davis-Monthan. Author

158963 with an identity crisis! Looking more than a little the worse for wear, the aircraft was cleaned up and is now on display at MCAS Cherry Point. Author

---

VIFFing and the Combat Plug

Maj Harry W. Blot, the Marine Corps Harrier Project Officer, was always keen to explore new facets of VSTOL operations and to survey the possibilities of 'VIFFing' (vectoring in forward flight) which he understood to be common practice among RAF Harrier pilots. The VIFF was a flying technique whereby the pilot suddenly swivelled the engine nozzles downward, thus endowing the Harrier with a new force in air combat. Blot decided that the only way to test theory was to try it, so on a test flight he decided to go for full reverse while flying straight at 500kts. To Blot's amazement the aircraft decelerated at an alarming rate; the AV-8 stayed in the air and the engine did not fall apart. By 1972 an impressive array of VIFFing techniques had filtered down to squadron level. Further VIFF trials were undertaken with the XV6A Kestrels, which achieved 'extraordinary' results when pitted against such aircraft as the T-38 Talon. Those obtained against other 'aggressor' aircraft were equally impressive and at low level were certain to make an unwary adversary fly straight into the ground.

What the Harrier needed, all combat pilots agreed, was an extra burst of thrust to combat the modern, low-wing loaded fighters. The engine nozzles were beefed up to alleviate tiresome restrictions imposed on VIFFing, which led to some improvements; enter then the 'combat plug'. This was a screw in the turbine temperature control fuse that allowed the pilot to pull out significantly more thrust when wing-borne; but with one disadvantage: it could be used for only 2.5 min at a time, which by coincidence was the length evaluated by the US Marine Corps as the duration of the average dogfight. The aircrew deemed it an excellent solution and soon showed that when used it 'did everything you asked of it'. Further tests confirmed there was no longer any question about what the Harrier might be capable of – the possibilities were said to be 'mouth watering'.

Camouflage and Markings

The AV-8A generally wore the standard US Marine Corps colours of dark green, FS 34079, and dark sea grey, FS 36118, in a disruptive pattern on the uppersurfaces, and light grey, FS 36440, on the lower surfaces, some aircraft wearing temporary 'Artic' white finish for winter exercises. All lettering was generally in black, with full-colour or plain black national insignia on the intakes and wings. Each squadron personalized its aircraft with colourful rudders, such as the 'Flying Tigers' golden-yellow saw-toothed design and the VMA-231's black ace of spades on a white background. Two Harriers, based at Patuxent River around 1976 carried high visibility, orange panels (FS 38903) on their wings and tailfins.

The 'Gun Squadrons' – a Short History

VMA-211 'The Wake Island Avengers': began as Fighter Squadron 4M in 1937, flying the Grumman F-3F at NAS San Diego. Redesignated VMF-211 to fly Wildcats in World War II. The squadron flew twelve Wildcats from the USS Enterprise at Wake Island, where a heroic battle was fought against the Japanese and seven of the aircraft were destroyed while inflicting twenty-one losses on the enemy. Following a move to Palmyra Atoll it adopted the name 'Avengers' in memory of those lost or captured at Wake Island. It ended the war flying F-4U Corsairs, and following the war was redesignated again as VMA-211.

VMA-214 'The Black Sheep': commissioned as Fighter Squadron-214 in 1942 at Ewa, Oahu, in the Hawaiian Islands. In August twenty-seven men under the leadership of Maj Gregory 'Pappy' Boyington formed the 'Blacksheep' of VMF-214. They fought their way to fame flying the F-4U Corsair, piling up a record 197 enemy aircraft destroyed or damaged in only eighty-four days. Boyington was awarded the Medal of Honor in 1945 as the leader of 'Pappy's Black Sheep'. The unit took part in the Korean War and in Vietnam, flying the A-4 Skyhawk, before converting to the Harrier.

VMA-311 'The Tomcats': originally commissioned at Cherry Point in 1942, it began to fly the F-4U in 1943. In 1948 it introduced the first jet aircraft to the Marine inventory, the Shooting Star, followed by the F9F-2 Panther. About this time it also acquired the 'WL' tailcode, which led to the name 'Willy Lovers'; this reportedly inspired the heart on the unit's insignia. It began to be known as the 'Tomcats' with the coming of the Cougar and was designated Marine Attack Squadron 311. It flew the A-4 in Vietnam and returned from Iwakuni to Yuma in 1988, converting to the Harrier soon after.

VMA-542 'The Flying Tigers': commissioned as a night-fighter squadron in 1944, it flew the Grumman Hellcat, operating in the west Pacific during World War II. After the war it moved to El Toro flying the Tigercat as VMF(AW)-542, until it received the Douglas Skyknight in 1951;1958 saw the arrival of the Skyray. The Squadron converted to the F-4 Phantom, which served throughout the Vietnam War. It received the AV-8A at MCAS

Beaufort before moving to its current home at Cherry Point in 1975, also operating the AV-8C, before acquiring the AV-8B in 1986.

VMA-223 'The Bulldogs': commissioned in May 1942 at Ewa, Oahu, with the Brewster Buffalo and originally known as the 'Rainbow' Squadron until 1943 when it adopted the name 'Bulldogs'. Flying the Wildcat and the Corsair it acquitted itself admirably during World War II, and returned to El Toro and later to Cherry Point to fly the Panther. Deploying to Atsugi an 1953, it returned to El Toro and the FJ-4B Fury in 1954, later taking on the Skyhawk in 1961 which it used throughout the Vietnam War. It converted from the 'Scooter' to the A-4M, moving to Cherry Point again in 1977, and then converted to the Harrier.

VMA-231 'Ace of Spades': began life as the 1st Division, Squadron 1 of the Northern Bombing Group of France in 1918. In 1973 the oldest Marine Corps Squadron took on the newest aircraft when it converted to the Harrier and VMA-231 was in the thick of the action during Desert Storm.

VMA-331 The Bumblebees': originally commissioned at Cherry Point in 1943 as Marine Scout Bomber Squadron-331, flying the Douglas Dauntless. Decommissioned after World War II, it flew Hellcats, Corsairs and Skyraiders following reactivation for the Korean War. The following years saw the introduction of the A-4E and the A-4M , and the unit moved to Beaufort in 1975 before returning to Cherry Point on the Harrier; it was the first unit to receive the Harrier II. As part of the post-Cold War reductions the Squadron was de-activated after the Gulf War.

VMA-513 'The Flying Nightmares': first commissioned at Oak Grove flying the Hellcat in 1944, moving on to the Corsair later that year. Following World War II, it operated the Skyknight, and was credited with the first ever night radar kill during the Korean War. It returned to El Toro with the Skyray and was redesignated VMFA-513 with the arrival of the F-4 Phantom, which it flew in combat operations over Vietnam. It received the Harrier in 1971, moving to MCAS Yuma.

Marine Corps Trainer: Harrier TAV-8A

To assist in the training of US Marine Corps Harrier pilots, the service placed an order with BAe for eight two-seater trainers to carry the designation TAV-8A (BAe Harrier Mk.54). For reasons of funding, these were delayed until the order for the last batch of AV-8As had been placed. A direct derivative of the RAF's T.Mk.4, the TAV-8A was fitted with the Pegasus 103 engine, and its equipment was appropriate to the specification applied to the 'Baseline' attack system of the AV-8A, together with the same Stencel ejection seats, mechanical, electrical and weapons-carrying modifications, as well as a full set of tactical VHF and UHF radios which had independent control from the rear seat.

The TAV-8A was demonstrated aboard the USS *Franklin D. Roosevelt* in 1976. However it spent its entire working life land-based , operating solely with VMAT-203 at MCAS Cherry Point, where the aircraft first began its training role in 1975. As a development of the AV-8A, the

engine, wing, centre fuselage, horizontal tailfins, rudder and landing gear were common to both types. The second crew member was accommodated by moving the front cockpit forward 47in and inserting a second station behind it. Both cockpits had dual flight controls, with those in the rear seat (the instructor's) overriding those of the front seat (the student's). The handling characteristics were similar to those of the AV-8A, and all phases of the training envelope could be explored and monitored from the rear seat, with flight information being projected on to the instructor's HUD.

Camouflage

The TAV-8A carried the dark sea grey, FS 36118, dark green, FS 34079, disruptive upper surfaces, and gull grey, FS 36440, undersides in a colour scheme familiar to the AV-8A, as well as the RAF's GR.1/3 and T.4. The white 'KD' tailcode was stylized on the tailfin, and full-colour 'stars and bars' were worn on the intakes, and upper and lower wings. VMAT-203 letter-

ing was also in white, as were the two-digit nose numbers, with the 'Marines' legends on the tailfin and wings being in black. At some point the rudders were painted with red, white and blue stripes, with the tip of the tailboom being bright red.

'Interim Upgrade': US Marines AV-8C

During the prototype development phase of the YAV-8B, it was discovered that the original AV-8A's lift could be increased with the minimal amount of difficulty, thereby improving the aircraft's abilities until the Harrier II programme was brought to squadron service. It was from an intriguingly titled USMC report *Operation Frosty Nozzle* that it came about. From an operational exercise entitled 'Palm Tree 2-77', in which the AV-8As were tasked with 'fire support in a high threat SAM and communications scenario', it was noted the Harrier lacked any ECM equipment, and had no RHWR and no secure voice radios.

A TAV-8A from VMAT-203 awaits its next 'customer'. Denis J. Calvert

The CILOP (Conversion In Lieu Of Procurement) programme was therefore initiated to give the AV-8A more of a fighting chance. As it turned out, the upgrading was significant event, leading to a new designation the AV-8C. The programme incorporated all the improvements that had already been already included in the previous AV-8A production batch, consisting of formation lights, CCIP, modification to the HUD, improvements to the hydraulic systems and the addition of a Stencel SIIIS.3 ejector seat. Added to this was a KY-28-TSEC secure voice radio set, together with an ARC-159 UHF, ALE-39 chaff and flare launchers, ALR-45F/45F antennae patterns, ALR-45F/APR-43 RHWR, updated later to ALR-67 (with its antennas located on the wingtips and tailboom), an ALQ-126 DECM pod, on board oxygen generating system (OBOGS) in place of the LOX (liquid oxygen) system, a 12kVA electrical system, attitude director indicator, horizontal situation indicator, outrigger wheel fork, yaw autostab actuator, ASN-116 AHRS and I/WAC.

In addition to this were the lift improvement devices (LIDs), which consisted of strakes attached to the Aden gunpods and a retractable 'fence' that could be extended between the front portion of the pods. With the airbrake lowered and landing gear extended, this formed a 'box' to trap air, thus enhancing the engine's lift in the ground-effect regime and reducing exhaust ingestion back into the engine. To complement the additions to the airframe, there were also notable deletions. These included the removal of the ram air turbine (RAT), the detachable strakes, the fire extinguisher system, ARC-150 UHF radio, sound recorder, ID-1329X-ADI, ID-1013A-HSI, standby sight and nose oblique camera. The net result of the programme was a far more capable Harrier, for the addition of only 197lb weight. The modifications were introduced in a three-phase sequence, which was set to convert all of the AV-8As. However, only forty-seven eventually received the CILOP fit, owing to a continuing high attrition rate and the introduction of the Harrier II.

McDonnell Douglas tested the modification 'kits' on two AV-8As, 158384 and 158387, with a further airframe 158706 being used as a demonstrator for the final operational fit. The work was undertaken by the Naval Air Rework Facility, located at Cherry Point. The first aircraft to appear as an AV-8C was 158384, which flew on a development basis on 5 May 1979, and featured a spectacular red, white and blue paint scheme. Trials took place aboard the USS *Saipan* in October, but unfortunately the aircraft was lost in a non-fatal accident during further tests from the USS *Tarawa*. The main recipient of the 'C' model was VMA-513, the 'Flying Nightmares' at Yuma, which began receiving the aircraft in 1983, and VMA-542, the 'Flying Tigers' at Cherry Point in 1984. VMA-513 was an entirely converted AV-8C unit when it retired the aircraft for the Harrier II in 1987, whereas VMA-542 operated its aircraft alongside the 'A' model until converting to the AV-8B in 1986.

YAV-8C Harrier Colour Scheme: the prototype colour scheme was overall white with red stripes on the fin, tailplane and atop the fuselage. Fuselage stripes were blue with a red outline, with red intake lips and wingtips. The engine access panel lines were grey and all lettering was in black as was the anti-glare panel above the nose.

(Above) **AV-8C being readied for flight; note the faired-over F.95 camera port in the nose, one of the distinguishing features of the 'C'.** Denis J. Calvert

A NASA AV-8C at the Ames Research Center; of note is the all-white with blue stripe scheme, the LID dam behind the nosewheel and the lack of the spine-mounted VHF aerial. Rolls-Royce

NASA AV-8C Colour Scheme: NASA-719 wore an all-over white scheme with medium blue stripes along the fuselage and strakes. The 'NASA' logo is red, with black fin number and anti-glare panel. It was also 'zapped' on the intake; the legend reads 'Thank GOD I'm BRITISH', in black and red.

Typical AV-8C Operational Scheme: Harrier No.159370 in service with VMA-542, the 'Flying Tigers' carries a three-tone scheme of dark green, FS 34064, and dark grey, FS 36099, disruptive upper surfaces, and gull grey, FS 36440, lower surfaces. All other markings are in black.

CHAPTER FOUR

From the Arctic to Belize

Snow Birds: Harriers in the Arctic

As part of their duties as a key element of the NATO RF(Air) [Reaction Force (Air)], No.1 (F) Squadron from RAF Wittering is tasked with providing support to NATO's ground troops in Norway. To provide additional security for their aircraft against the Arctic scenery they began the tradition of applying a unique winter camouflage scheme in order to make them less visible.

The first generation of Harriers, GR.1/GR.3, wearing the 'standard' RAF paint, and where the green extended to undersurfaces the white covered these areas as well. The 1988 exercise *Snow Falcon* was a good example of the GR.3s' operations in the snowy wastes. Arriving on 5 February, No.1(F) Squadron was greeted by temperatures of –25°C, yet,

Seen in the UK before deployment to Norway in 1988: a winter Harrier GR.3 from No.1 Squadron taxis out to Wittering's main runway. Author

Northern Flank, and accordingly deploys its aircraft to Norway for winter training exercises. As early as September 1970, only weeks from the Squadron's being declared operational, a detachment of six Harrier GR.1s exercised with ACE Mobile Force camouflage scheme of dark green, medium sea grey and, before the adoption of the grey/green wrap-around style, light aircraft grey, the green (not the grey, as other sources have stated) was overpainted with a water-based, soluble, white despite the extreme cold, the unit maintained an excellent 95 per cent availability rate, flying over seventy-five sorties. The pilots revelled in the opportunity to fly at low-level, down narrow twisting valleys, hugging the terrain for cover.

With the introduction of the second generation of Harriers, the GR.5 and latterly the GR.7, once again it was necessary to deploy these assets to the north, not only to continue with the development of the aircraft as a weapons system but also as part of the annual reinforcement exercises, to provided a strong, visible deterrent and give credence to the GR.5/7's ability to match and exceed the older GR.3 in all theatres of conflict. It was November 1989 when No.1(F) Squadron first took four of its new GR.5s to Norway for a brief work-up with the Royal Norwegian Air Force at their Bardufoss base near Tromsø, 150 miles inside the Arctic circle. Four months later, on 8 March 1990 they returned to Bardufoss to take part in the NATO exercise *Cold Winter*, bringing a total of eight

Harrier GR.5s and a single two-seater T.4 borrowed from No.233 OCU.

The aircraft operated from snow- and ice-packed sites, and in all their serviceability was reported as being excellent. Six of the GR.5s were painted in a new variation of the winter camouflage scheme, while the other two and the two-seater carried their normal schemes. On the GR.5 there is no two-colour disruptive pattern such as was found on the GR.3, so the white over-wash was applied to form a mottled effect on the top, side and undernose surfaces, with at least one aircraft having the pattern applied to its wing undersides. Most of the six had the white paint applied with a 'hard' edge, although one aircraft was noted to have some areas sprayed with soft edges. The scheme was intended to

Two Harrier GR.3s take on fuel from an RAF VC.10 tanker en route to winter training exercises in Norway. BAe

Arctic Schemed GR.5: Exercise Cold Winter 1990	
ZD350/05	white camouflage applied to tail only
ZD355/01	white camouflage applied to undersides of wings and pylons
ZD400/02	
ZD403/08	
ZD404/07	white paint noted as streaked along the intakes
ZD409/06	white camouflage had soft edges

(Above) **ZD403/08 emerges from a HAS at Bardufoss; despite the harsh conditions GR.5 and GR.7 both performed very well, pilots reported take-offs to be 'sporty'!** BAe

A rather grubby looking GR.3 taxis out for a Norwegian sortie; note in the background the Arctic-camouflaged two-seater. Denis J. Calvert

A Harrier GR.7 pilot and ground crewman run through final checks before an Arctic sortie.
BAe

break up the outline of the aircraft and make use of the local terrain and peculiar Arctic light to make the aircraft more difficult to see. However, no matter how attractive it made the aircraft look, the scheme was less successful than that applied to the GR.3. Although it blended well against the multicoloured, snow-covered landscape, the aircraft were easy to detect when they moved over a plain, dark area of ground or headed out across the sea.

The scheme was therefore short lived, and deployments since that time have featured the standard camouflage green/grey scheme; however, it should be noted that the newer medium-level, two-tone greys seem to work admirably against the Norwegian backdrop. The Harrier GR.7s gradually became involved in winter exercises, with a Boscombe Down-based Strike Attack OEU GR.7 being deployed to Bardufoss for cold weather evaluation, and, taking advantage of the NATO exercise *Teamwork '92*, to hone its skills further. At this time it shared the ramp with VMA-

331's AV-8As which used the base as a forward refuelling and rearming centre.

For the purposes of *Cold Winter 1990*, the Harrier GR.5s of No.1(F) squadron carried 350-gallon fuel tanks, two Sidewinder AAMs and empty 25mm Aden gun pods, with a single Phimatt chaff dispenser being housed on the starboard outer pylon.

No.1(F)'s Harrier GR.7s began their Norwegian visits in the mid 1990s and continue to carry out valuable work guarding NATO's frozen north.

Combat Zone #1: Crisis Management in Belize

A crisis in the former colony of British Honduras, now Belize, in Central America, led to the Harriers' first 'out of area' deployment. As a response to Guatemala's threatened invasion, a garrison of 1,000 British troops, was dispatched, supported by six Harrier GR.1As from No.1(F) Squadron.

The aircraft flew out from RAF Wittering on 5 November 1975 under the codename Operation *Nucha*, being air-refuelled by Victor tanker and making two stop-overs en route before taking up station at the Belize International Airport. The detachment was, however, short lived and in April 1976 the aircraft were dismantled and returned to the UK by RAF Belfast, having lost one of their number XV788 on 1 December 1975 through a bird strike, its pilot Flt Lt Scott ejecting successfully. During the latter part of 1975 the detachment Harriers were all given names; one of these has since regrettably been forgotten, however, XV795/05 gained the name 'The Intruder' on its tail. Another sported the logo 'Hod Carrier' (later retained on GR.3 XZ971) and yet another of the GR.1As, XV787/02, acquired the title 'Hot to Trot' just below the windshield. The logo itself was painted on to a 2ft-square panel in a bright shade of red, applied with the paint used to add the tail code. An interesting note is that the Harriers arrived in Belize wearing their standard UK design of

XZ996/F carrying the name of the first and last CO of
1417 Flight seen on patrol over Belize. BAe

The 'Hot to Trot' logo applied to XV787/02.
Colin Watson via IPMS Harrier SIG

green/grey topsides and light grey undersides; but XV787/02 received a locally applied grey/green wrap-around scheme.

July 1977 saw a return to tension across the Belize border, and as a result four Harrier GR.3s were again flown out under the aegis of the 'Strike Command Det', and were piloted and maintained by personnel drawn from the three operational squadrons, to be manned subsequently on a three-months rotational basis, with No.233 OCU also taking a turn in March 1978. The need to maintain a more formal presence was accepted, and in March 1981 1417 Flight was created to operate the four aircraft, carrying a white 'sailfish' motif in a red circle flanked by red and blue bars beneath the cockpits. The Harriers were tasked with air defence, reconnaissance and close air support, and most had received the Phase 6 modifications which enabled them to carry AIM-9G Sidewinder AAMs, along with the more usual bombs, Aden cannons and SNEB rocket pods. Conditions were hot and humid, the aircraft operating from two hide sites on either side of the main airport runway. Operations were conducted from air-conditioned Portakabins, before more permanent buildings were erected in 1986.

No.1417 Flight continued its tasking until its eventual withdrawal in July 1993, when it had the honour of being the RAF's last operational GR.3 unit. With the introduction of the GR.5 to squadron service, a small pool of GR.3 pilots was kept current by the Harrier OCU, until the decision to withdraw the GR.3s was made in February 1993. Three of the four aircraft, ZD667/C, ZD670/F and XZ971/G (as already noted, suitably marked with the 'hod carrier' logo on its fin) were led home by the first, and coincidentally, the last CO of 1417 Flight, Sqn Ldr John Finlayson, returned to Wittering on 8 July 1993; the fourth aircraft ZD669 remained in Belize as a gate guard.

To show that Belize could be reinforced quickly if need be, four Harrier GR.7s from No.4(AC) Squadron undertook the first RAF detachment there since the withdrawal of the GR.3s. The '4 from IV' flew out from RAF Laarbruch in Germany on 6 September 1993 with VC-10 tanker support, stopping over at Goose Bay in Canada and Key West in Florida. Belize is similar in size to Wales and an excellent low-flying area, with few restrictions. The jungle, however, is an unwelcoming sight to any ejectee, who would more than likely have

Close-in detail of the 'sailfish' emblem applied to the Harriers of 1417 Flight.
f4 Aviation Photobank

to lower himself to the ground using a 'treescape' system carried in his 'g-suit'.

The climate in Belize causes storage problem for weapons, and No.IV Squadron was more than happy to assist in the turnover of stocks in the bomb dump. Live 1,000lb bombs were delivered from both low and high level, and HE SNEB rockets were used on the New River Lagoon and Seven Hills weapons ranges, the targets – painted-up scrap vehicles, or at least the ones that had not been stolen by the locals – took a severe pounding. The brief detachment ended on 7 October.

CHAPTER FIVE

Sea Harrier

Jack Tar's New SHARs: Sea Harrier FRS.1

The Fleet Air Arm surely reached its lowest ebb when it launched its last fixed-wing aircraft, a Phantom FG.1 from HMS *Ark Royal*'s catapult on 27 November 1978. This followed the then Labour government's decision to end the Navy's fixed-wing capability, having already cancelled the P.1154RN and a new carrier destined to replace *Ark Royal*. The decision-makers settled instead for helicopter-based 'commando carriers' or 'through-deck cruisers' (more commonly known as 'see-through cruisers' as they were so obviously designed with the Harrier in mind). The first of these ships was ordered from Vickers in April 1973, to be named HMS *Invincible*, with a second, *Illustrious*,being laid down by Swan Hunter in June 1976. Both were fitted with Harrier 'ski-ramps' in the light of successful shore-based trials; these are dealt with below.

The Harrier had been flying off ships since the early 1960s; Bill Bedford had 'cushioned' P.1127 XP831 on to the *Ark*'s deck on 8 February 1963 while she anchored off Lyme Bay, and the Kestrel had undertaken deck trails from HMS *Bulwark* in 1966, ably demonstrating that VSTOL could be used as a 'stand-alone' force or integrated with other assets. Land-based Harriers were operated from the Navy's carriers in the following years, GR.1s completing trials aboard HMS *Eagle* as well as *Ark Royal*, and the 'Crabs' of No.1(F) Squadron (Navy-speak for anyone not wearing blue) received their service clearance to operate from decks in 1970, a clear pointer to the future.

During 1971 a Naval Air Staff requirement was developed for a seagoing aircraft based on the RAF's Harrier GR.3 and Hawker Siddeley were given a contract to study and develop a suitable design. There were two major hurdles for the HSA team to overcome in order to meet the Navy's requirements. First, as the aircraft's primary role was to be that of air defence, it had

to be fitted with radar and, secondly, it was necessary to replace components in the GR.3's make-up that would be prone to salt-water corrosion. Additionally one of the Navy's stipulations was that the aircraft should be able to carry two Sea Eagle missiles. One of the P.1127(RAF) airframes, XV277, was modified as a trials aircraft to show that the Harrier could carry such a weapon. It was decided that XV277 should fire a Martel ASM as a demonstration, and the aircraft gained a new nose section (similar in shape to that of the future Harrier II Plus) as a mock-up of what a seagoing Harrier might look like. Following a successful study, an order for twenty-four 'Sea Harrier FRS.1s' was announced in May 1975, and the need for four two-seat trainers was also established. A subsequent order followed in 1982 for seven attrition replacements, and a further order was forthcoming in 1984 for another nine. The 'FRS' designation stood for Fighter, Reconnaissance and Strike, the last referring to the aircraft's ability to carry nuclear weapons or nuclear depth charges should the need ever arise.

To save costs, the Sea Harrier was to be what was later frequently referred to as a

'minimum change' derivative of the GR.3. However, the FRS.1 introduced a number of new and key features. First the cockpit floor was raised by 10in to provide more equipment space thus allowing, for the first time in a Harrier, some semblance of a decent downward view over the massive intakes. This revision was further enhanced with the fitting of a 'bubble' canopy, which gave a better all-round view as well. The radar was a miniature masterpiece called Blue Fox, developed by Ferranti, and a version of their ARI.5979 Sea Spray set already in service and fitted to the Navy's Lynx helicopter fleet. This I-band pulse modulated set was designed for air-to-air interception and air-to-surface search and strike with ground-mapping abilities; this was fitted into a pointed radome that folded sideways for space saving aboard the carriers. To avoid the problems of setting up the inertial platform on a moving deck, the FE.541 INS was replaced by a twin gyro platform and a Decca 72 Doppler, giving a very small navigational error after a typical 50-min sortie. In the cockpit a new Smiths Industries HUD was fitted, driven by a 20,000-word digital computer; as well as displaying its symbology it also served as a weapon aiming computer (WAC) for air-to-air and air-to-surface deliveries. Tie-down lugs were fitted to the mainwheels and outriggers, and an enhanced water injection system to aid carrier recovery was added. The ejector seat was replaced by a Martin-Baker Mk.10 and a revised RWR was also fitted, as was a radio altimeter and starboard F.95 oblique camera in the nose; the moving map display of the GR.3 was deleted. Because of its primary role, the Sea Harrier was fitted out to carry Sidewinder AAMs on LAU-7A/5 launch rails on the outer pylons and retained the Aden cannons on their underfuselage stations. The engine was a Pegasus Mk.104, an especially developed and 'navalized' version of the Mk.103, eliminating the major magnesium components and having a similarly rated thrust as the Mk.103 at 21,500lb.

Specification – Sea Harrier FRS.1/FRS.51	
ENGINE	One 21,500lb (9,800kg) Rolls-Royce Pegasus 104 turbofan.
WEIGHTS	Empty 14,000lb (6,400kg); loaded 26,200lb (11,900kg).
DIMENSIONS	Span 25ft 3in (7.65m); length 47ft 7in (14.42m).
PERFORMANCE	Max level speed at sea level: 638kts (1,180km/h); climb to 40,000ft (12,000m): 2min 23sec; combat radius, STO with 3,000lb of stores: 250nm (460km); ceiling: 51,000ft (15,500m).
ARMAMENT	2x30mm Aden cannon, Sidewinder AAMs, Sea Eagle ASMs, bombs, CBUs, RN rockets.

ZA450 the first Sea Harrier FRS.1 to fly takes off from Dunsfold in 1980; this particular aircraft was lost in the Falklands, having been pressed into service from its development flying programme. Hilary Calvert

The first production Sea Harrier FRS.1, XZ450, took its maiden flight from Dunsfold on 20 August 1978 with test pilot John Farley at the controls, and within two weeks it was ready to make a spectacular debut at the Farnborough Airshow. Three development aircraft came a little later, XZ438 on 30 December 1978, XZ439 on 30 March 1979 and XZ440 on 6 June 1979. The first Sea Harrier handed over to the Royal Navy was XZ451, which was delivered to RNAS Yeovilton on 18 June 1979. The first unit to form on the new aircraft was No.700A Intensive Flying Trials Unit (IFTU) during May 1979, in anticipation of the arrival of their first aircraft. At its zenith, 700A operated five Sea Harriers, and developed the operational techniques required for safe VSTOL operations at sea, embarking aboard HMS Hermes in October of that year. In March 1980, 700A disbanded to become No.899 Squadron, the Headquarters and Training Unit for all naval Sea Har-

riers and their pilots. The 899 Squadron 'Mailed Fist' emblem, which had last adorned their Sea Vixens, was reinstated on the Harriers' tails and their camouflage scheme of extra dark sea grey and white was firmly re-established in the Navy's tradition.

HMS Invincible was commissioned in 1980, but to accommodate the shortfall of available carriers from which to operate the new Sea Harriers, HMS Hermes went through a refit programme in 1979–80, adding a 12-degree ski-jump to her bow in order to fill the gap created by HMS Illustrious's not being available until 1982.

Plans were laid to equip three front-line squadrons, Nos 800, 801 and 802, each having five Sea Harriers, and a Harrier OCU. In the event, only Nos 800 and 801 were commissioned. However, No.809 Squadron saw a brief return to duty during the Falklands conflict. In April 1980 the first front-line unit was commissioned, No.800 Squadron, under Lt Cdr Tim Gedge, with

its extremely flamboyant tail markings of a red arrowhead, edged in white on which a gold trident with crossed swords was placed. These smart adornments were short-lived. Meanwhile, 899's aircraft had made the first ski-jump launches at sea in November 1980, and 800 Squadron embarked on HMS Invincible in January 1981. The Squadron did sterling work in developing the Sea Harrier's tactics, and on 16 June 1981 Invincible was declared 'operationally ready'. Her first cruise, which included an Operational Readiness Inspection, took place later in June, and by this time the second of the Sea Harrier Squadrons, No.801, had been commissioned with Lt Cdr 'Sharkey' Ward at the helm. 801, with its traditional 'Winged Trident' motif in a white disc on the tail, was the embarked squadron for Invincible's deployment. During the second half of 1981 she took part in Ocean Venture and Ocean Safari, followed by Alloy Express in early 1982.

XZ499/255 on the Yeovilton ramp during July 1982, resplendent in its light grey scheme; the higher canopy gave the Sea Harrier much better visibility.
Denis J. Calvert

XZ489/001 from 800 NAS on the deck of HMS Ark Royal. Denis J. Calvert

Ski-Jumping

A study which evolved from an idea by a Naval officer, Lt Cdr D.R. Taylor, was undertaken at Southampton University in 1972. This was to have a great impact on the Sea Harrier's ability to carry a heavier load direct from the ship, thus increasing its effectiveness. He showed that an appreciable advantage could be gained by launching a VSTOL aircraft from a flat deck with an upward inclined ramp at the end. RAE Bedford undertook to try out the theory, building an adjustable, scaffolded ramp, and between August 1977 and June 1978 tested it at inclinations varying from 6 to 20 degrees, with Bill Bedford making the first 'leap' in XV281, followed by the two-seater XW175. The idea was that the pilot would start a 90ft run, and the ramp would impart a ballistic trajectory to the aircraft, while the pilot would select 35 degrees down nozzle to arrest the aircraft's sink rate as the 'white line' at the end of the ramp passed the edge of his peripheral vision, before he gradually moved the lever aft as the aircraft achieved wingborne flight. The gear came up as the aircraft reached 220 kts pulling 12 degrees AOA (angle of attack): a simple yet devastating answer to a big VSTOL headache. Thus for any Harrier take-off weight, the launch speed could be about 25 kts or less than from a flat deck. This also then translates into a 50 per cent shorter take-off run, or more importantly 30 per cent more fuel or weapons can be carried. So conclusive and impressive were the test results that the Navy took the decision to incorporate a ski-jump on the Invincible class carriers, where for reasons of self defence (mainly due to the position of the forward Sea Dart launchers) they were initially set at 7 degrees, but during *Hermes*'s refit her ramp was set at what was considered to be the optimum, 12. The ramps were later revised to a 12-degrees fit on *Ark Royal*, *Invincible* and *Illustrious*.

Looking 'down the line' as a Sea Harrier FRS.1 makes an impressive ski-jump. f4 Aviation Photobank

Ski-jump. BAe

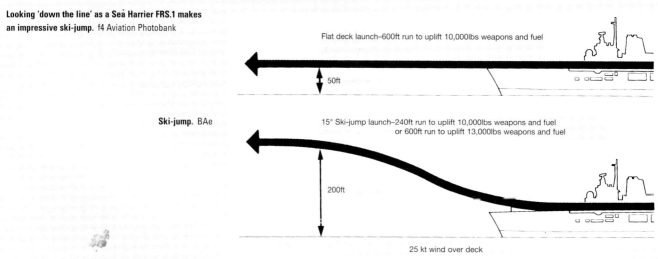

Flat deck launch–600ft run to uplift 10,000lbs weapons and fuel

50ft

15° Ski-jump launch–240ft run to uplift 10,000lbs weapons and fuel
or 600ft run to uplift 13,000lbs weapons and fuel

200ft

25 kt wind over deck

Her refit and sea trials over, HMS *Hermes* embarked No.800 Squadron as her first air group with five Sea Harriers. The intention had been for the Royal Navy to have two operational carriers, commissioning *Ark Royal* in 1985, selling Invincible to the Australian Navy (on the understanding that it would go hand-in-hand three *Invincible* class carriers, finally selling *Hermes* to the Indian Navy, with the Australian deal falling by the wayside. So, currently the Royal Navy continues to fulfil its NATO requirements in having two carriers at sea and one in 'maintenance'.

The arrival of the BAe Sea Eagle missile added another string to the Sea Harrier's 1982. One of the more interesting events after the war was on 7 March 1983, with the unscheduled landing by ZA176 from No.801 Squadron on the freighter *Alraigo* after the pilot Lt Ian Watson became separated from his carrier by a NAVHARS failure and ran short of fuel. Pilot and aircraft survived and after repair ZA176 was

A crowded scene as deck crews prepare to launch Sea Harrier FRS.1s from No.800 Squadron.
Neil 'Joe' Mercer

with an order for Sea Harriers) and retiring *Hermes*. To this end, the third planned Fleet Air Arm Harrier squadron was never formed. However, the Falklands war brought with it substantial changes, and as a direct consequence the Navy retained its bow. This anti-shipping, sea-skimming missile, of which two would be the normal warload, led to an intense period of work for the pilots but one which made the aircraft a very competent and flexible weapons platform that proved its worth in returned to service, being later converted to F/A-2 standard. Some notable losses were of ZD609 which made an unfortunate wheels-up landing at the 1986 NAS Pensacola Airshow; ZA191 which hit *Ark Royal*'s mast during a fly-past in 1989; and

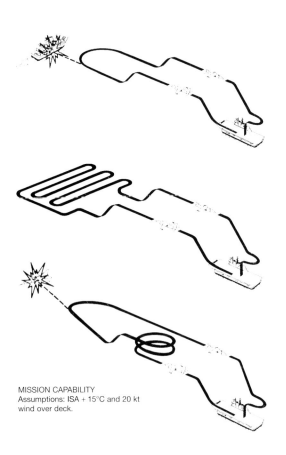

MISSION CAPABILITY
Assumptions: ISA + 15°C and 20 kt wind over deck.

Mission Surface Strike

Profile Li-Lo-Hi

Warload 2 × 30mm Aden guns
2 × air-to-surface missiles

Mission Reconnaissance and Probe

Warload 2 × 30mm Aden guns
2 × 190 Imp gal (860 litre) drop tanks

Mission Air Defence

Warload 2 × 30mm Aden guns
2 × AIM9L Sidewinder air-to-air missiles
2 × 190 Imp gal (860 litre) drop tanks

SURFACE STRIKE

Radius of action to low-level missile launch 210nm (390mkm) with two 30mm Aden guns and two Sea Eagle air-to-surface missiles.

RECONNAISSANCE AND PROBE

Medium/high level – radius of action 560nm (1,040km).

Low level – 28,000nm² (96,000km²) covered in 1¾ hours, with two 190 Imp gal (860 litre) drop tanks

AIR DEFENCE

Endurance 1¾ hours on combat air patrol at 100nm (185km) with two 30mm Aden guns, two Sidewinder air-to-air missiles and two 190 Imp gal (860 litre) drop tanks.

Mission capability. BAe

(Opposite) **The Blue Fox radar was a masterpiece of compact design in fitting such a versatile set into such a small space.** Neil 'Joe' Mercer

Armament BAe

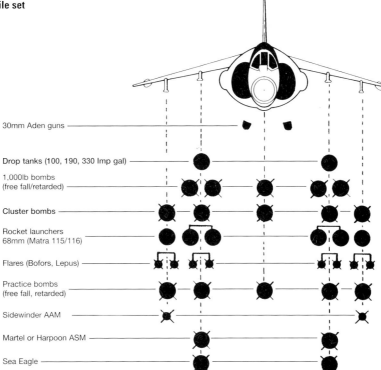

30mm Aden guns

Drop tanks (100, 190, 330 Imp gal)

1,000lb bombs (free fall/retarded)

Cluster bombs

Rocket launchers 68mm (Matra 115/116)

Flares (Bofors, Lepus)

Practice bombs (free fall, retarded)

Sidewinder AAM

Martel or Harpoon ASM

Sea Eagle

Mk 83 LDGP free fall
Mk 82 Snakeye retarded 500lb
Mk 81 Snakeye retarded 250lb
Mk 81 LDGP free fall 250lb
Mk 82 LDGP free fall
LAU-69A rocket launcher
LAU-10A rocket launcher
LAU-68A rocket launcher
Mk 77 firebomb
APAM cluster/Mk 7 dispenser
Rockeye II cluster/Mk 7 dispenser
PMBR practice bomb rack.

(Below) **Sea Harrier FRS.1 '38' replaced XZ450 '40' lost in the Falklands, and continued the latter's development programme; seen here carrying a pair of Sea Eagle missiles.** BAe

AIM-9L/M Sidewinder Missile

Third-generation AAM introduced in 1976; the warhead is a sheathing of preformed steel rods triggered by a Hughes DSU-15B active optical proximity fuse which incorporates a ring of eight gallium arsenide laser-diode emitters and one of silicon photodiode receivers to provide better manoeuvring and better detonation. The AIM-9M improved on this platform with a better smokeless motor, better seeker sensitivity and greater resistance to countermeasures.

Sidewinder missiles ready to be loaded. Author

XZ499 which tore off an outrigger wheel during a launch off the coast of Australia.

In the period following the Falklands War the aircraft all visited the paint shop to emerge in a Fleet-wide scheme of dark sea grey, BS.381C:638. Other shades were also tried, but it would be difficult to note all the various marking and colour permutations of the Sea Harriers in this period. Roundels also became more standardized at this time at 18in equal red and blue applied to the intakes and above and below the wings; also featured was a solid black 899 Squadron winged fist motif. The Squadron badges became much less colourful, being universally plain and black. Variations did occur, however: 801, for example, went from plain Squadron trident; to plain trident with wings; to plain trident with black chequerboards added to the rudder; to slightly more colourful trident with wings and black and white chequerboards.

Squadron Histories

800 Squadron: motto: *Nunquam non paratus*, 'Never unprepared'; formed on the Osprey and Nimrod biplanes; during World War II flew Sea Skuas in a bombing raid on the Königsberg. Operated Hellcats and took part in the Tirpitz raid; flew Seafires in Malaysia, and became the first FAA jet Squadron with the Sea Hawk FGA.1, progressing through the Scimitar and Buccaneer before disbandment in 1972; reformed with the Sea Harrier in 1980, and took part in both the Falklands and Bosnia campaigns; trident with crossed swords emblem.

801 Squadron: motto: *On les aura*: 'We'll get them'; formed at Netheravon on the Fairy Flycatcher and Nimrod, seeing service with HMS *Furious* and later flying Sea Gladiators; post-war flew the Sea Hornet and Sea Hawk; after the Aden operation took on charge the Buccaneer; disbanded in 1970 to be reformed eleven years later on the Sea Harrier, deploying to the Falklands aboard HMS *Invincible*; winged trident and chequerboard emblem.

899 Squadron: motto: 'Strike and defend'; formed at Hatston in 1942 with the Seafire IIC, and embarked aboard HMS *Indomitable* in 1943; disbanded after the Suez crisis, it was back in action with the Sea Vixen FAW 1 and 2 as the Headquarters and Training Squadron, making occasional deployments to sea before disbandment again; reformed as 700A Squadron and regained its full status as an HQ and training unit for the Sea Harrier FRS.1 and F/A-2, with an interlude in the South Atlantic; mailed fist emblem.

fast jet route, finally ending at Wittering for conversion to the Harrier. After that they were posted to No.899 Squadron, the Sea Harrier Operational Flying Training Unit (SHOFTU) at RNAS Yeovilton for the dedicated SHAR training phase. The RAF-based T.4 trainer 'owned' by the Navy, XZ445, first flew on 12 March 1979 and joined the HOCU at Wittering on 2

with the avionics of the single-seat FRS.1, making pilot conversion and training much easier. These aircraft carried the 'navalized' Pegasus Mk.104 engine and were painted in all-over extra dark sea grey, each sporting a black 'false radome' to add a similarity to the Sea Harrier FRS.1, a feature that also distinguished them from the T.4A. All carried the 899 Squadron's mailed fist emblem on

The 'full set': No.899 Squadron display the complete Sea Harrier FRS.1 training programme aircraft; nearest the camera is XW266/719, a T.4N, then a Hunter T.8N, XL603/724, used for Blue Fox radar training, and finally Sea Harrier FRS.1, ZE890/711. Neil 'Joe' Mercer

Royal Navy T.4N

Following the original order for twenty-four Sea Harrier FRS.1s in 1975, the follow-on order increased this figure to thirty-four single-seaters, adding one T.4A for initial VSTOL training at RAF Wittering and a further three T.4Ns (N for Navy) to acquaint pilots with the Sea Harrier's avionics; these last were based at RNAS Yeovilton. Initial Harrier pilot training for the Fleet Air Arm flyers began with the students going through the standard RAF

May, as its contribution to the Harrier training syllabus. This 'dual base' situation continued until 1989 when the Royal Navy's *ab initio* training was passed fully to No.899 Squadron, which then had its three T.4Ns on strength, together with the temporary loan of an RAF T.4, XW927, and also received a further two ex-RAF T.4As in 1989.

To duplicate the Sea Harrier's cockpit and systems, less the radar, the three Harrier T.4Ns serial numbers ZB604, ZB605 and ZB606 had their front cockpits outfitted

their tails in black, with all codes and markings also being in black and with full-colour red and blue roundels. One of their number ZB606 was written off in a crash near Yeovilton in 1985, and was replaced by T.4A XZ445 from Wittering, which was painted up for delivery in a semi-matt medium grey scheme with pale pink and pale blue roundels and pale pink warning, access and fire-panel markings. Another T.4N, XW268, also crashed in the Yeovilton area in June 1994 and XZ455 met a sad end over the Blackdown Hills on 21 February 1996,

(Above) **More or less the same as the RAF's trainers, the glossy grey scheme suits the T.4 well; note the MDC chords on the canopies.** Author

(Below)**XL603/724 in EDSG finish with full-colour tail marking; the Hunters played a vital role in the training of the SHAR pilots.** Steve Gensler

killing both crew. T.4N XW266 was withdrawn from service in November 1995 and then used for spares. The T.4Ns lacked radar, and rather than develop a radar-equipped aircraft, a trio of Hunter T.8s were converted to serve as radar trainers, being fitted with the full Blue Fox avionics of the Sea Harrier FRS.1. The T.8s XL580 and XL602 had been previously used in the development of Blue Fox. Students spent about 28 hrs flying the T.4A, 8 hrs 10 min with the T.8M, 11 hrs 15 min aboard the T.4N, and 72 hrs 10 min in the Sea Harrier FRS.1. The remaining T.4Ns have now been converted to the latest T.8 standard.

CHAPTER SIX

War Birds: The Falklands

Combat Zone #2

It hardly seems conceivable that in 1982 a small group of subsonic, relatively lightly armed aircraft could operate thousands of miles from home in a hostile environment and play a major role in recapturing a group of invaded islands without losing a single one in aerial combat. Such was the feat of the UK Harrier Force dispatched to the South Atlantic to retake that small and relatively unknown British outpost, the Falkland Islands. Within a few weeks the campaign catapulted the Sea Harrier FRS.1 and the RAF Harrier GR.3 into the world's headlines and the aircraft quickly ceased to be regarded as British novelties and undoubtedly became two of the most flexible and capable fighting machines

ever devised. The word 'Harrier' seemed to be recognized everywhere and most notably it became etched into the minds of the Argentinians, for whom it had taken on a whole new meaning: *La Muerta Negra* – the Black Death.

When Argentina invaded the Falkland Islands on 2 April 1982, the Royal Navy had just thirty-one of its latest (and still under development) acquisition, the Sea Harrier FRS.1 on strength, with seven in storage and four engaged in trials work. By contrast, Argentina had around 180 combat aircraft, which were calculated to outnumber the British contingent by a ratio of 10:1. The RAF, on the other hand, had been operating the land-based versions of the Harrier, the GR.1 and then the GR.3, for some ten years, but it had yet to use them in anger.

Sea Harriers

A Task Force was assembled under the aegis of Operation *Corporate* to recapture the Islands, and included in the flotilla of warships were the two carriers HMS *Hermes*, the flagship, and (on the verge of being sold to Australia) HMS *Invincible*, both of which embarked Harrier Air Groups. When the Task Force sailed on 14 April it took with it twenty Sea Harrier FRS.1s drawn from the two operational units, Nos.800 and 801 Squadrons, and the shore-based training establishment, No.899 Squadron. HMS *Hermes* carried twelve FRS.1s from No.800 Squadron, commanded by Lt Cdr Andy Auld, augmented by pilots from No.899 Squadron, including their CO, Lt Cdr Neil Thomas.

Aboard HMS Hermes **XZ497/27 is readied for a CAP launch; the aircraft, with Lt Cdr Mike Blissett is credited with despatching an A-4C with a 'winder' and damaging a second with gunfire.** FAA Museum

HMS Hermes *initial Air Group*:
XZ450/50 (first Sea Harrier to fly; then undertaking Sea Eagle trials), XZ455/12, XZ457/14, XZ459/25, XZ460/26, XZ492/23, XZ494/16, XZ496/27, XZ500/30, ZA191/18, ZA192/92 (taken out of attrition storage at St.Athan), ZA193/93 (taken out of attrition storage at St.Athan).

HMS *Invincible* sailed with six FRS.1s embarked, to be joined by a further two as she sailed down the English Channel; these aircraft were from No.801 Squadron, led by Lt Cdr Nigel 'Sharkey' Ward, again augmented by No.899 Squadron.

HMS Invincible *initial Air Group*:
XZ451/006, XZ452/007, XZ453/009, XZ458/008, XZ493/001, XZ459/003, XZ498/005, ZA175/004.

Additionally a further Sea Harrier unit was hastily formed, bringing together all the airframes that remained in the UK, except for four that were to stay at RNAS Yeovilton for training purposes.

Harriers that remained in the UK:
XZ440, XZ438 (crashed testing long-range tanks), XZ439 and XZ497.

This new unit saw the reformation of No.809 Squadron under the leadership of Lt Cdr Gedge; it took its eight aircraft to the South Atlantic aboard the container ship *Atlantic Conveyor*. On arrival four of the aircraft joined HMS *Hermes*'s Air Group: XZ499/99, ZA176/76, ZA177/77 and ZA194/94; and four joined HMS *Illustrious*'s Air Group: XZ458/007, XZ491/002, ZA174/000 and ZA190/009.

As they left the UK the aircraft of Nos. 800, 801 and 899 Squadrons all wore the 'standard' scheme of the day, dark sea grey upper surfaces and white lower surfaces, with full-colour unit markings and national insignia. *En route* the on-board paint shops worked overtime to produce an all-over, single-colour finish, which gave each aircraft initially deployed on the two carriers a 'war paint' camouflage of glossy extra dark sea grey, with toned down red and blue type 'B' roundels and black code numbers. All of the unit markings were obliterated as were the Royal Navy legends; the only visible markings were those for the emergency escape systems.

No.801's aircraft were all resprayed at Dunsfold in a much lighter (and as it turned out far more visible) scheme of medium sea grey upper surfaces and barley grey under the wings and tailplanes. They also wore a pale pink and pale blue phoenix badge on their tails, pale blue Royal Navy tiles on the tailfin (these were overpainted on reaching the war zone), and pale pink and pale blue roundels on the forward fuselage and wings. The first six aircraft flew out from the UK on 30 April, refuelled by Victor tanker to Ascension Island. This small British outpost was the only 'friendly' base in the area and

Returning from a CAP sortie to HMS Invincible; **the hot gas from the rear nozzle of the lead aircraft ZA495/003 contrasts with the sea, while ZA175/004, the aircraft used by 'Sharkey' Ward to down a Dagger waits its turn to come aboard.** FAA Museum

One of 809 Squadron's Sea Harriers (the Phoenix barely visible on the tail) aboard HMS Hermes, **a shot that typifies the conditions; the aircraft is credited with damaging an A-4B and strafing the** Rio Iguazu. BAe

roughly halfway between the UK and the Falklands Two more aircraft followed on 3 May. The aircraft then embarked aboard *Atlantic Conveyor* which took them on the final leg to meet up with the Task Force. One Sea Harrier was kept on alert, fully fuelled and armed on a purpose-built landing pad at the prow of the ship, in case it was necessary to provide air defence.

The Sea Harriers received several modifications for their war role; the attack system was altered to allow for loft bombing from an IP (initial point) offset, and to permit blind delivery against ground targets. The aircraft were also cleared for higher take-off weights using the larger 330 gallon ferry tanks. Some aircraft also received a Tracor AN/ALE-40 chaff/flare dispenser fit behind the airbrake. Those not so fortunate rammed as much chaff into the airbrake well as possible, allowing for a 'one-shot' dump; smaller amounts of chaff were liberally stuffed between weapon and pylon

on the wings and centreline. The Harriers had an intensive work-up on their way south, making live firings against towed targets and Lepus flares.

'First contact' by the Task Force with Argentine aircraft was made on 21 April when XZ460 from 801 Squadron flown by Lt Simon Hargreaves was dispatched to 'Hack the Shad' – a FAA 707-320B surveillance aircraft, known colloquially as 'The Burglar'. It was not fired upon, but it was made known through diplomatic channels that other incursions into the Task Force's zone would lead to a more aggressive response. Once within the Falklands area the Task Force set up a TEZ (Total Exclusion Zone) around the islands and prepared to use whatever means were necessary to enforce it.

The air war began on the 1 May with a night-time 'Black Buck' bombing raid by an RAF Vulcan. This was followed by a dawn strike against Port Stanley airfield by nine

800 Squadron aircraft, eight each armed with three BL.755 CBUs and one with three 1,000lb bombs, and a three-ship attack on Goose Green, ably supported by nine air-defence configured Harriers from 801 Squadron. ZA192, flown by Flt Lt Dave Morgan, took a shell hit in the tailfin, which was quickly repaired once it was back on the carrier. No aircraft had been lost in the attack, much to the relief of the commanders, who had expected to lose at least three. The Sea Harriers took up CAP (combat air patrol) stations, flying at 15,000ft where the performance of the Mirage would be degraded if it engaged in air combat. Flt Lt Paul Barton and Lt Cdr John Eyton-Jones were soon vectored to intercept two 'bandits' detected by one of the radar piquet ships. The Mirages seemed reluctant to come down from their 34,500ft altitude, as they obviously wanted to tempt the Sea Harriers into a high altitude fight, but the experienced SHAR pilots would have none of it.

Eventually fuel became critical and the enemy turned away. Later that afternoon Lt Cdr Sharkey Ward, and Lt Mike Watson from No.801 Squadron were vectored to intercept three Beech T-34C Turbo-Mentors who were about to make an attack on the British warships. The Argentine aircraft soon departed for the protection of the Port Stanley defences on catching sight of the Sea Harriers. Returning to their CAP station, they were again vectored to another threat; Ward thought that he had spotted contrails from Argentinian aircraft and tried to lock up one of his Sidewinders; however, they turned out to be smoke trails from missiles fired at them, the attack was ineffective and Ward reported seeing one of the missiles fall harmlessly into the sea.

Wild Weasel GR.3?

It was reported, that following the *Black Buck* Shrike raids, a GR.3 was modified to carry a pair of the American anti-radar missiles, and a modification kit was flown out to HMS *Hermes*. A single GR.3 'Wild Weasel' modification had been completed just as the war ended.

9L while flying in XZ455, followed shortly afterwards by Lt Al Curtiss from 801 Squadron dispatching one of three Canberra bombers from Grupo 2. For their air defence role the Sea Harriers were armed with two AIM-9 'Lima' Sidewinders, two wing tanks and twin 30mm Aden cannons.

killed. Two SHARS also attacked and disabled the trawler *Narwal* with bombs and cannon fire. On 21 May the Task Force went ashore at San Carlos, which provoked the Argentinians into a concerted attack pattern. However the Sea Harriers were more than a match for them. Lt Cdr Ward started the most successful day for the SHARs, destroying a Grupo 3 Pucara with 30mm cannon fire, while flying XZ451, and 800 Squadron's Lt Cdr Mike Blissitt in XZ496 and Lt Cdr Neil Thomas in XZ492 each downed an A-4Q Skyhawk and Rod Fredriksen took out a Dagger from Grupo 6. These were followed in short order by a further two Daggers from the same unit dispatched by 801 Squadron's Steve Thomas in ZA190 and a third by Sharkey Ward in

Ships under fire from Argentine aircraft in 'bomb alley'. BAe

The first air to air kill of the war fell to Flt Lt Paul Barton of 801 Squadron flying XZ452. Barton splashed a Mirage III from Grupo 8, which 'exploded in a brilliant blue fireball' and a few minutes later his wingman Flt Lt Steve Thomas in XZ453 damaged another Mirage, which attempted an emergency landing at Port Stanley only to be shot down by very nervous AAA gunners, a classic 'own goal'. Barton was later quoted as saying 'The Argentinians were good "stick and rudder men" but their tactics were awful, I don't think the leader realized he was under attack until I had fireballed his wingman.' The third kill of the day was that of a Dagger from Grupo 6, 'shredded' by Flt Lt Bertie Penfold's AIM-

May also saw the first Sea Harrier loss of the conflict when Lt Nick Taylor, flying XZ450, was making a low-level attack on Goose Green. Radar-directed Oerlikon AAA fire reportedly hit his wing tank, totally destroying the aircraft.

This loss led to a rethinking of tactics, and from that point the Sea Harriers would no longer overfly heavily defended targets and their operations would be in the height range 18,000–20,000ft, making wings level bomb deliveries or 'toss bombing' from outside the Argentine defensive envelope. The Sea Harrier Force was also dealt a double blow when 801 Squadron's Lt Cdr Eyton-Jones in XZ452 and Lt Curtiss in XZ453 collided in thick fog, both pilots being

ZA175. For good measure, Lt Clive Morrell caused an A-4Q from 3 Escuadrilla to break in half and severely damaged a second with cannon fire while flying XZ457; his wingman, Flt Lt John Leeming, 'cannonized' a third, bringing the day's total to an impressive ten for no losses.

The Force lost a further two Sea Harriers in non-combat accidents: Lt Cdr Gordon Batt of 800 Squadron was killed when ZA192 exploded and hit the water following a night launch, and on 29 May Lt Cdr Mike Broadwater's ZA174 slid off *Invincible*'s deck, Broadwater ejecting safely.

'Bomb-alley', as San Carlos water had become known, continued to come under Argentine air attack, but 23 May brought more successes: Rod Fredriksen and Martin Hale strafed and beached the patrol vessel *Rio Iguazú*, and 800 Squadron's Dave Morgan in ZA192 and John Leeming in ZA191 attacked and destroyed an A109 helicopter on the ground with cannon fire and spiralled a Puma into the dirt in their wake. A second Puma was damaged by Morgan and was subsequently finished off by Tim Gedge of 801 Squadron, flying ZA494 and ably assisted by Lt Cdr Dave Braithwaite in ZA190. Later in the day Lt Hale from 800 Squadron shot down a Dagger from Grupo 6 in ZA194, and on 24 May Lt Cdr Andy Auld in XZ457 took out two more Daggers, while his wingman Dave Morgan in ZA193 hit a third. The Argentine night-time Hercules resupply effort was a constant irritation to the Task Force, so it was with some pleasure that in daylight on 1 June Sharkey Ward shot down a C-130E, with two Sidewinders and 200 rounds of cannon fire, prising off the aircraft's wing and sending it tumbling into the sea. Later that same day Flt Lt Ian Mortimer in XZ456 was hit by a Roland SAM; Mortimer ejected to be picked up by a No.820 Squadron Sea King.

By 5 June 'HMS *Sheathbill*', an 850ft aluminium-planked, refuelling strip had been laid near San Carlos, making life a little easier for the combined Harrier Force. The final air engagements of the war took place on 8 June, when Dave Morgan, flying ZA177, shot down two A-4Bs from Grupo 5, and Lt Dave Smith in XZ499 got a third. Despite the Sea Harriers' success in air combat, the work they undertook before the arrival of the RAF's GR.3s in providing reconnaissance and in bombing operations should not go unreported.

Aircraft began to sport 'kill markings' in the shape of either black or white silhouettes of Dagger/Mirages, Pucaras or Skyhawks. Examples are XZ457, 'Black 14', with two Mirages and one Pucara credited; ZA177 with two Mirages credited; and ZA194 with one Dagger. After the war, the 809 Squadron Sea Harriers deployed to HMS *Illustrious* between August and December; all sported names in small back script below their canopies, although it seems that only 'Ethel' painted on XZ499/255 survived once back in the UK.

A Harrier GR.3 makes a run in to deliver a brace of BL.755 cluster bombs on to an Argentine position. BAe

The results of an attack on Goose Green: Argentine Pucaras that were most definitely out of the war. BAe

Other 'names' were still just discernible, having been through the official 'censor'; one example was XZ459/256, which bore the name 'Emmanuelle' with a small heart. Also of note was the short-lived practice of stencilling the names of the deck crews on the nosewheel doors and the last digit of the aircraft's code inside the rear face of the airbrake.

RAF Harrier GR.3s

The decision to deploy RAF Harriers to the Falklands was taken in order to bolster the small number of Sea Harriers, since attrition replacement was thought to be a high priority early in the campaign and there were more GR.3s available than the very small number of 'irreplaceable' FRS.1s, and give the former an air-defence role, a task which had always been part of US Marine Corps Harrier doctrine. Following trials, the air-defence scenario was

certainly feasible with the GR.3, and the fitting of outboard wing pylons to carry Sidewinder launch rails was quickly undertaken. The AIM-9G version of the AAM, Tracor AN/ALE-40 chaff/flare dispensers were also made available, some twenty being at hand by mid May. The aircraft were also fitted with a transponder to enhance their appearance on the carriers' radar, which resulted in a pronounced bulge beneath the aircraft's LRMTS. Operations were also greatly assisted by Ferranti's invention and swift delivery of their FINRAE (Ferranti Inertial Rapid Alignment Equipment) system, which allowed for the fast setting up of the aircraft's INS platform on a rolling and pitching deck. Extra drain holes were placed to aid the clearing of salt water from the airframe, and tie down lugs were added to the outrigger and main wheels. In all fourteen late production models were eventually prepared for deployment; the aircraft all retained their grey/green wrap-around

camouflage schemes, with the squadron insignia overpainted, although the yellow outrigger numbers remained. Roundels and fin flashes were retained on some aircraft and overpainted on others.

No.1(F) Squadron received the call that they were to deploy aircraft to the Falklands on 8 April, and Wg Cdr Peter Squire set about finding the best airframes fitted with the most powerful engines. Eventually six were found with No.1 Squadron with six from Nos.3 and 4 Squadrons and 233 OCU. Crash courses in ski-jump techniques were taken at RNAS Yeovilton, three 'jumps' per pilot were scheduled but in the event just one proved sufficient, and clearance trials were undertaken with Navy 2in rocket pods and 1,000lb Paveway LGBs (laser-guided bombs). Subsequently nine Harrier GR.3s left RAF St Mawgan on 3, 4 and 5 May (although one turned back with mechanical trouble) and with Victor tanker support flew the 4,260 miles to Ascension Island. Two of their number remained on the

Sea Harriers and GR.3s being prepared for a launch from HMS Hermes. BAe

A crowded deck scene aboard HMS Hermes, **with both SHARs and 'Muds' being readied.** BAe

Island to provide air defence; the other six boarded the *Atlantic Conveyor* on 6 May, shielded from the elements by two rows of containers at the edges of the deck and wrapped in temporary Driclad plastic covers. They joined the Sea Harriers already embarked for the trip. Four other GR.3s made the flight to Ascension, with two making the final 3,529-mile hop direct to HMS *Hermes* arriving on 1 June. A second pair made the trip out to *Hermes* on the 8th, arriving in the middle of an air raid. The six GR.3s aboard *Atlantic Conveyor* transferred over to *Hermes* on 18 May .

As the Sea Harrier losses were much lower than had been expected, the GR.3s did not have to use their new-found 'interceptor' abilities, and discarded their Sidewinder launch rails in favour of their customary 'mud-moving equipment', thus releasing the Sea Harriers for their practised air defence role. The first Harrier GR.3 attack took place in the afternoon of 20 May, when a three-ship formation led by Wg Cdr Squire dropped BL.755 CBUs on an Argentine fuel dump just outside Fox Bay. Next day a group of GR.3s attacked and destroyed a number of aircraft on the ground near Mount Kent. On that day there was also the first GR.3 casualty, when Flt Lt Jeff Glover, flying XZ972 in a reconnaissance run, was hit by a Blowpipe SAM near Port Howard. Glover ejected and was taken prisoner. On 21 May Flt Lt John Rochefort returned to *Hermes*

from a sortie in XZ997, still fully armed, and landed his aircraft with the port outrigger over the edge of the deck, making it lurch over and coming to rest on one of its weapons. No serious damage occurred and the aircraft was soon back in the air. Further GR.3 losses occurred when on the 27th Sqn Ldr Bob Iveson, flying XZ988, was hit by Skyguard-directed AAA fire while attacking Goose Green. He ejected, managed to evade capture, and was picked up two days later by a Royal Marines helicopter. Flt Lt Peter Harris and Flt Lt Tony Harper eventually silenced the Goose Green guns with BL.755 CBUs; they were followed by Jerry Pook who launched sixty 2in RPs (rocket projectiles) into the 'nest'. On the 30th Flt Lt Pook, flying XZ963, took hits from small arms while attacking a gun position at Mount Harriet. Pook tried to nurse his stricken aircraft back to the carrier but was forced to eject, being picked up by a Sea King helicopter.

Once a beachhead had been established at San Carlos, and 'HMS *Sheathbill*' had been instituted, the Harriers became regular customers for fuel and weapons. Two much needed replacement Harriers arrived during the first days of June, followed by two more on the 8th. The latter, XW919 and XZ992 had 'Blue Eric' ECM jammers and Tracor AN/ALE-40 chaff and flare dispensers fitted. The 'Blue Eric' jammer was modified Skyshadow ECM equipment fitted into one of the two Aden

cannon pods. These new fits, however, did not prevent XW919 and its pilot Flt Lt Murdo McLeod from sustaining small arms hits on 12 June, causing a fire on recovery and effectively ending the career of one of the replacement aircraft. During the final days of the conflict the GR.3s flew daily attack missions in support of the advancing troops.

The final GR.3 to be 'lost' was XZ989, flown by Peter Squire, which suffered a power loss on returning to the matted landing site; his aircraft hit the ground rather hard, irretrievably damaging it. The final attacks of the war were made with Paveway LGBs, which had been unsuccessfully tried in the preceding days owing to a lack of suitable designation from the ground. This time, however, the targets were well 'illuminated' by ground-based FACs. Wg Cdr Squire scored a direct hit on a company HQ on Mount Tumbledown with one of his two Paveways on 13 June, and later Jerry Pook was able to place an LGB direct into a gun emplacement. The final attack on the 14th was to be flown by Sqn Ldr Peter Harris against the Argentine HQ on Sapper Hill, but this was called off within moments of its planned delivery, when white flags suddenly appeared from the Argentine positions. At the end the statistics were impressive: twenty-three Argentine aircraft confirmed as kills in the air, plus three other 'probables', and fifteen destroyed on the ground. No aircraft was lost in aerial combat.

Sea Harriers from No.809 Squadron and Harrier GR.3s from No.1 Squadron seen on the deck of the Atlantic Conveyor at Ascension Island; they would soon be wrapped in their protective coverings, save for one, which would occupy the 'alert' station on the currently empty landing pad on the prow. BAe

After the Surrender

When the hostilities ceased, the GR.3s were quickly re-roled back to air defence and given two Sidewinders as a safeguard. Two Sea Harriers nominally from No.809 Squadron aboard HMS *Invincible* went ashore to Port Stanley to provide day and night, all-weather air defence until October when the airfield had been extended and modified to host the Phantoms from No.29 Squadron. It interesting to note that the two Sea Harriers were now armed with four AIM-9 Sidewinder missiles, two on each wing pylon, and carried enlarged combat wing tanks. Reborn on the tail was again the 809 'Phoenix' emblem with all other markings being in black. The main shore-based defence was established on 26 June and was provided by four Harrier GR.3s from HMS *Hermes*, and four 'fresh legs' brought south on board the container ship *Contender Bezant*, which also served as the floating HQ for the officers and men. The shore-based element was initially referred to as the RAF Stanley 'HarDet', its GR.3s now armed with the combat-proved AIM-9L Sidewinder, and on 20 August 1983 it was officially redesignated 1453 Flight, complete with a shield motif on the nose and a single-letter tailcode. It was manned on rotation by all the Harrier Squadrons, including 233 OCU, before being eventually disbanded with the opening of Mount Pleasant airfield on 12 May 1985. HMS *Hermes* left the Falklands on 4 July, and HMS *Illustrious* later came on station to relieve HMS *Invincible*. On its return to the UK, No.809 Squadron stood down and was disbanded again on 17 December 1982 – a short rebirth, but a job well done.

(Right) One outcome of the conflict was the addition of twin Sidewinder missiles to the Sea Harrier's outer pylons. Author

CHAPTER SEVEN

Harriers for Sale

'El' E/AV-8S: the Spanish 'Matador'

As a maritime nation, with a mainland bordered by two oceans and having a number of major islands to protect, it was considered a natural progression that Spain should decide to operate a credible aircraft carrier force. Its first carrier, the *Dédalo* (RS01) was a purchase from the USA,

being the former World War II escort carrier *Cabot*, which was transferred to Spain in 1967, and tasked as being solely an ASW platform, equipped with the SH-3 Sea King helicopter. In October 1972 Hawker's Chief Test Pilot John Farley made an impressive series of demonstrations with the British Harrier from the deck of the *Dédalo* while it was operating in the Mediterranean. The undoubted success

of the US Marine Corps LPH and LPD assault carriers, which were successfully operating the AV-8A, led the Spanish government in 1973 to approve the purchase of two TAV-8A two-seat trainers and an initial batch of six single-seat AV-8As under the designation AV-8S, and the local designation VA.1 (single-seat) and VAE.1 (two-seat) Matador, these being almost identical with their US counterparts.

Undergoing maintenance at the Rota naval base, three AV8-S Matadors in varying states of repair; note that 01-809 is minus its nose cone. BAe

Due to the prevailing political climate at the time, the six aircraft were built by BAe at Kingston and shipped to the United States as part of the USMC's Harrier purchase and from where the initial aircrew conversion was to take place. One of their number – AV-8S 008-5 – was lost during a formation take-off incident in the United States. The initial batch of ten pilots, all of whom had prior helicopter experience, went through VMAT-203at Cherry Point in 1976, after which they and their aircraft boarded the *Dédalo* and formed *Escuadrilla 008* at Mayport in Florida on 29 September 1976, before returning to their home port of Rota near Cadiz in early 1977. Two USMC pilots stayed with the embryo squadron, helping it to achieve IOC (initial operational capability) in March 1977. Also in 1977, a further batch of five AV-8Ss were ordered and delivered direct to Spain from Dunsfold. A second group of Harrier pilots, this time without rotary experience, began transition at Cherry Point before transferring to RAF Wittering to complete their training. Following that interim programme, aircrew training moved to Rota in Spain. For normal operations *Dédalo* carried up to six Matadors and its usual complement of ASW helicopters. *Escuadrilla 008* had the honour of being the first Harrier unit to operate the aircraft regularly at sea.

The *Dédalo*, with its wooden deck, narrow beam, limited flightdeck and amidships metal landing pad, continued in service until June 1989 and was the replaced by the *Príncipe de Asturias* (R11), laid down at the Empressa Nacional Bazan shipyard in 1977, launched in May 1982 and commissioned in May 1988. Better able to handle the Harrier and equipped with a 12-degree ski-jump, as well as carrying a full array of sensors, command and control facilities and armed with the point defence Meroka 20mm gun system, she received her first complement of Harriers in late1988. The vessel was able to carry a twenty-strong air group, which included the ability to operate both the AV-8S and the new EAV-8B variants, four of each type being carried as normal (up to twelve EAV-8Bs could be accommodated alongside the AV-8S), as well as the usual Sea King helicopter element. The complement of EAV-8Bs was increased to six during the carrier's participation in *Deny Flight* operations in 1994. One of the biggest advantages of the new carrier was its ability simultaneously to launch and

recover aircraft, something the *Dèdalo* was unable to achieve.

The Armada has always enjoyed a close relationship with the US Marine Corps, and regularly undertook exercises with them, a collaboration which began in 1981 with cross-decking operations during exercise *Ocean Safari 81*. With the arrival of the US Marine Corps AV-8B Harrier II, the Spanish military could see the advantages of the second-generation aircraft, and as a result ordered twelve EAV-8Bs (Matador II) in March 1983 and formed *Escuadrilla 009* to operate the new aircraft in 1987. The first three aircraft were delivered direct to Rota from McDonnell Douglas on 6 October 1987, with the final ones being delivered in September 1988. The service also took delivery of a Celeas-built EAV-8B simulator during April 1987. Work-up began on the *Príncipe de Asturias* during 1989, and by the mid 1990s it had become the centrepiece of Spain's carrier battle group, alongside four *Santa Maria* class frigates. During June 1988 the Armada pilots had deployed to RNAS Yeovilton to undertake ski-jump training, and BAe test pilots Steve Thomas and Heinz Frick made ski-jumps from the *Príncipe de Asturias*'s deck, clearing the way for the Spanish operators.

One of the most important factors for the future of the Spanish Navy and its fixed-wing component was the addition of a radar-equipped aircraft not only to provide better air cover and offensive capabilities but to make use of the new carrier's night-operating facilities. In 1993 Spain awarded McDonnell Douglas a $257 million contract to supply eight FLIR- and radar-equipped EAV-8B Harrier II Plus aircraft, the first being delivered in January 1996, with the final assembly being contracted to the Spanish aerospace company CASA. Spain plans to have her remaining eleven EAV-8Bs remanufactured to the II Plus standard. The remaining original AV-8S aircraft have since been retired, and because of their relatively low airframe hours they have been sold as a package to Thailand. Training on the EAV-8 II Plus's radar- and night-attack systems began at Rota in 1995.

The final flight of *Escuadrilla 008* took place on 21 October 1996 in 01-808, a two-seat TAV-8B (callsign 'Phoenix') on an instrument-rating sortie. The unit was officially decommissioned on 24 October 1996, having logged over 24,244 hrs with its original Harriers. The same day that the

remaining seven AV-8S and two TAV8-S aircraft were transferred to the Thai Navy, *Escuadrilla 008*'s final nucleus of seven pilots moved to *Escuadrilla 009*.

AV-8S

Almost identical to the US Marine Corps' AV-8A with Baseline nav/attack kits, the AV-8S differed only in the fitting of radios to conform to Spanish Navy standards. The aircraft delivered to the Navy were painted in standard high gloss USMC light gull grey, FS 16440, topsides and white undersides, with a hard demarcation line. Markings were full-colour, as were the large yellow and red roundels. Aircraft numbers were carried on the intakes, with the last one or two digits repeated on the tailfin with the black 'Armada' legend being clearly applied to the rear fuselage and the wings, top and bottom (the original aircraft carried the legend 'Marina'; this was changed on the second batch and retro-painted on the others). With their primary role being that of air defence, the aircraft were from the outset armed with two AIM-9 (P and L) Sidewinder AAMs and two standard 30mm Aden cannons. The secondary mission was that of supporting the Spanish Marines, and therefore the Matador was capable of carrying the full range of American conventional weapons, including 500 and 1,000lb high and low drag bombs, CBUs and 2.5in Zuni rockets. Upgrades to the aircraft have included the addition of formation flying lights, a new CCIP weapons computer and the Marconi Skyguard radar homing and warning system. TAV-8S 01-808 was given the nickname 'The Shark' because of its appearance, and in keeping with that received a colourful set of 'fangs'.

Escuadrilla 008 AV-8S losses

008-2 10 June 1976: crashed on take-off from Whiteman AFB; the pilot Lt Trujillo ejected safely.

008-4 28 May 1980: crashed into sea near Caberra operating from *Dèdalo*; the pilot Lt Jaurergui killed.

01-810 13 May 1994: crashed into sea after technical failure operating from *Príncipe de Asturias*; the pilot ejected.

01-812 30 June 1986: engine failure at Rota; the pilot ejected.

An AV8-S in its gull grey and white colours. BAe

EAV-8B

The 'E' designation on the aircraft refers to 'Espana', and its duties are similar to those of the AV8-S. Painted in a low-visibility, two-tone finish of matt light grey, FS 36495, and matt pale grey, FS 36622, with a soft demarcation line, the 'Armada' markings of FS 36375, now on the nose as well as on the tailfin, have become almost invisible, as have the caution and warning marks, changes made in an effort to tone down the aircraft's appearance; however, the national insignia remain full-colour. The aircraft carry the full range of American-built weaponry and countermeasures, including AIM-9M AAMs and the GAU-12 Gatling gun, as well as DECS-equipped engines.

EAV-8 Harrier II Plus

Like the EAV-8 before it, the II Plus is exactly the same as its American counterpart and carries the same camouflage scheme as the standard EAV-8. It is fitted with the APG-65 radar, which the Spanish military already have extensive experience in operating as it is virtually the same set as is fitted to their EF-18 Hornets. It also has the more powerful Pegasus 11-52 engine, making it a highly capable seaborne fighter. Prospective Harrier II Plus pilots were posted to *Escuadrilla* 152 at Zaragoza from September 1994 to gain experience with the radar system.

Sea Harriers for the Indian Navy

The Indian Navy currently operates two aircraft carriers, the INS *Vikrant* (formerly HMS *Hercules*) and the INS *Viraat* (the

(Above) **With a rather worn-looking camouflage scheme, symptomatic of the combination of low-visibility grey paintwork and the effects of sea water, an EAV8-S recovers to a vertical landing following a training sortie from its home base of Rota.** BAe

The high tech 'office' of the Spanish Harrier II Plus. Salvador Mafe Huretas

former Falklands flagship HMS *Hermes*); the former was commissioned in 1961 and the latter in 1987. With the *Vikrant* due for decommission in the late 1990s, its replacement is still under consideration. In the early 1970s the Sea Hawk FGA.6s then in service were fast approaching the end of their lives and efforts were being made to identify potential replacements. Studies

began between Britain and India for the purchase of a number of the aircraft; these eventually led to an initial order for six Sea Harrier FRS.51s and two two-seat Harrier T.60s trainers on 29 November 1979.

The first batch of personnel headed for the UK in September 1980 to form the Sea Harrier Project Team (SHARP) at BAe Kingston. The first pilots arrived in April

course, to be managed by the newly formed IN Training Unit.

The first Indian Navy Sea Harrier, coded IN601 arrived on 27 January 1983, and, by using a mixture of aircraft, including IN601, G-VTOL, an RAF T.4 and a Hunter T.8, the training continued apace. Deck landings were made on HMS *Hermes* and RAF Canberras provided the 'targets' for use with

A quartet of FRS.51s in close formation on a 'pre-delivery'sortie. BAe

were made of the A-4 Skyhawk and the Super Etendard. However, the Indian Navy had always maintained a liking for the British Harrier, having had Hawker Siddeley's two-seat demonstrator G-VTOL operating from the *Vikrant* in July 1972. With the ordering of the Sea Harrier FRS.1 for the Royal Navy, serious negotiations

1982 at RAF Brawdy in South Wales for a brief familiarization course before being dispatched to RAF Wittering and No.233 OCU for basic conversion to the Harrier. Following this the pilots moved to Dunsfold before going to what was to be their main base, RNAS Yeovilton, for the Sea Harrier operational flying training

the Blue Fox radar. By November 1983 the first flying course had been completed and with IN603, IN604 and IN605 ready for delivery to India, pilots Lt Cdr Taylor Scott, RN, Cdr Arun Prakash and Lt Cdr Sanjay Gupta made the 5,000 mile trip via Luqa, Luxor and Dubai to arrive at Goa on 16 December 1983. The first two Sea Harriers

A near-plan view of an Indian FRS.51. BAe

IN601 and IN602 remained at Yeovilton for the second Indian training course. To facilitate the arrival of the Harriers, Indian Naval Squadron 300, the 'White Tigers' was reformed at INS *Hansa*.

The first T.60, IN651, arrived at Goa on 29 March 1984 and the first fully Indian conducted training course started in July 1984. With the arrival in India of IN602 and IN606, the 'White Tigers' were declared operational. A Singer Link-Miles mission simulator was installed in March 1984 at INS *Hansa*, and the eighth and last Sea Harrier FRS.51, IN652, arrived at Goa on 18 April.

The Indian government ordered a further ten Sea Harrier FRS.51s and a single T.60 on 25 November 1985, followed by another batch of seven FRS.51s and

another T.60 on 9 October 1986, bringing the total Sea Harrier complement to twenty-seven. A further batch of twenty-one Harriers, seventeen single-seaters and four two-seaters were delivered between 1989 and 1992. The SHOFTU began regular flying courses at INS *Hansa* in April 1990.

The Indian Navy Sea Harriers are basically the same as the Royal Navy's FRS.1s apart from their LOX system being replaced by an on-board oxygen generating system (OBOGS). Matra R550 Magic AAMs were acquired as the standard missile because of an embargo placed by the US government on the AIM-9 Sidewinder. Other changes included alterations to the to the IFF and the radar systems, together with pressure reductions to the water injection system. The T.60s were, similarly,

essentially naval T.4N trainers equipped with the Pegasus Mk.103 engine and cockpit revisions to suit the FRS.51. Additional armament for the FRS.51s also included the BAe Sea Eagle missile.

By the middle of the 1990s the Indian Navy began to explore ways of giving its Harriers a mid-life update (MLU), and possibly replacing the Blue Fox radars with

---

Matra R.550 Magic missile

Developed in 1968 as a competitor to the AIM-9 Sidewinder, this has a genuine all-aspect ratio, a digital autopilot and an active proximity fuse. It carries a 27.6lb warhead and is powered by a SNPE Romeo single-stage, solid-propellant rocket motor. The missile is 9ft 1in long; 6.18in in diameter, and weighs 198lb.

Coming into the hover, IN617/17; note the Hindi for 'Navy' on the tailfin. BAe

Showing off its original colour scheme and markings, while his wingman banks away. BAe

the latest set fitted to the Royal Navy's Sea Harrier F/A.2s, the excellent Blue Vixen. However, the lengthy and costly overruns that affected the Royal Navy's Sea Harrier update, together with the Indian Navy's not being cleared to use some hardware and software (such as the Sidewinder and the AIM-120 AMRAAM missile) led to another player entering the picture – Israel Aircraft Industries (IAI), which is reportedly working in conjunction with BAe to provide a low-cost upgrade package for the Indian Navy.

This is understood to include the Elta Electronics ELM/2032 radar, which will be integrated with the BAe ASRAAM missile project, together with an Elta 8420 EW suite, plus cockpit, structural and other improvements to maintain the aircraft until at least 2010. A further purchase is also possible with the Indians needing to replace two Harrier T.60s lost in accidents. The possibility exists for them to purchase two ex-RAF T.4s which have been delivered to Dunsfold, or a proposed sale of five ex-USMC TAV-8As from the AMARC storage facility.

The Indian Navy Sea Harriers carried the same dark sea grey with white undersides scheme that originally applied to the Royal Navy's aircraft before the Falklands campaign, although it does appear that this scheme has been subtly changed to more of a slate grey colour in recent photographs. The aircraft have roundels on the intake sides and above and below each wing. The 'White Tiger' emblem, originally applied to the tail, has since been moved to the forward fuselage, just behind the radome. The original numerical code numbers on the intake sides have now been changed from three characters to two.

The Italian Navy: Harrier II Plus

The Italian Navy finally entered into the VSTOL business in August 1991, with the arrival of two TAV-8B Harrier IIs. It had been a long road for the service which had been forbidden by law since 1929 from operating fixed-wing aircraft at sea, being allowed to fly only helicopters in Navy colours. As far back as 1967, when the Harrier was demonstrated aboard the *Andrea Doria*, the Italian Navy had expressed an interest in purchasing VSTOL aircraft and in 1983 stated its desire to buy twelve Sea Harriers from the UK but was balked by the legal wrangle. However, the arrival of the Navy's new aircraft carrier the *Giuseppe Garibaldi*, launched on 4 June 1983, signalled the Navy's future hopes, as it was fitted with a 6-degree ski-jump at its bow; explained at the time as being needed to 'protect the flight deck from excessive spray in high sea states'.

After much lobbying, the Italian Parliament passed the law on 1 February 1989 that finally allowed the Navy to rejoin the fixed-wing market, and the MMI chose to purchase the AV-8B Harrier II Plus, with its powerful radar, FLIR, defensive and offensive systems, and the Rolls-Royce Pegasus 11-61 engine. The order was for two TAV-8Bs and sixteen of the uprated Harriers, with an option on eight more aircraft.

Initially the purchase of the two TAV-8Bs (MM55032 and MM55033) was for pilot training based out of MCAS Cherry Point, with trainee pilots converting through VMAT-203 and VMA-233. They made their first deck landings on the *Giuseppe Garibaldi* on 23 August 1991, when the carrier was off the coast of Norfolk, Virginia. The aircraft then formed the basis of The 1st *Gruppo Aerei Imbarcati/Gruppo Aero* (*Grupaer*) at the land base of Grottagile near the *Giuseppe Garibaldi*'s home port of Taranto, being officially handed over on 16 January 1995. The first three of the Harrier II Plus aircraft, MM7199/7200/7201, diverted from the FY91 USMC allocation, arrived at Grottagile on 3 December 1994, and the last of the ordered aircraft was expected to enter service by the end of 1997. The two-seater trainers also received

Seen in 1991 on a pre-delivery sortie, the second of the Italian Navy's TAV-8B Harrier trainers is put through its paces. McDonnell Douglas

An Italian Naval TAV-8B lands on the deck of the Giuseppe Garibaldi; **note the white 'intake' warning markings.** BAe

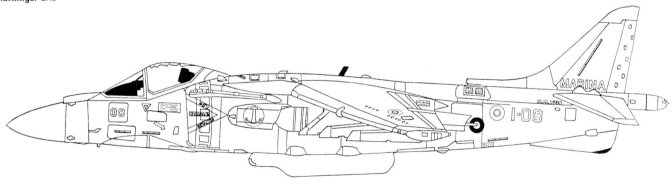

Italian Navy Harrier II Plus I-08. Nils Mathisrud

the uprated F402-RR-408 engine in 1994 to improve their hot weather performance.

The involvement of the US Marine Corps in training the Italian pilots continued, with work taking place on how to 'fly and fight' the new radar-equipped version. Instructor pilots were suitably trained, returning to Italy to bring to bear their training on the aircraft's armament, ground attack, missile firing and air combat capabilities and on carrier operations.

On 18 January 1995 the Giuseppe Garibaldi sailed from Taranto to add its assistance to the United Nations peacekeeping effort in Somalia, and carried with it three Harrier II Plus types from 1 Grupaer along with helicopter support. Together with five US Navy vessels the group were to cover the withdrawal of forces, and the Italian Navy Harriers worked in close concert with their Harrier counterparts from the US Marine Corps, standing on 20 min readiness alert.

Armed with 200 rounds of ammunition in their Equaliser gun pods and their flare ejectors filled, the Italian aircraft flew mostly reconnaissance missions, the pilots using hand-held video camcorders and 35mm still cameras, mapping troop placements with their radar screens and thus providing invaluable intelligence for the operations commanders. The Navy's Harriers had logged 102 sorties by the time the withdrawal from Somalia was completed. The Giuseppe Garibaldi took part in exercise Tridente 95 before making its return to Taranto.

I-02 lets it all hang down as it comes to the hover; the II Plus represents a major step in capability for the Italian Navy: the first three aircraft were assembled in the USA and the remainder of the order by Alenia.
McDonnell Douglas

I-08 waits for its next sortie, with the Italian Alps as backdrop. via Paul J. Perron

The Italian Harriers carry similar grey camouflage colours to those used on the US Marine Corps aircraft, these being FS 595a 36231 topsides and FS 595a 36320 undersides. The TAV-8As have high-visibility white intake warnings and the single-seaters have low-visibility grey. National insignias are in full colour on the upper and lower wings and rear fuselage sides, and the 'Marina' titles, code numbers and letters are in white, their last two digits being repeated on the nose with the naval anchor badge on the intake sides. The single-seater aircraft have begun to receive a 'false canopy' on their undersides, painted in dark grey and designed to confuse an opponent during combat; these have been noted on I-07 and I-08.

Harriers for Thailand

Thailand joined the Harrier 'club' at the end of October 1996, when seven low-hour single- seater AV-8As and a pair of dual-control TAV-8A trainers joined the Royal Thai Navy (RTN). The aircraft were all ex-Spanish Navy AV-8S air-frames, refurbished by CASA in Spain and former residents with *Escuadrilla 008* at Rota, the aircraft being purchased by the Thai government for the express task of patrolling the coastline for pirate vessels.

Navy in March 1997, and was due to take on board her air contingent in the autumn, after the completion of her sea trials. The carrier, which is fitted with a 12-degree ski-jump is similarly styled to the *Príncipe de Asturias*, but weighs 12,284 tonnes rather than the 16,700 of the *Príncipe*, and additionally carries ample living space for the Thai Royal Family.

The initial batch of Thai Navy pilots (their full complement being fifteen air-crew) began their Harrier training at Rota in 1996 following basic aviator courses

changed to 301, and coincidentally adopt-ed the same 'Phoenix' callsign as the air-craft's previous owners in Spain; it is to be shore based at U-Tapao.

The single-seat aircraft have received an all-over colour scheme of medium grey, applied by CASA in Spain; however, the white underside of the original Spanish scheme is still slightly visible, showing through as a 'demarcation' line. The Thai national insigne is carried on the intakes and wings, and the Thai flag with the wording 'Royal Thai Navy' on the tailfin;

Thai Harrier AV-8S 3107/7 (ex-01-809) was the first of the naval aircraft to receive the full marking suite.
Jorge Flethes

The aircraft form No.301 Squadron and are the strike fighter element for the air group aboard the *Príncipe de Asturias* class aircraft carrier the RTNS *Chakri Naruebet*, which was built by the Empressa Nacional Bazan company in Spain. The *Chakri Naruebet* OPC 911 (Offshore Patrol Craft) was officially handed over to the Thai

with the US Navy, with their training courses lasting 100 hrs. The Thai Harrier pilots began their work-up aboard the car-rier during May and June 1997, gaining their initial sea qualifications while the ship sailed the waters of the Gulf of Cadiz. Originally the RTN unit was to have been designated No.105 Squadron, but it was

the Navy title in Thai script is repeated on the rear fuselage. All caution and warning markings are in black, as are the 'jet intake' stripes; the engine access and fire panels have 'no-step' footprints in red with yellow crosses over them. The aircraft carry the designation 'AV-8A' next to their former US BuNo on the extreme lower

Thai Fighters			
Type	Former Armada No.	US BuNo	Thai Navy No.
TAV-8AS	01-807	159563	3101
	01-808	159564	3102
AV-8AS	01-803	159559	3103
	01-804	159560	3104
	01-805	159561	3105
	01-806	159562	3106
	01-809	161174	3107
	01-811	161176	3108
	01-814	161178	3109

portion of the rear fuselage. Interestingly, the Harriers have been given a black 'false radome' which bears more than a passing similarity to that of the Sea Harrier FRS.1. The first two aircraft to receive the new paint scheme were 3107 and 3109, with the others quickly following suit.

The two-seaters retain their former Spanish colours of gull grey and white, with the Thai markings applied as for the single-seater, apart from the absence of intake warning stripes and the original red engine access and fire panel marks; the tip of the tailboom is painted bright orange. Several redundant AV-8A/C airframes are reported to have been purchased from the United States' 'AMARC' facility for spares, along with three spare Pegasus engines and a large stock of equipment from Spain.

One of the duo of TAV-8S two-seaters, still in its original Spanish scheme but now with Thai markings. Jorge Flethes

The Nearly Machines: Harriers for Sale?

Despite the Falklands campaign, the Gulf War and the advent of the far superior Harrier II Plus, VSTOL export sales have been disappointing to say the least. Hawker Siddeley did all that it could to promote the Harrier in its early guises, sending its company-developed G-VTOL (see Chapter 1) on many export drives. Possibly it was felt that in the 1960s and the 1970s the whole concept was perhaps premature, or perhaps it was simply viewed as only a novelty. France was a distinct possibility, despite their setbacks with the Balzac project. G-VTOL was demonstrated on the French carrier Foch in 1973 to no immediate avail, although the French did consider leasing Sea Harriers to bridge the gap between the Crusaders' retirement and the arrival of the Rafale.

West Germany may have been a possibility too; however, its withdrawal from the Tri-Partite unit and the generous support of the United States in offering bargain-priced, conventional aircraft as a sweetener for the use of German bases proved too good to reject. Switzerland, an operator of British aircraft since 1946, seemed another likely customer, but despite sending along Harrier GR.1 XV472 coded G-VSTO to allow for Swiss military rulings and a calendar full of demonstrations, the government chose the American F-5 Tiger. Argentina was a regular attender at the early Harrier trials and, having acquired the *Vienticinco de Mayo*, it was hoped that it would be in the market for a seaborne Harrier. GR.1 XV757 flew from the Argentine carrier, and one wonders what might have been had both sides in the Falklands conflict been armed with Harriers?

Chile was seen as a potential purchaser in 1990, and two GR.3s visited the FIDAE at Santiago, but no orders appeared. The African nations were also considered, but showed no interest in such a 'complex' aircraft as the Harrier. An RAF GR.1 demonstrated at Japan's Nagoya Airshow in 1971, and the Japanese have expressed an interest in the Harrier II Plus, a project which in mid 1997 was still under consideration. China had also approved of the Harrier following a demonstration by GR.3 XV762 and further flights arranged with G-VTOL. However, currency problems ruled out any sales.

CHAPTER EIGHT

US Second Generation

Harrier II: the Next Generation – Developing the Concept

The operational success of the AV-8A/C had confirmed the US Marine Corps' belief in VSTOL technology and its advantages for its particular type of warfare. What was needed now was a follow-on aircraft that met its future requirements for a 'light attack' aircraft that carried a big punch and ensured the achievement of the stated goal of having a 'total VSTOL light attack force by the 1990s'. This gathered together studies undertaken by McDonnell Douglas, following their aborted collaborative AV-16 effort with the UK, and then led on to the AV-8B Advanced Harrier Program, originally proposed in 1973 and formalized by the Defense Armed Services Committee in March 1976.

Central to this new breed of Harrier was an advanced 'big-wing', originally proposed by Hawker and then derived from NASA-

<table>
<tr><th colspan="2">Harrier II Specification</th></tr>
<tr><td colspan="2">LENGTH: 47.75ft;</td></tr>
<tr><td colspan="2">WIDTH (wingtip to wingtip): 30.33ft;</td></tr>
<tr><td colspan="2">OPERATING WEIGHT (empty): 14,867lb;</td></tr>
<tr><td colspan="2">MAXIMUM USEFUL LOAD: 16,133lb;</td></tr>
<tr><td colspan="2">MAXIMUM TOW: 31,000lb;</td></tr>
<tr><td colspan="2">MAXIMUM EXTERNAL LOAD CAPABILITY (including gun and ammunition): 13,234lb</td></tr>
</table>

Cutaway schematic view of the AV-8B. McDonnell Douglas

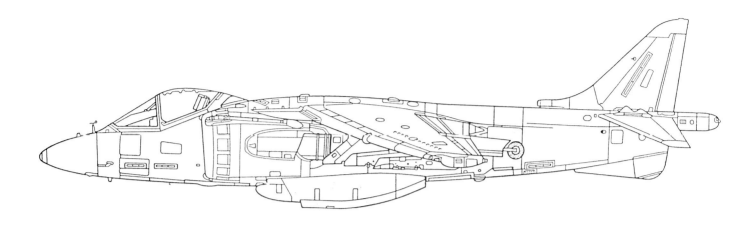

AV-8B Nils Mathisrud

Highly colourful YAV-8B caught during a RVTO (rolling vertical take-off). Rolls-Royce

based technology of supercritical aerofoils, where the drag was reduced and the lift increased. To achieve the maximum benefits in terms of weight saving, advanced structural materials were used instead of traditional metal, and the unique graphite epoxy construction gave the AV-8B the first carbon-fibre technology wing fitted to a military aircraft. At the rear of the wing a large, single, slotted flap was integrated to support the jet efflux from the engine nozzles, which increased take-off lift and helped to arrest the loss of performance during vertical landings. The outrigger wheels were also moved inboard the better to facilitate rough field work, and the 'elephant's ear' engine intakes were also redesigned and increased in size, initially with a double row of suction relief doors (later revised to a single row) and the forward cold-air nozzles reshaped to a 'zero-scarf' design; these two features alone added an amazing 800lb of thrust.

Part of the original Phase I of the 1976 Advanced Harrier Program was the production of two Harrier Technology Demonstrators, as well as a full-scale wind tunnel test with the use of the old AV-8A 158385; this was successfully completed in late 1976. The primary element of Phase II of the Program was to test the theories behind the AV-8B in a flight programme; to accommodate this, two AV-8As were remanufactured as YAV-8B test aircraft. YAV-8B No.1, 158394, was completed on 1 September 1978, with its first flight on 9 November, and the second, YAV-8B, 158395, flew on 19 February 1979; however, on 15 November with test pilot Jackie Jackson on board the engine flamed out and he was forced to eject. The modifications to the aircraft incorporated the new supercritical wing, improved inlet system and positive circulation flaps. The engine was the Pegasus 11 F402-RR-404 with 21,700lb of thrust, which included a new gearbox and zero-scarf forward nozzles and the same LID improvements that were added to the AV-8C. The main fuselage of the aircraft remained largely unchanged from the standard AV-8A and included the under-fuselage Aden gun packs with strakes. McDonnell Douglas also produced a full-scale mock-up 159234/20 to show what the AV-8B might look like, using parts from a crashed AV-8A with the new wing; this too still used the basic Harrier I fuselage. The trials were impressive, going through the full scope of the flight envelope and weapons capacity; there was no doubt that the AV-8B would provide the much needed improve-

ments in warload and radius of operation that the Marines required. YAV-8B No.1 was deployed aboard USS Saipan for seagoing trials in October 1979 together with the development version of the AV-8C. The promise of the next generation was huge in terms of performance and payload, and with the latest state of the art avionics the US Congress ordered four Full Scale Development (FSD) Aircraft, under the full designation AV-8B. Following the completion of the test programme YAV-8B No.1 joined the NASA Test Fleet as N704NA.

Flight Colours

Both the YAV-8B aircraft were painted up overall gloss white with a medium blue spine band, pitot tube, canopy frame, wing tips and tail band. Side flashes were red, as were also the tail, wing and stabilizer bands. The 'Marines' legend, anti-glare panel and ID numbers were all in black, with full-colour national insignia on the wings and the US flag on the tailfin. On the intakes, contained inside the red fuselage stripe, was a white 'AV-8B' in an italic type, although on the aircraft's first flights the AV-8B was in roman type.

Into Service: the AV-8B, Harrier II

Following on from the two YAV-8Bs and the FSD aircraft came an initial batch of twelve production AV-8Bs and a limited run of a further twenty-one. The first of the FSDs, 161396, made its first tentative hover flight on 5 November 1981. The AV-8B was a totally changed aircraft compared with the YAV-8. McDonnell Douglas produced the first batches of aircraft in St.Louis, before a work-share agreement with British Aerospace came on line. BAe were responsible

Specification – AV-8B Harrier II/EAV-8B	
ENGINE	One F402-RR-406 Pegasus turbofan.
WEIGHTS	Empty 13,000lb (6,000kg); loaded 31,000lb (14,100kg).
DIMENSIONS	Span 30ft 4in (9.19); length 46ft 4in (14m).
PERFORMANCE	Max level speed at sea level: 570kts (1,060km/h); range (typical): 400nm (740km); ceiling: 50,000ft (15,000m).
ARMAMENT	1xGAU-12/U Gatling cannon, Sidewinder AAMs, bombs, CBUs.

161396 first of the FSD AV-8Bs; note the twin row of 'blow-in' doors, the instrument boom and the lack of the LERX on the wings. USMC via Tony Thornborough

for the centre and rear fuselage sections, the fin and rudder, the centreline pylon and the reaction control system, and Rolls-Royce had the very important role of supplying the Pegasus engine. The wing was by now well refined with the LERX (leading edge root extension) added to the roots and a completely new tailplane fitted, again using carbon fibre technology. The forward fuselage also took a large area of carbon fibre components and, benefiting from the Sea Harrier's experience, enjoyed a redesigned and raised 'bubble' canopy with a wrap-around windshield, lifting the crew position by 10.5in, thereby giving a much better view and providing room below for the some of the new avionics. The ejector seat fitted was the UPC/Stencel 10B, with zero-zero capabilities.

The avionics themselves were in the main new brand new although some were unashamedly borrowed from other McDonnell Douglas programmes. In the nose was a Hughes ARBS (Angle-Rate Bombing System), originally developed for the A-4M Skyhawk, with a TV and dual mode tracker facility, projecting its information on to a Smiths Industries upgraded SU-128/A HUD or on to the MFD (multi-function display) in the cockpit on the pilot's left, on which can be shown sensor information, nav/mission plots, ARN-118 TACAN information and engine data, and the SAAHS (stability augmentation and attitude-hold system). Such systems assist the accurate delivery of laser-guided as well as 'dumb' bombs. Some of the cockpit interfaces were borrowed from the F-18: items such as the improved HOTAS (hands-on-throttle-and-stick) controls, the AYK-14 mission computer, the ASN-130 INS, the Lear Siegler AN/AYQ-13 stores management system, and the ECM-resistant fibre optic cables. The RWR and underfuselage AN/ALE-39 chaff and flare dispensers are the same as those used in the CILOP AV-8C programme. All the aircraft information is fed through a 1553A databus and in front of the pilot beneath the HUD is his UFC (up front controller), his link with the computer system. Also fitted is a Sperry Auto Pilot. Communications were provided by two ARC-182 wide band UHF/VHF radios, and the ECM suite includes the highly efficient AN/ALR-67 RWR system. The entire cockpit was of a more ergonomically satisfactory design than in any previous Harriers.

To add more muscle to its attack potential a new gun, the General Electric GAU-12A Equaliser was developed, replacing the Aden packs, with the new

An AV-8B from VMA-331 takes on fuel en route to an overseas deployment. Curtiss Knowles

gun being fitted with strakes for better LID effect, as was demonstrated on the AV-8C. The gun is housed in the left-hand pod, with 300 rounds of ammunition in the right-hand pod, fed over to the gun via a bridge across the underfuselage. The gun is able to discharge 3,600 rpm, driven by bleed air from the engine. The four FSDs, the twelve 'initial production' and the twenty-one 'limited production' aircraft were fitted with an interim F402-RR-404A engine, before the production batch proper were fitted with the definitive F404-RR-406, with zero-scarfed front nozzles and the DECS engine controls.

The first aircraft that would bear the name 'Harrier II' was FSD.1, which was officially rolled out on 16 October 1981 and used to undertake the initial hovering trials and the basic flight characteristics tests, wearing the 'traditional' dark grey/dark green/light grey camouflage. This aircraft was not fitted with the LERX and still carried the YAV-8B-style double

row of intake doors. The second aircraft, FSD.2, 161397, was the first to be fitted with the new 'bolt-on' retractable IFR probe, and undertook aerial tanking trials, at first being demonstrated in a garish scheme of white fuselage, red wings, tailfin and tailplanes, dark blue fuselage and fin bands, trimmed with gold. This aircraft also introduced the LERX and the single row of blow-in doors on the engine intakes and was used for fuel, engine and intake design tests. FSD.3, 161398, undertook avionics and weapons trials wearing a light grey and dark green wrap-around scheme, while FSD.4, 161399, which flew in June 1983 and was as near to a 'production' AV-8B as possible, was painted up in an overall light grey scheme. The aircraft were based out of Patuxent River and undertook these operational tests while being in the service of VX-5. The range and weapons trials gave some superior results, as did the handling and flight tests, and paved the way for the next batch of twelve aircraft.

Broken probe – Harrier refuel incident

Captain 'Blade' Bonner of VMA-231 was part of a 'routine' section of Harriers meeting a KC-130 tanker after simulated air-to-air combat manoeuvres. Bonner took the hose to the port and began to take on board 3,000lb of fuel. During the disengagement the hose separated from the tanker, and the basket and 83ft of hose remained attached to the Harrier. Bonner and his wingman turned toward Pohang, Korea with the hose wrapped round the port stabilitor. During the descent the hose broke away from the stabilitor and whipped around wildly; he was advised to climb and eject. However, Bonner continued his approach He found it difficult to control the aircraft and decided on a dog-leg approach; going to full power and nozzling down to 60 degrees he regained full control and made a safe 135kt landing with the Harrier undamaged.

VMAT-203 received its first AV-8B in a ceremony on 12 January 1984, when it was officially handed 161573/KD-21. VMAT-203 was given most of the early production models for pilot training and conversion at

MCAS Cherry Point. VMA-331, 'The Bumblebees', was the first unit of the front-line 'gun squadrons' to get its hands on the AV-8B, having traded in the trusty A-4M Skyhawks to fly the Harrier in 1985. It was followed at Cherry Point by VMA-231, VMA-223 and VMA-542, while at Yuma VMA-513, which stood down the Marines' last AV-8C in August 1986 for the AV-8B; VMA-211 and VMA-311 also traded-up for the Harrier II. VMA-311 conducted an extended deployment aboard the LHA USS *Belleau Wood* during the first six months of 1987, flying some 950 sorties. AV-8Bs regularly attended NATO exercises, as well as establishing new techniques and procedures, such as combined operations with the US Army's Apache helicopters at Fort Hood, with the AH-64s being used as designators for the Harriers carrying LGBs. The AV-8Bs have also been successful in DACT (dissimilar air combat training) sorties against the high-powered US Navy jets. Assault tactics were also developed to support the Marine on the ground; as one Harrier pilot put it, 'We are the artillery for the Corps, the grunts need to know we can respond quickly and effectively. If they're dug in trying to push a breach through enemy defences – funnelling in asshole to belly-button and they need air support, we will be there – in double quick time because we are on the spot, not based on a carrier hundreds of miles off the coast!' So far only one Harrier unit has been stood down in consequence of the post-Cold War cutbacks: the AV-8Bs of VMA-311 were decommissioned in October 1992.

Camouflage and Markings

Until the start of the Gulf War, the AV-8Bs were fairly universal in their use of a three- or two-tone camouflage scheme. The former was dark green, S 34064, dark grey, FS 36099, and light gull grey, FS 36044. This gave way to the grey and green being used in a wrap-around style in the mid 1980s, although light grey schemes were also trialled in the early 1990s, before the Gulf War. One of the test AV-8Bs assigned to Edwards AFB was noted with wingtip Sidewinder rails and carrying a red arrowhead diagonally down the wings from the centre of the spine.

Training to Fly Harrier II: US Marine Corps TAV-8B

Because of the success of the TAV-8A, the US Marine Corps was not in favour of purchasing a dedicated Harrier II training vehicle, as they considered that the current system was more than adequate for their needs. It soon became clear, however, that the handling characteristics of the AV-8B were totally different to those of the AV-8A, and the Marines chose a trainer version that would faithfully replicate the abilities of the Harrier II. With the addition of an order for two trainers from Italy, the TAV-8B was designed and added to the production lines at McDonnell Douglas. The first TAV-8B, 162747, made its first flight on 21 October 1986, and was then the sixty-fifth Harrier II produced from an order of twenty-two for the Marines and two for Italy, the first production example, 162963, arriving at the Marines' training unit VMAT-203 on 24 July 1987.

The TAV-8B featured an additional cockpit which gave it the unorthodox 'T-Bird' appearance, with an enlarged tailfin to counteract the new fuselage arrangement

An AV-8B from VMAT-203 showing the three-tone camouflage. Author

Good planform shot of the AV-8B, rolling in on target. McDonnell Douglas

and an improved internal bird-strike-proof windshield in front of the instructor's rear cockpit. The rest of the airframe bore all the characteristics of the single-seater AV-8B, but dimensionally the TAV-8B was 3ft 11in longer than the single-seater. The aircraft also carried two types of ejection seat, the Stencel SJU-13 in the front and the SJU-14 in the rear, the difference being that in the event of an ejection the front seat would diverge to the right and the rear seat to the left, ensuring that the occupants did not collide. The front cockpit is identical to that of

the AV-8B, so that when the 'student' eventually goes solo there is no difference (except the lack of an instructor in the back), and, like the AV-8B, does not posses a colour moving-map display, the track information being shown on a DDI, (digital display indicator).The instructor's rear suite contains full flight and engine controls, with further improvements including SAAHS and DECS-controlled engines. Because the TAV-8B was purchased solely as a training aircraft, it has only two underwing pylons fitted; for the tactical weapons phase of the

Harrier syllabus these are used to carry practice munitions such as six Mk.76 Practice Bombs, LAU-68 rocket pods or two 250-gallon tanks. The underfuselage cannon armament is also available, but it is more usual to see the aircraft with the LID strakes fitted.

Development TAV-8B, 162747

The aircraft's first flight was at the hands of test pilot Jackie Jackson who took an hour's sortie to pronounce that the new T-bird was going to be a success. The aircraft

TAV-8B 162747. McDonnell Douglas

A good view of the TAV-8B's side-hinging canopy and rounded nose section without the ARBS of the single seater. Author

A superb study of a brace of Warden-prepared Harriers, both showing signs of 'paint fatigue' and each carrying a single four-round CVR-7 rocket pod on the starboard side and a single CBLS on the port; note the size and position of the serial numbers. Sgt Rick Brewell

(Below) **Inching over the rear deck, an AV-8B positions for landing.** Author

Complete with high visibility tail marking, a GR.7 from No.4(AC) Squadron flies over a lagoon during the Squadron's brief deployment to Belize in 1993. Sqn Ldr Andy Suddards

Carrying a pair of live 1,000lb bombs, XZ498/124 skirts the edge of Split during one of the regular CAS patrols over Bosnia. Neil 'Joe' Mercer

A fine study of grey-clad GR.7 ZG503/74 from No.3 Squadron. RAF

Skimming across the Arctic countryside, the Harrier's camouflage seems at first glance to be ideal; but this was not the case when set against a uniformly dark background or the sea. BAe

One of the Indian Navy's Sea Harrier FRS.51s, with ferry tanks and the latest lighter grey camouflage scheme; the 'White Tiger' motif is now to be found on the nose and the 'Navy' lettering has changed from its original white to black. BAe

(Right) **A line-up of Falklands Harriers on the deck of HMS** Hermes: **first a GR.3 (note the transponder fairing under the nose), secondly a light grey-painted Sea Harrier and finally an EDSG-coloured Sea Harrier.** BAe

An AMRAAM-armed F/A.2 launches from the deck of HMS Illustrious **while an RAF GR.7 sits on the foredeck.** HMS Illustrious

Both Italian Harrier TAV-8 trainers visited RNAS Yeovilton in 1996 to support the annual air day; a now rather worn looking '01' may be seen sporting a darker nose section, reportedly as an aid for Harrier II Plus training. f4 Aviation Photobank

Practice, especially when going into a war zone, is all important; here we see a grey-clad GR.7 ZD376 firing off a practice CVR-7 high velocity rocket from a four-round pod. Sgt Rick Brewell

The LRMTS housing or the so-called 'Snoopy-nose' that makes the GR.3 so distinctive. Author

(Below) An AV-8B from VMAT-203 showing the original three-tone camouflage. Author

(Right) ZD405/34 making a stop-over at Aviano AFB in Italy during a visit to show the US forces based there the finer points of the GR.7. Author

(Left) A grey-clad GR.7 is 'pushed' into its hide by the ubiquitous Unimog tractor. Author

(Left) **An aerial study of the F/A.2 showing its new radome housing the excellent Blue Vixen radar set.** BAe

Wittering's warriors: a T.10 and GR.7 from No.20(R) Squadron in formation with a GR.7 from No.1(F) Squadron. BAe

AMRAAM trials Harrier F/A.2 XZ439 shows its teeth on the ramp at Boscombe Down. Author

(Below) Reportedly the only time that all four of No.899 Squadron's T.4Ns were ever captured in the air together; the two aircraft nearest the camera are both marked to proclaim the fiftieth anniversary of the Squadron. Neil 'Joe' Mercer

was painted in the standard USMC grey/green wrap-around colours, with a test boom fitted to the nose. 162574 was about 1,400lb heavier than the equivalent squadron model owing to its test instrumentation and wiring, which for evaluation purposes were equated to a similar weight in ordnance.

The task of producing pilots for the TAV-8B falls on Marine Attack Training Squadron 203 (VMAT-203), 'The Hawks', who are based at Cherry Point. It bridges the gap between the 'rookie' flyer and the

States. VMAT-203's history may be traced back to 1927, and subsequently it has had various designations: VMT-1, VMT-203 and VMAT-203. VMT-1 began to train pilots on the TR-9J Cougar and the T-33 Shooting Star until 1967, when it received its first TA-4J Skykhawks, and was then redesignated VMT-203 in April 1968. May 1972 saw a further redesignation to VMAT-203, when it took on charge a mix of TA-4J and A4M Skyhawks, being tasked to train replacement pilots for fleet duty. April 1975 heralded the arrival of the

During the Gulf War VMAT-203 was a very busy unit, being tasked with supporting the 'shooters' in the battle area, keeping them fully mission-capable in the combat zone, often by trading their good aircraft for damaged ones, and augmenting the front-line units with additional pilots drawn from the instructor staff. As a result a few AV-8Bs could be seen with an extra squadron designation stencilled on their rear fuselages, in the shape of a white 'VMAT-203'. VMAT-203 operates a mix of AV-8As and TAV-8Bs, and the previous

The 'boss-bird' of VMAT-203, denoted by the '00' on the nose. Author

competent aviator with one of the seven prestige gun squadrons. The unit is unique in that it not only trains the pilots but also all the maintenance personnel as well. The 'Hawks' pioneered the training mission during the Marines Corps' transition from the 'straight-liners' to the VSTOL regime and has the distinction of being the only Harrier training unit in the United

AV-8A Harrier, and with it came the dedicated two-seater TAV-8A in October. The unit continued with these aircraft until the arrival of the AV-8B, when it had the dual role of training pilots on both the AV-8C and the B model until 1985 when its last 'C' pilot completed his course. From then its sole mission has been that of training on the AV-8B.

tree-top level scheme of dark gull grey, FS 32631, and European green, FS 34092, camouflage has been replaced by the universally adopted Harrier Tactical Paint Scheme (HTPS) of dark sea grey, FS 36118, applied to the top of the wings and fuselage, dark gull grey, FS 36321, on the outer sections of the upper wings and fuselage sides, and dark ghost grey, FS 36230, to the underfuselage, with the darker shade on the upper fuselage rounding over the back of the raised rear cockpit.

Markings for VMAT-203 aircraft, both single- and two-seater types, are currently, as might have been expected, subdued. The 'stars and bars' on the intakes and wings are in the appropriate contrasting shade of grey for their position, as are all of the caution and warning markings, together with the aircraft's ID number and squadron description. The tail code 'KD' is in white, as is the two-digit aircraft code on the nose and on the upper inboard wing

black, including the national insignia and tailfin 'Marines' logo; however, like the current grey-clad machines, the tail codes and aircraft numbers were in white.

Harrier II Training Course

The instructor pilots of VMAT-203 are highly experienced aviators most of whom have in excess of 1,000 hrs on the Harrier, many having flown combat sorties in the Gulf. On strength at the close of 1996 were twenty-four instructor pilots and more than thirty maintenance instructors. Not only

of qualified pilots to operate them. In the early days, from the introduction of the AV-8B, conversion was initially undertaken on the TAV-8A, before the 'B' trainer arrived. The Harrier selection process takes only the 'high flyers' of above average ability and they embark on an intensive fifteen-week course which gives them 70 hrs of flying, plus simulator work. Having started dual, they will have gone solo and qualified in formation flying, tactics and weaponeering. Only then do they reach 'combat capable' status, before going on to being declared 'combat ready' and being dispatched to one

From this view the aircraft seems to be a little 'nose heavy'; it also affords a view across the top of the wing; note that the KD marking is grey not white. Author

flap section; this code is repeated in miniature on the tip of the tailfin. But maintenance personnel are not always favourable to standardization so that there are always some 'modifications' around. In their previous incarnation of grey and green, all the TAV-8B and AV-8Bs' markings were in

does VMAT-203 train *ab initio* students, but also converts those switching to the Harrier from other aircraft or helicopters and trains foreign aircrew, such as the Spanish and the Italian Navy's aviators. With the introduction of the AV-8B, the 'Hawks' came under pressure to turn out a high rate

of the gun squadrons. To aid in the preparation for shipboard operations, the Marines have built a dummy LHA deck site at MCALF Bogue Field, some 20 miles from Cherry Point, where carrier landings can be practised, a site shared with the other Marine striker, the F-18 Hornet.

(Right) Poking its nose out of the 'shed', '13'
undergoing maintenance. Author

All set, as TAV-8B taxies out for a training sortie.
Author

Carrier Harrier: Embarking with VSTOL on the USS *Guam*

On a dull, grey, overcast April morning, in conditions more reminiscent of the North Sea than just a few miles off America's sunshine coast, the characteristic whine of Rolls-Royce Pegasus engines starting up

from Walsh, and the launch officer waits the 'commit' signal from the Fly-co. A final check, nozzles set ...Go ...the throttles are snapped to the stop, brakes off and a plume of steam and spray explodes across the deck as the Harrier hurtles down and away. Clearing the bow, it seems to 'hang' momentarily as the nozzles are rotated

assault vessels, and along with another five *Tarawa* class ships serves as one of the Marines' main manoeuvre platforms. Typically the *Guam* would carry from twenty to twenty-four Sea Knight helicopters and four Sea Stallions. It is not unusual to find a mix of types such as the AH-1, UH-1, CH-46 and CH-53 embarked as a compos-

(Above) **The USS** Guam. Author

(Right) **Captain Walsh waits his turn to launch from the** Guam. Author

signals the beginning of another day's flying operations aboard the assault ship USS *Guam*. Marshalled into their 'starting' positions, two AV-8B Harrier IIs from the US Marine Corps Attack Squadron 542, the 'Flying Tigers', prepare for their launch sequence. The morning's task, to practise take-off and recovery procedures around the ship, before an Atlantic deployment. In the lead aircraft, Captain John 'Vapour' Walsh, experienced Harrier jockey and Gulf War veteran, takes the helm of 'Tiger Zero-One'. He is marshalled into the correct position by the deck crew. The FDO (flight deck officer) takes the 'OK' signal

back and the thrust from the Pegasus engine is converted to winglift. The aircraft is quickly cleaned up, gear and flaps cycle in, and just a faint haze of smoke is evident as the Harrier powers away, banking left and gaining height before disappearing into the gloom. The deck cleared, and John Walsh's wingman is the next to go: an ear-splitting scream, a rain-splattered blast and 'Tiger Zero-Two' forces out into the murky sky...

A typical launch from the *Guam*. One of six *Iwo Jima* class ships, the *Guam*, LPH-9, displaces 19,300 tons fully laden and was one of the world's first helicopter

ite unit. She can also carry a small number of OV-10 Broncos if neccessary and would normally play host to six AV-8 Harriers. The ship's complement is 680; she has a top speed of 23kts with a range of 10,000 nautical miles, drawing power from a 23,000shp twin-shaft turbine engine. Self-defence weapons comprise two Vulcan Phalanx CIWS (close-in weapon system), two eight-tube Sea Sparrow launchers and four dual-purpose guns. Her flight deck is a modest 602ft long and 104ft wide, but, unlike the British, the Spanish and the Italian carriers, does not have the added benefit of the ski-jump.

...In the distance the roar of engines announces the return of the 'Tigers'. They make a low fly-past, just above deck level, and break hard to bleed off speed as they turn away. Approaching the stern, Walsh begins to ease the nozzles forward, making the transition from forward flight to the near hover, matching his speed with that of the ship. With the Harrier now 'standing' on its engine thrust abeam the port side of the ship, he gently eases the aircraft over the deck. Keeping an eye on the 'weather vane' in front of him, and watching the JPT (jetpipe temperature), he reduces power and the Harrier sinks on to the deck, the undercarriage absorbing the landing shock. The engine is dropped to idle, and once established on the deck, a slight increase in power, and he is marshalled away behind the island to make way for his No.2.

(Right) **An excellent view of the Harrier hovering over the deck during the final seconds before landing; note the 'fire truck' in the foreground, just in case.** Author.

(Below) **Last few feet, the throttle gradually eases off, the pilot looks to the gear to absorb the final 'shock' on the deck.** Author

Grey sea, grey skies, grey Harriers …
Author

(Below) **A typical Harrier launch from the assault ship** Belleau Wood. McDonnell Douglas

Combat Zone # 3: 'Storm Birds' – Harriers in the Gulf

2 August 1990, the day Iraq invaded Kuwait, was the start of a campaign that would pit the AV-8B Harrier II of the US Marine Corps in combat for the first time. Within days of the invasion, Marine air and ground units were on their way to Saudi Arabia to forestall any attempted move on Kuwait's neighbour. The first Marine Corps tactical aviation to arrive in theatre were the AV-8Bs, who were to be tasked with providing their own brand of CAS (close air support). When the invasion of Kuwait occurred, the last two of the MCAS Yuma-based Harrier units were in the middle of converting from their AV-8Bs to the new night-attack Harrier and,

Once the 'alert' had been sounded, USMC squadron personnel worked round the clock to get the men and machines ready for action. Those aircraft scheduled for deployment were repainted in a two-tone, grey camouflage scheme, more suited to the desert skyline, and munitions and spares were loaded on to transports for the trip out to Saudi Arabia. On 18 and 19 August Yuma-based VMA-311, 'The Bumblebees', led by Lt Col Dick White, and Cherry Point-based VMA-542, under the command of Lt Col Ted Herman (swapping some of their jets for the DECS-equipped aircraft from VMAT-203) headed out across the Atlantic, refuelling at night from USAF KC-10s. Carrying two external tanks, gun pods and Sidewinder AAMs, the aircraft stopped

AV-8Bs were ready for their part in Operation *Desert Shield*.

After a short stay in Bahrain, VMA-311 moved to King Abdul Aziz Air Base (KAAAB), which was located next to a soccer stadium and described as 'an extremely austere setting', although it was said to be much better than the unit's previous surroundings, added to which it was ideally situated, being just 100 miles from the Kuwaiti border. Another 'Tent City' was soon established, as were the maintenance sites and fuel and armament compounds. Four clamshell hangars were erected to allow the aircraft to be maintained away from the rigours of the desert winds. Once facilities had been established, the 'Flying Tigers' also made the move from Bahrain to KAAAB in November, bringing the Harrier comple-

One of the instant hangars erected by the Marines to try to alleviate some of the problems of the sand and desert wind (not that successfully, it has been reported). J. S. Walsh

with VMAT-203 solely charged with training, this left only five fully operational units for the Marine commanders to deploy: three at Cherry Point, one at Yuma and one on deployment in Okinawa.

off at Rota in Spain before continuing on to Sheikh Isa AB in Bahrain, arriving on 20 August. Within 48 hrs of their arrival, the aircraft were sitting on alert, and flying their first desert training missions: the

ment up to forty. In mid August, VMA-331 had also arrived, under the leadership of Lt Col Gerry Fitzgerald, and deployed aboard the assault ship USS *Nassau*, where it undertook a number of amphibious exercises designed to convince Saddam Hussein that an amphibious assault might be made.

The second wave of twenty Harriers to arrive were from VMA-231, under the command of Lt Col 'Rusty' Jones. The Squadron had been on deployment at Iwakuni in Japan since June 1990 and made the trip to the Gulf via MCAS Cherry Point in early December, arriving at KAAAB later that month. Six more Har-

To the north the Marines had established a FARP (Forward Area Rearm/Refuel Point) at an Aramco helicopter base at Tanajib, from where the aircraft could refuel and rearm, and, because it was only 5 min flight time from the border, this meant that the Harriers could provide a rapid response to any call for assistance.

When the United Nations' patience with the Iraqi leadership's failure to with-

artillery battery shelling a US Marine position at the nearby border town of Khafji. The four VMA-311 aircraft on alert were launched, followed swiftly by VMA-542 and VMA-231, and successfully attacked and silenced the guns with 1,000lb bombs and cannon fire. From then on the Harriers carried forward their attacks on Iraqi elements right up until the cease-fire was eventually called on 28 February.

163201 WH/02 being armed with Mk.20 Rockeyes and Mk.77 fire bombs. J. S. Walsh

riers also arrived from the Yuma-based VMA-513 (Det. B) and deployed ashore at KAAAB from the assault ship USS *Tarawa* as part of the 5th MEB (Marine Expeditionary Brigade); the remainder of VMA-513's Harriers moved to Japan to replace VMA-231. By mid January KAAAB was a hectic place, with some 3,500 Marines, sixty-six Harriers and twenty OV-10 Bronco FAC aircraft. A parallel taxiway had been constructed and a 3,500ft AM2 matted dispersal area laid.

draw from Kuwait finally ran out, the night of 17 January 1991 lit the fuse for Operation *Desert Storm*. While Coalition jets hit targets in Iraq and Kuwait, the Harriers were held in reserve during the first phase of the air war to be used in the preparation of the battlefield for the ground war. Each of the Squadrons was, however, required to stand four fully-armed aircraft on 'ground alert' during this time. Just after dawn on the first day of the war an orbiting Marine Corps OV-10 Bronco spotted an Iraqi 122mm

The Harriers carried a variety of weaponry; it was said that you could 'dangle an encyclopaedic variety of death and destruction from the wings of the AV-8B'! During the early days of the war the Harriers carried AIM-9M Sidewinders on their outer wing pylons, but, as the air threat was virtually non-existent, they were discarded in favour of more air-to-ground weaponry. Similarly, they also deleted the multiple ejector racks in favour of the single-weapon installation. Mk.20 Rockeye

Heading out over Kuwait, WH/17, loaded for 'bear' with six Rockeyes. J. S. Walsh

Typically chaotic sight at Sheikh Isa AFB in the early days of the Marine Harrier deployments; WH/40 is being marshalled on to the runway for a 'delivery run'. J. S. Walsh

cluster bombs, Mk.82 500lb and Mk.83 1,000lb bombs, and AGM-65 laser guided Maverick missiles were the primary warloads, as well as Snakeye retard bombs and silver-clad Mk.77 Mod.5 fuel/air explosive bombs. Extra fuel tanks were seldom carried as the aircraft were so close to their operating bases, but the GAU-12 cannon was present on every mission, as was a full loading of chaff and flares. Occasionally the aircraft would also carry an ALQ-164 ECM pod on the centreline.

VMA-311's Harriers aboard USS Nassau, although not used as much as they would have liked to be in the early days of the war, played a major role in a diversionary attack on the Failaka Islands on 20 February during Operations *Desert Dagger* and *Desert Slash*, and were fully involved once the ground war got under way. The shore-based Harriers flew a variety of tasks from helicopter escort to interdiction, working in conjunction with other Marine assets

such as FAST-FAC F-18D Hornets. In the early days the pairing got off to an uneasy start, but by the end of the war they had forged a lethal partnership. The FAST-FACs marked targets inside 15 miles by 15 miles-square 'kill boxes' with 9in Zuni rockets fitted with white phosphorus heads, Harriers following in the mark hit hard with their weapons. By far the most devastating attack was perhaps the 'turkey shoot' along the Basra road on 26 February when, along with other aircraft, the Harriers bombed and strafed retreating Iraqi convoys along the so-called 'Highway of Death'.

Final Figures

The US Marines' AV-8B Harriers flew 9,353 sorties, consuming over 11,120 hrs and dispatched in excess of 6 million lb of ordinance in 3,380 combat missions, and fulfilled every requirement they were tasked with.

Harriers lost

Five Harriers were lost, four to SAM attacks and the fifth flew into the ground during a night raid; an additional Harrier was lost from USS *Nassau*.

162954	VMA-311	1st Lt Manuel Rivera: killed in night-training accident
163518	VMA-311	Capt Michael Berryman: POW
162081	VMA-321	Capt Russell Sanbourn: POW (callsign Shank)
161573	VMA-542	Capt James Wilborne: killed (callsign LZ)
163190	VMA-542	Capt J. Scott Walsh: rescued
163740	VMA-331	Capt Reginald Underwood: killed

One of the Harriers' many tasks was to provide air cover for the twelve EA6-B Prowlers deployed to Desert Storm, a valuable asset and prized target; here a Sidewinder-armed 'Tiger' escorts a 'Playboy' on another trip; note the 'dual' identity aboard WH/40: carrying VMA-542 and VMAT-203 on the rear fuselage.
J. S. Walsh

Harrier mission: 'One pass – haul ass'

Captain John Scott 'Vapour' Walsh flew with 'The Flying Tigers' during *Desert Storm*. He recounts what it was like on a 'Harrier hop':

The first thing we did each morning was to study the day's ATO to see our objectives – perhaps flying into Kuwait or being turned on to 'armed alert status'. We knew we had our FARP at Tanajib so fuel was never a consideration, but we spent time checking out our IFF and the codes on our ciphered radios. We would decide on the best weaponry for the job, either 'slicks' or CBUs, unless we were 'torching trenches', when fire bombs were the only choice. We look at our mutual support, what calls we would give if one of us went down, set our delivery angles, and made sure we were fully stocked with expendables.

Personally, I put on my survival vest – with water, mirror, space blanket, candle, matches, extra water, camouflage paint and flares, plus my trusty 9mm pistol. Once the walkround is done, and I am strapped in, the armourers and the plane captain give the OK, and our formation heads out into Kuwait. We would contact the Direct Air Support and Fire Control Center to tell them we were up, who we were and what we were, and they would hand us off to a Marine ANGLICO (Air and Naval Gunfire Liaison Company) who would handle our mission. Once targeted, they read us the standard 'nine-line brief':

> Initial Point to hold
> Heading to target
> Target Elevation
> Target co-ordinates
> Target description
> Type of mark on target
> Friendly forces location
> Egress direction
> Time hack

We hit our stopwatches, enter the co-ordinates into the computer, ensure the ECM/RWR is on line, expendables programmed and weapons armed. The ANGLICO team then 'paint' the target with laser, which we pick up in the ARBS/DMT, and begin our run from 20,000ft at 480 kts. As I roll in for a steep delivery, my wingman takes 'shotgun'; he tells me my 'six' is clear as I accelerate to 600kts at 45 degrees. The flare/chaff program pumps out the decoys, because for about 20 to 30 sec I am in the 'box' for the AAA and hand-held SAMs. I tell the ANGLICO I am wings level in the dive, and he gives me a 'clear and hot' call – and with laser lock I go for an 'auto-delivery'. I press the pickle button, get a tone in my headset and the bombs fly. My wingman gives me calls as I pull up, and I then take cover as he rolls in for his attack. He can now see my bombs going off and the ANGLICO FAC corrects his descent accordingly. After the strike we egress back to Tanajib, refuel, rearm, this time with Rockeye CBUs and return to the fray. This time we are picked up by a FAST-FAC F-18D who has a convoy of Iraqi trucks to deal with. He reads us the nine-line brief and I pick him up as he rolls in watching the flash from Zuni rockets as he launches the mark. He pulls off, popping out flares and I roll in squeezing off a long burst of 25mm cannon before releasing the weaponry. The Rockeye has 247 anti-armour bomblets and you can see the pattern spread out, explosions in their wake.

Lucky escape – desert ejection

As well making a valuable contribution to the bombing effort, Walsh was also entangled in an incident during a raid into Iraq. On 25 February and on his thirty-ninth combat mission, flying 163190 12/WH, operating out of Tanajib, he was taking part in an attack on an armoured column in bad visibility. Having lost sight of the formation leader, he took an IR SAM hit into the right-hand rear exhaust nozzle. Walsh contacted the orbiting F-18D FAST-FAC Hornet and he directed him out of the area, with the Harrier's wing well on fire. On finding a deserted desert airstrip Walsh attempted a landing; however the 'gear' did not work and he ejected. Uninjured, but shaken he was picked up by a USMC truck and returned to duty in a couple of days.

John 'Vapour' Walsh Posing beside an inscribed Rockeye. J. S. Walsh

Camouflage scheme

The two-tone grey evolved from the need to have a camouflage scheme that did not make the Harriers stand out against the desert sky, which their traditional green scheme would have done with potentially devastating effects. Some of the Harriers belonging to VMA-513 had already received the new HTPS (Harrier tactical paint scheme) so they were in effect ready for action. The other units, VMA-331, VMA-311 and VMA-542, all paid visits to Cherry Point's NADEP to receive their new camouflage, which came from standard gunship grey, FS 36118, and dark gull grey, FS 36231, paint stock, although at least two examples from VMA-542 (162945 being one) were noted at Cherry Point carrying overall light ghost grey, FS 36375. VMA-231 were not so fortunate in being away from home and had to make alternative arrangements. Lt Col Rusty Jones gave this explanation for the new colours:

We took the light ghost grey from the Hornet squadrons and sprayed it as the base color. Then we took another can of ghost grey and dumped a coffee cup full of black

into it, which made a contrasting shade of grey (nearest comparison dark ghost grey, FS 36320), and we then followed the contours of our original scheme. We also painted the interior of the intakes gloss white to kill any shadow and make us harder to see from head-on.

The personal mount of the 'boss' of VMA-231 or 'Shark-01' had a neat black shark's mouth and eyes painted on the nose of his Harrier and a personalized 'Venom' nametag painted beneath the canopy. This goes some way to explaining the differences in the tones of paint applied to the Harriers, although there were several variations in colours between aircraft in the same squadron. Some Harriers in addition to carrying the VMA-513 wording also carried the VMAT-203 legend on the rear fuselage. This was to denote the role played by a number of instructor pilots from the unit who had deployed to the Gulf to bolster the available aircrew. All the aircraft's markings were in black or grey, with squadron motifs being present on most.

62964 CG/08 in a lighter scheme of dark and light ghost grey; note the bomb-mission symbol under the windshield and the Arabic script for 'Free Kuwait'. Author

(Below) 163515 CG/18 gives us a good view of the camouflage scheme applied to VMA-231's aircraft. Author

The 'buddy' pose, as Capt Walsh (right) gets one for the album with wingman Capt Jeff 'Delta' Burke.
J. S. Walsh

(Below) A pair of 'Night Stalkers' from VMA-211, the only unit to retain the old-style 'Star and Meatball' insignia, found under the windshield; the 'Avenger' in the foreground carries LAU rocket launchers; the one in the background carries Snakeye retard bombs; both carry inert Sidewinders. McDonnell Douglas

AV-8B(NA): Yuma's 'Night Stalkers'

The ability to operate their Harriers 'after dark' was of great importance to the US Marine Corps philosophy. Its interest was awakened to the possibilities of nocturnal forays enhanced by forward looking infrared (FLIR) as a result of trials carried out at China Lake, where a TA-7C Corsair was fitted with a pod-mounted system, complemented with NVGs. A 'proof of concept' aircraft, AV-8B 162966, complete with night-attack suite, was produced and fitted with a GEC Sensors FLIR, mounted in front of the cockpit, atop the nose section and above and to the rear of the Hughes AN/ASB-19 Angle Rate Bombing System (ARBS), and within near direct line of sight for the pilot. Trials were then undertaken in its new guise after its first flight on 26 June 1987. After successful examination, a production programme was introduced to deliver a new version of the Harrier based on the systems included in the development aircraft. The first production aircraft to be completed was 163853 which was first flown on 8 July 1989 and delivered into squadron service on 15 September of that year.

Originally the aircraft type was to be designated the AV-8D; however AV-8B(NA) is what it has become formally known as. The AV-8B(NA) carries modifications that improve its capability and survivability, some of which went on to serve with the radar-equipped Harrier II

exploding in close proximity to the Harrier will at the very least take the wing off; a direct hit is something else!' Other improvements saw the introduction of a Honeywell digital moving map display, something deleted from the original AV-8A concept, fed by laser CD and able to be

Island Avengers', which converted straight to the Night Attack Harrier from its A-4Ms in spring 1990. It was followed by VMA-311, 'The Tomcats', which traded up its 'vanilla' AV-8Bs for the AV-8B(NA) in May 1992, and VMA-513, 'The Flying Nightmares', which also traded up in September

Night Attacker from VMA-513, 'Flying Nightmares'; this 'factory fresh' example made a welcome stop-over at March AFB during 1995; the VMA-513 legend was yet to be applied, but the aircraft did show off the latest incarnation of the Squadron's emblems. Author

Plus. In addition to the FLIR, which gives a 22-degrees field of view, is a Smiths Industries wide-angle HUD and cockpit lighting compatible with the GEC Cat's Eyes NVG. Also included were upward and downward firing AN/ALE-39 chaff and flare dispensers, the upward firing ones being scabbed on to the topsides of the rear fuselage (an unusual concept for America aircraft, but found on the MiG-29 and the Su-27) fitted perhaps in the light of the Soviet experience in Afghanistan. As one US Marine pilot explained, 'Good decoys are vital to us – because of the position of the Harrier's engine exhaust any SAM

controlled by HOTAS 'switchery' and the '100 per cent LERX' at the wing roots. From March 1990 the production standard of the Night Attack Harrier was also raised by the fitting of the Rolls-Royce F402-RR-408 11-61 engine, the first aircraft to receive the new powerplant being 163873.

The majority of Night Attack Harriers were to be found at MCAS Yuma in Arizona, and the first unit to take on charge the new breed was VMA-214, 'The Black Sheep', on 1 September 1989, which took its new mounts on deployment to Iwakuni in October 1991. Hot on the heels of 'The Black Sheep' came VMA-211, 'The Wake

1992. VMA-233 was the only Cherry Pointer to have the night attack model from 1992 until converting to the Harrier II Plus in June 1994.

VMA-211 was deployed alongside other 'vanilla' AV-8Bs aboard USS *Tarawa* during the summer of 1992, aiding in Operation *Restore Hope* in Somalia and being relieved by USS *Tripoli* before the action began.

Current Camouflage

Night Attack Harriers all currently carry the standard HTPS paintwork.

Development aircraft: 162966 markings

The first version of the AV-8B(NA) was initially delivered to China Lake for an intense three-months evaluation period. During this time it was painted in the traditional US Marine Corps grey and green wrap-around camouflage scheme, with the stylized black tail markings of VX-5, 'The Vampires'. All other markings, including national insignia, were in black, and on the nose a white bird logo was applied with the words 'Night Attack' to the rear.

The first AV-8B(NA) 162966 on a test flight over Missouri in 1987. McDonnell Douglas

GEC Cat's Eyes night vision goggles

The Cat's Eye NVGs are fitted with prismatic lenses with clear glass to allow the pilot to 'look through' at his HUD and instruments. The actual NVG binocular lenses are at forehead level.

'Cat's Eyes': US Marine Corps Harrier II Plus

The original concept of a radar-equipped Harrier was first mooted in a 1988 Marine Corps requirement for an upgraded AV-8 that could carry out attacks by both day and night, without regard for weather conditions. By combining the interest of the Navies of Spain and Italy, which also had a requirement for an aircraft that could carry out fleet defence and attack with the 'off the shelf' proven abilities of the APG-65 radar system and the capabilities of the

FLIR-equipped Night Attack Harrier, an MoU (Memorandum of Understanding) was signed with the governments of Spain and Italy in 1990 jointly to fund radar integration and development for a new variant of the Harrier. McDonnell Douglas was thus awarded a contract on 3 December 1990, and the first Harrier II Plus, 164129, fitted with an APG-65Q4 radar took to the air on 22 September 1992, with test pilot Jackie Jackson at the helm. With the concept having been proved, a second MoU was signed for the production of the Harrier II Plus in 1992, and manufacture

Harrier fleet, and for twenty-seven new airframes to be produced. The reality of the situation was only seventy-three rebuilds were authorized from a total of 144 aircraft. However, the reworked AV-8Bs would have the benefit of the stronger, new-build Night Attack Standard fuselage, while retaining the original wings, tailfin, tailplane and undercarriage. The only objection to the remanufactured aircraft was that the reuse of their original wings without internal modification prevented the fitting of the extra outrigger pylons, as seen on the Night Attack, II Plus and RAF aircraft.

Specification – Harrier II Plus	
ENGINE	One F402-RR-408 Pegasus turbofan.
WEIGHTS	Empty 14,600lb (6,600kg); loaded 31,000lb (14,000kg).
DIMENSIONS	Span 30ft 4in (9.2m); length 47ft 9in (14.5m).
PERFORMANCE	Max level speed at sea level: 600kts (1,100km/h); range (typical): 450nm (830km); ceiling: 50,000ft (15,000m).
ARMAMENT	1xGAU-12/U Gatling cannon, Sidewinder AAMs, bombs, CBUs

The first Harrier II Plus making its inaugural flight on 22 September 1992 over southern Missouri.
McDonnell Douglas

began with aircraft 164548 which made its first flight on 17 March 1993, with the first deliveries to US squadron service beginning in June 1993.

The US Marine Corps programme had called for all its remaining original AV-8B airframes to be converted to the II Plus standard in a concerted effort to standardize the

The capability upgrade was a major advance even when measured against the Night Attack Harrier, giving the users a greater operational scope. The addition of several new and key systems has given the jet a much wider envelope of 'missions in conditions'. For the US Marines, it is what they always desired: VSTOL with 'eyes',

and for the first time the ability to operate their Harriers in all elements.

The Harrier II Plus retains all the avionics of the successful Night Attack Harrier, including the FLIR and upward and downward firing Tracor AN/ALE-39 chaff/flare launchers scabbed to the upper and lower rear fuselage. It also has the benefit of the

APG-65 Radar

The central element for the Harrier II Plus is the radar: the Hughes APG-65Q4, an extremely versatile and compact Doppler set which is already in service with the McDonnell Douglas F/A-18 Hornet, and has been cleverly squeezed into a radome that is even smaller that of the F/A-18, running flush with the Harrier's fuselage. The APG-65Q4 is fully integrated into the existing nav/attack system through the MIL STD 1553 databus, has a jam resistant capability and, even though it is reportedly degraded by 10 per cent in the air-to-air mode compared with its counterpart in the Hornet (due to a size reduction in the dish to accommodate it to the radome), it still offers more than impressive all-weather tracking, even against hard manoeuvring targets, and has search, track, track-while-search and air-combat modes – providing information for SARH (semi-automatic radar homing) missiles for BVR (beyond visual range) engagements, as well as rapid acquisition for Sidewinder and 25mm cannon fire. In the air-to-ground mode it can ensure the successful delivery of a huge variety of weapons, and has modes for high-resolution, long-range surface mapping, as well as the detection and tracking of both land- and sea-based targets, whether moving or stationary. The radar can be overlaid by the FLIR image, thus giving a true 'near daylight' picture, and this can be projected on to the SU-158 wide-angle HUD or viewed on one of the two cockpit MPCDs. The night systems of the Harrier II Plus are completed by the pilot-worn Cat's Eyes NVG, with the Harrier having NVG-compatible cockpit lighting.

(Top) **The compact APG-65 radar, seen here in the nose of an F-18.**
McDonnell Douglas

(Left) **Capt. Mike Richardson demonstrates the Cat's Eye NVGs.**
Author

powerful Rolls-Royce Pegasus F402-RR-408 engine, the installation of the 100 per cent LERX, GPS receiver and provision for the AIM-120 AMRAAM missile, as well as a proposed reconnaissance pod. For the pilot it means the advantages of a laser disk-generated colour moving map, a Card File computer system and a portable DSU (data storage unit).

The DSU has taken away the need to feed flight information into the aircraft's computer while the pilot is sitting in the cockpit; this can now be done in the squadron's operations centre at the mission-planning stage. The pilots spend a great deal of time in the planning phase at the MOMS (maintenance operator and mapping station), which is a computer set up to calculate timings, fuel, threat sector and navigational planning. The computer then provides the ingress and egress routes, required fuel, the positions of the known threat corridors, weaponeering, moon or sun angles, communications, AN/APX-100 IFF settings, flight 'cards' and load-outs. Once completed, the information is stored on a 3.5in floppy disk and then transferred to the DSU for the pilot to take with him to his aircraft. Card File is an integrated computer system which allows the pilot to 'write' via the planning aid all his mission data on to files which can be accessed during flight on either of the MPCDs.

The digital colour moving map is tied to the INS, and has given the Harrier a 'paperless cockpit' – no longer does the pilot need

Flying the Harrier II Plus

Like the other Harriers before it, the II Plus has its function in the supporting of the Marine on the ground. The aircraft is so designed as to provide its pilot with mission and flight data at all times, and the pilot must know how to interpret this information to the best advantage. The radar can be used to verify the INS for position, target location and to 'sanitize' enemy airspace for fighters, for instance. The FLIR, HUD and NVGs aid safe flight control, visual detection and ID on targets. As the selected target is approached, final radar verification of the INS is undertaken, weapons armed and further 'sanitization' carried out. Using a combination of FLIR, radar and INS the target is acquired, the computer works out the delivery solutions and the weapons are released. As Marine pilots such as Captain Mike 'Shooter' Richardson are at pains to point out: 'It's as simple as that!'

Inside the roomy cockpit with systems fired up; on the left MPCD is the FLIR picture, on the right MPCD is the moving map. McDonnell Douglas

the obligatory 'legful' of flight papers, as the aircraft's position is on constant view, in several scales from 1:1,000,000 down to 1:50,000, and relevant mission data, such as fuel, timings, threat data, navigation cues and 'reminders' may be marked on the map display.

The GEC Sensors FLIR is housed in an angular 'box' fairing in the centre of the nose section set back above the radome, and is just lower than the pilot's actual line of sight, thus giving him a far more realistic view forward than that provided by wing or fuselage mounted pods. The FLIR can be set to either white equals hot or black equals hot, depending on the pilot's choice, and is capable of piercing through all but the most severe rainstorms, which can degrade its performance. Its view forward can be projected on to the Harrier's wide-angle HUD or on to one of the two MPCDs, allowing the pilot to conduct 'day' tactics after dark. As a result of the introduction of the new nose shape, the Harrier's familiar 'yaw-vane' has been relocated to the right-hand side of the nose just in front of the windshield. Also included in the armoury of the Harrier II Plus is a Missile Approach Warning System (MAWS), the external 'eye' of which can be found in a faceted sensor beneath the aircraft's nose. This sensor detects 'flashes' and missile plumes by scanning in the ultraviolet and providing both a visual and an audible warning in the cockpit.

Future enhancements planned for the Harrier II Plus include an ATHS (Automatic Target Hand-off System) system, which will enable other elements such as ground-based FACs to have a direct link to the aircraft's systems to feed target information to the on-board computer, and wing-tip Sidewinder stations to free up underwing pylon space. Other options for the Harrier II Plus take their lead from the 'flexible basing' scenarios. Because the Harrier does not require an external power source the possibility exists for many types of vessel to carry Harriers: towed or anchored barges, cargo ships, even platforms on oil tankers have been discussed.

Harrier II Plus – New Build

With their $20 million contract in hand, McDonnell Douglas set about modifying AV-8B 164129 into a full-scale development airframe, as a precursor to an order for twenty-seven aircraft. It was flown ahead of schedule by 'Jackie' Jackson on 22 September 1992, and was passed to the Naval Air Weapons Center for airframe and systems trials in early 1993 before being transferred to China Lake for radar evaluation. The second 'brand new II' was dispatched to VX-5 for further trials, while a third, 164548, was tested for carrier work before being delivered to its new masters VMA-542 at Cherry Point in June 1993. The first aircraft was painted in the HTPS of dark sea grey, FS 36118, applied to the top of the wings and fuselage, dark gull grey, FS 36321, on the outer sections of the upper wings and fuselage sides, and dark ghost grey, FS 36230, on the undersides. The aircraft carried national insignia and 'Marines' titles for its maiden flight and had the national flags of the USA, Spain and Italy applied to the sides of the nose just below the windshield. The paintwork was, as would be expected, flawless: the radome being a satin finish compared with the matt of the rest of the airframe. No. 164129 also had its upper chaff/flare launchers faired over, did not carry the MAWS fitting and carried strakes instead of the gun pack.

Harrier II Plus – Rebuild

As mentioned above, the rebuild programme centred around a new fuselage, which was a cheaper option than actually extending and modifying the existing structure. The rebuild process takes about a year per airframe and the contract is set for completion in 2002. An important work-share

Low-angle view of the nose of the II Plus on the Cherry Point ramp. Author

arrangement was developed between the Naval Aviation Depot (NADEP) which is located at MCAS Cherry Point, where the AV-8 aircraft are assembled and inspected, and McDonnell Douglas's St Louis facility to perform the work on the aircraft.

It was on 29 November 1995 that 'Jackie' Jackson flew the first remanufactured Harrier II Plus, a/c 263/165305 (formerly 168782) from St Louis with no problems, and within three months the first of the rebuild aircraft were entering squadron service. The first flight was made in an 'unpainted' state, with only 263 165305 visible, stencilled on the rear fuselage.

Harrier II Plus in USMC service

The Harrier II Plus is concentrated at MCAS Cherry Point in North Carolina, where the first unit to receive the new aircraft was VMA-542, 'The Flying Tigers', taking 164548 on charge in June 1993, followed by deliveries to VMA-223, 'The Bulldogs', in June 1994 and to VMA-231, 'Ace of Spades', later that year.

VMA-542's 'The Flying Tigers' aircraft carry the HTPS with their familiar yellow 'tiger' markings applied to the rudders. A low-visibility tiger's head emblem has been applied to the nose, and all markings are in low-vis FS 36320; the tail code is WH.

VMA-223's 'The Bulldogs' aircraft also have the HTPS and continue to carry the

rudder art which dates from when it was VMF-223, the 'Rainbow Squadron', in 1943, although now it is only seen as dark grey over light grey on the rudder. The name VMA-223 is just ahead of the chaff/flare dispensers and the word 'Bulldogs' is painted on the upper rear fuselage. The Squadron insignia of a boxing glove-clad bulldog may be found on the nose,

either in low-vis or full colour; the tail code is WP.

VMA-231's 'Ace of Spades' aircraft also carry the HTPS and are the most colourful of the three units, having a very dark grey rudder with 'Ace of Spade' characters picked out in lighter grey. The Squadron's logo of an 'Ace' playing card is in a dark grey circle on the nose; the tail code is CG.

(Above) **A brace of 'Tigers' take on fuel from a USMC KC-130 Hercules.** McDonnell Douglas

(Below) **Two 'Tigers' from VMA-542.** McDonnell Douglas

A brace of 'Bulldogs' with high-vis Squadron emblems. McDonnell Douglas

A 'Bulldog' banks away, giving a good view of its underside; note the Equaliser cannon, its ammunition pod and 'bridge link' between the two, plus the typical Harrier engine exhaust stain pattern.
McDonnell Douglas

'Ace from the pack', a II Plus from VMA-231. McDonnell Douglas

A II Plus from VMA-231 releases a pair of iron bombs from a shallow dive on one of the range targets.
McDonnell Douglas

Pilot Profile

Captain Mike Richardson, callsign 'Shooter', is a Marine pilot of thirty-five from Hamilton, Ohio. He was commissioned as a Second Lieutenant in the USMC in 1987, completing his primary jet training on the T-34 in 1988. Intermediate jet training took place in the T-2, and advanced flying in the A-4 Skyhawk from 1989 to 1990. He converted to the AV-8B in November 1990 and served with VMA-542 as Harrier II Plus Standardization Officer from 1994 to 1996. He comments: 'The Harrier II Plus is what we always wanted, and it's a quantum leap for the Marine Corps.'

Capt Mike Richardson poses in front of a Harrier II Plus on the Cherry Point flightline. Author

Harriers...Break!! McDonnell Douglas

Harrier Ejector Seats

Harrier Type	Seat Type
P1127	Martin-Baker Mk4B
Kestrel	Martin-Baker Mk6HA
P1127(RAF)	Martin-Baker Mk6HA
GR.1/1A	Martin-Baker Type 9A Mk.2
GR.3	Martin-Baker Type 9A Mk2
T.4	Martin-Baker Type 9D1 Mk2
	Martin-Baker Type 9D2 Mk2
T.8	Martin-Baker Type 9D2 Mk2
	Martin-Baker Type 9D2 Mk2
GR.5	Martin-Baker Mk12
GR.7	Martin-Baker Mk12A
T.10	Martin-Baker M12A
	Martin-Baker Mk12B
FRS.1	Martin-Baker Mk10H
F/A-2	Martin-Baker Mk10H
AV8A up to 159259 then retrofitted	Stencel SIIIS-3
AV8C	Stencel SIIIS-3
TAV-8A	Stencel SIIIS-3
AV8B	Stencel SIIIS-3 AV8B
TAV-8B	Stencel SIIIS-3 AV8B
Indian FRS.51	Martin-Baker MkIOH
Indian T.60	Martin-Baker Type 9D
	Martin-Baker Type 9D
Spanish AV8A AV8B AV8S TAV-8A	Stencel SIIIS-3
Spanish EAV-8B	Stencel SIIIS-3 AV8
Italian AV8B + TAV-8B	Stencel SIII3-S AV8

(Top) **Martin-Baker Mk12 High performance ejector seat with the capability of sensing airspeed and adjusting its operation to suit. The Mk12 was fitted to the GR.5.** Martin-Baker

Probably the only recorded photograph of a pilot ejecting from a Harrier; captured by Robin Adshead of the Military Picture Library, this stunning image shows the pilot of Harrier GR.1A XV739/V banging out; he was involved in rehearsal for an airshow at Episkopi in Cyprus and went out of control through an excessive pitch down from a vertical climb. The photographer reports that, contrary to other published reports that the pilot sustained a broken leg, in fact he suffered a broken ankle after been forcibly removed from the ground by an overzealous airman.
Robin Adshead MPL

CHAPTER NINE

UK Second Generation

RAF Harrier GR.5

Essentially an 'Anglicized' AV-8B, the RAF's Harrier GR.5 represented a major technological leap for the UK's Harrier Force – with the further promise of even greater things to come. In 1981 the MoD confirmed an order for sixty Harrier GR.5s with a further two examples to be acquired for pure development work. The GR.5 was purchased through a programme that continued the partnership between British Aerospace and McDonnell Douglas which had been so successful with the AV-8A/B. For the GR.5 however, the balance moved in favour of the UK, with an equal work-share in the GR.5, rather than a 60/40 share in the AV-8B. This had the effect of supporting valuable jobs for the UK aviation industry. In August 1981 an MoU was signed in which the RAF agreed to buy the developed version of the AV-8B.

The original Harrier had already proved that it was a small target to spot, the exhaust nozzles hidden under the high wings left little heat signature and the Pegasus put out little smoke, and it had an amazing reliability and turn-round time. A lot was expected of the new breed. Externally differing from the AV-8B only in the extreme nose section, the GR.5's main changes were internal. In the more spacious cockpit, the US AV-8B's Stencel ejector seat was replaced by a 'zero-zero' Martin-Baker Mk12. The cockpit layout was definitely of the next century when compared with the GR.3's. A Ferranti FIN.1075 INAS replaced the Litton AN/ASN-130 of the AV-8B (although early models carried the Litton system because of delays with the Ferranti model), providing a moving-map display on the right-hand side of the fascia, fed by cassette tape of the pilot's intended sortie area. An MFD occupied the left-hand side of the instrument panel. On the pilot's eyeline was a Smiths Industries HUD, below which was the pilot's UFC (up-front controller) – his interface with the aircraft's computer system. Traditional 'dials'

The modern cockpit of the GR.5, with its MPDC and colour moving-map. BAe

are conspicuous by their absence, except for the basic flight instrumentation such as altitude, speed AOA and a clock. The side consoles carried fuel switches and lighting,

oxygen and power supply switches on the right, with the HOTAS nozzle lever and the throttle lever on the left, along with other devices such as the SAAHS, an essential for automatic stabilization throughout flight, which also acted as an autopilot during take-off and landing. On the nose end of the GR.5 was the 'eye' for the Hughes AN/ASB-19 ARBS which also contained a Dual Mode Tracker (DMT), which in its TV mode projects target information and accurate angle-rate data to the pilot via his HUD or MFD, to ensure the best delivery for a single-pass attack. In its 'laser' mode it can detect and lock-on to targets being 'sparkled' by a ground-based or airborne FAC.

Like the AV-8B, the GR.5's use of composite materials was also an innovation, and the new 'big-wing' allowed for a much improved performance and increased the amount of weaponry that could be carried, with small LERX extensions (a British development originally destined for the GR.5(K)) at the wing roots. Under the wings themselves, instead of the five stations of earlier Harriers, the GR.5 had eight, with a pair of Sidewinder launch

rails being cleverly added to the front portion of the outrigger wheel fairings, thus not taking up valuable space needed for other weapons. In place of the AV-8B's GAU-12/U Gattling gun, the MoD selected twin Royal Ordinance 25mm Aden (AD from Armament, Design and ENfield) gas-operated revolver-cannons with NATO Stanag 4173 ammunition. Beneath the ARBS is a curiously shaped fairing for the proposed Miniature Infra-Red Linescan (MIRLS) system, which was to have provided an all-weather reconnaissance capability; however, costs and delays forced the project to be shelved, thereby effectively 'losing' the reconnaissance capabilities of the GR.5, which were not completely re-addressed until the advent of the GR.7. The IFF transponder was also changed from the Bendix type fitted to the AV-8B to a Cossor IFF.4760. The RAF's radio suite was provided by the GEC.

The engine chosen for the GR.5 was the Pegasus Mk.105, offering 21,750lb of

thrust, some 300lb more than the engine of the AV-8B. This also contained the DECS (digital engine control system) which monitored the performance of the powerplant and manages the propulsion systems. Developed jointly by Rolls-Royce, British Aerospace, McDonnell Douglas and Dowty/Smiths Industries, it automatically adjusts the engine's thrust settings, after taking into account the speed, altitude jetpipe temperature and acceleration, functions that previously had had to be monitored by the pilot.

A lengthy flight testing programme was undertaken with the initial development aircraft ZD318 (DB1), which first flew on 30 April 1985, with ZD319 (DB2) testing the engine, systems and ordnance trials. However, lengthy delays with the avionics fit and weapons clearances resulted in the first GR.5 not being delivered until May 1989. ZD318 was rolled out and flown with strakes not gunpacks in an unpainted state, the only concession to any type of

Forward fuselage undergoing inspection. BAe

commemorative marking was a large white 'Harrier' and a large red 'GR.5' on the nose and 'ZD318' roughly stencilled on the tail-fin. The RAF's order for sixty production aircraft was split into forty-one to be completed as standard GR.5s and the remainder as GR.5As. A major factor in the service delay was the sad and somewhat

had accidentally fired, dragging him out of the cockpit.

Following these unfortunate delays, RAF Wittering finally received its first GR.5, ZD323/A, on 30 April 1987, an aircraft which was intended for familiarization only and was immediately taken on charge by the GR.5 Conversion Team

The original plan was to equip the two RAF Germany squadrons with the GR.5 first, but this was thwarted by many factors, and the first unit to form up on 23 November 1988 was fittingly No.1(F) Squadron, which had been instrumental in bringing the Harrier GR.1 into service. It finally relinquished its GR.3s in the

ZD318, the first Harrier GR.5 flies in its unpainted state. BAe

bizarre loss of GR.5 ZD325 on its last pre-delivery trip on 22 October 1987 with Taylor Scott at the controls. While checks were being made over Salisbury Plain, contact was lost with the pilot although the aircraft continued to be tracked heading west. It was eventually sighted by a USAFE F-15 which reported that the canopy was shattered but the ejector seat – minus the pilot – was still in position. The aircraft flew on for another hour and a half before plunging into the sea. Scott's body was recovered from a small town in Wiltshire and investigations concluded that his ejector seat manual separation system

(GR5CT), a unit formed within No.233 OCU, flying its first sortie on 30 March 1988, with Sqn Ldr John Baynton at the controls. In all eight aircraft were received by the GR5CT. The Team's personnel were all trained by the US Marine Corps at Cherry Point, using their simulator and flying the AV-8B. On 28 September 1988 Wg Cdr Peter Day, AFC, the then OC of 233 OCU, climbed out of a Harrier GR.5 and into the record books as the first pilot in the world to complete 3,000 hours on the Harrier, with a special marking applied to the nose: 'Wg Cdr Pete Day 70–88 3,000hrs'.

early spring of 1989 and was fully operational with the GR.5 by 2 November 1989, after being declared to SACEUR's Strategic Reserve (AIR) on 2 October. No.1 Squadron also made the first live firing of a Sidewinder missile by an aircraft on operational duty when Flt Lt 'Spike' Jepson released an AIM-9L at a flare towed behind a low flying Jindivik drone over the Aberporth range in June 1989. Conversion by 233 OCU mirrored that of No.1 Squadron, the former also being 'operational' by April 1989, from which time deliveries switched to No.3 Squadron at Guterslôh, which received its first GR.5

(Above) **Flt Lt 'Spike' Jepson unloads a Sidewinder at a Jindivik drone over the Aberporth range.** BAe

A No.4 (AC) Squadron GR.5 comes in to land in a woodland clearing. BAe

(Above) **Toting a full load of seven BL.755 Inert Cluster Bombs, indicative of the aircraft's abilities but unlikely to constitute a typical warload.**
BAe

Rising up from an 'Ebhardt' site in Germany, the efflux from the Pegasus engine blowing spray in its wake. Denis J. Calvert

in December 1988, reaching operational status in April 1990. It was decided that No.3 Squadron's co-located sister unit, No.4 Squadron, should not get the GR.5 but go straight to the GR.7, receiving ZG473 in late December 1990. Another user of the GR.5 was the Boscombe Down-based Strike Attack OEU which had three GR.5s on strength during the early 1990s, one being ZD328. Harrier GR.5s also took part in the fly-past over Buckingham Palace of 168 aircraft on 15 September 1990 to mark the fiftieth anniversary of the Battle of Britain.

The 'Horsefly' trials

In the summer of 1989 three GR.5s from the Strike Attack OEU deployed to the US Weapons Center at China Lake to carry out an evaluation of the Marconi Zeus ECM system and the tailcone-mounted, semi-active Plessey MAWS, which is designed to warn of the launching of heat-seeking missiles, such as the Russian SA-7 Grail. These tests were described as 'convincing and effective' and concentrated on the testing of the threat-warning and active-jamming capabilities provided by the two systems. After the China Lake deployment, the aircraft relocated to MCAS Yuma where they flew on the ACMI range against US Marines AV-8Bs.

A huge leap forward for the RAF, the GR.5 was still only an interim model before the GR.7. Author

Flt Lt Gary Waterfall.
Author

VIFFing in the GR.5

'VIFFing is not the "square corner magic" you sometimes hear about', explains Flt Lt Gary Waterfall from No.20(R) Squadron,

it does, however, have some useful applications both on the offence and defence. On the offence, you want to improve your nose position for a gun attack or missile lock. At max-turn rate your wings are performing at the ideal AOA. Any more the drag increases, any less and the aircraft buffets, you loose airspeed and turn performance deteriorates. If you lower the nozzles, the wings are still carrying the same g-loading, but the vector changes, increasing the rate of turn. In other words, some of the thrust, instead of pushing the Harrier forward, pushes the nose upwards. Of course, the lack of forward thrust kills your airspeed, so it must be used at the right moment to give you a shot and not leave you a 'hanging target'. On the defence the same principles apply, if a bad guy is in your six and turning on to you in a shooting position,

you may be able to tighten your turn but this won't prevent him keeping his guns on you, especially if he's an F-16, but it might against a lesser aircraft. VIFF is very much a last ditch manoeuvre – when all else fails! In the ultimate you can be so slow, almost in the hover and just turn toward him making a difficult shot. Another variation is to 'bury the nose' and use the loss of forward thrust to stay slow, while the other guy overshoots, you tuck in behind – giving you a shot instead. This is of course if its one vs one; if its a pair, 'Plan A' is to get out – fast! Always remembering the Harrier is not a dog-fighter.

Camouflage and Markings

Both the development aircraft ZD318 and ZD319 were originally finished in a paint scheme that comprised dark sea grey, BS.381C-638, upper surfaces and medium sea grey, BS.381C- 637. For a short while ZD319 was noted with a 'false canopy' in back painted beneath the nose.

Front-line aircraft received a two-tone green scheme of NATO green upper surfaces and medium green lower surfaces, the upper surface colour 'wrapping under' the wing leading edges by 2in.

No.233 OCU Welsh wildcat emblem, flanked by red and blue (left) and black and yellow (right) bars on the nose; single letter tailcodes.

No.1 Squadron White disk containing red 'Winged 1' flanked by two white triangles on the nose; two-digit tailcodes in golden yellow.

No.3 Squadron Cockatrice emblem with green and yellow flanking bars, positioned on the engine intake sides; tip of the tail-fin has a thick green band flanked in yellow; two-digit tailcodes in black.

SAOEU Blue ring with red and white triple-swords superimposed over it on the nose; a single, pale blue tailcode letter.

After Dark Trials: Developing the System, 'Nightbirds and Night Vision'

Much of the work undertaken in bringing the Harrier GR.7 into service was assigned to the Strike Attack Operational Evaluation Unit (SAOEU, based at Boscombe Down in Wiltshire. The SAOEU is itself only a resident unit at the DTEO site and is part of the RAF's Air Warfare Centre (AWC), set up after the Gulf War at RAF Waddington in Lincolnshire. Early work in developing the Harrier's night-attack systems was undertaken using two Harrier T.4s (not T.6s, as may have been reported elsewhere) – XW267/SA and XW269/BD, of which XW269 was modified to a derivation called the 'Nightbird Harrier', (complete with a 'blindfolded crow' nose artwork). Along with a Buccaneer S.2, from the A&AEE, a Tornado GR.1 and a FLIR-podded-Jaguar T.2A it undertook the lion's share of the trials work. Although based at

Boscombe Down, much of the Nightbird Harrier flying took place at RAF Lyneham in Wiltshire; however, it was another Harrier that pioneered the earliest FLIR trials in 1983, when RAE Bedford's flying test bed XW175 was used to extend the then RAE Farnborough 'Nightbird' programme into the VSTOL regime. XW175 was fitted with a pod-mounted FLIR under its port wing, and night vision goggles were worn by the crew. This brief trial was concluded in December 1983.

The 'Nightbird' Harrier was fitted with an experimental FLIR system, housed in the nose section originally modified to carry the LRMTS in the Harrier GR.3 and T.4, and was further fitted out with a version of the Ferranti 4510 cursive/raster HUD and an FD.500 video camera. Trials began by the SAOEU in 1990 alongside the GR.7 programme, the unit then having three GR.7s assigned to it for evaluation. Work was also begun on introducing NVG-compatible lighting to the Harrier, with experimental operations being car-

Screaming around a headland, with vapour streaming from the wing just above the LERX, and SAOEU GR.7 makes a low-level dash; the aircraft carries the 'old style' nose markings, inert bombs, Sidewinder acquisition rounds and a Phimat chaff dispenser. Sgt Rick Brewell

Another 'testing' sortie over, ZG472/0 winds down its Pegasus engine on the Boscombe Down ramp; the aircraft carries wing tanks, CBLS pods, Sidewinder launch rails on the outer pylons and a BOL fitted launch rail on the No.2 wing station. Author

(Below) Close-up of the modified LRMTS fairing on the Nightbird Harrier; flight systems at Farnborough were responsible for the modification to the familiar 'Snoopy' nose to accommodate the FLIR. Author

ried out using the Nightbird T.4 which flew the initial NVG sortie on 11 December of that year. A new lightweight GEC Nightbird goggle set, on a swivel mounting attached to the pilot's helmet giving a 40-degree field of view, was tested.

Because of the 'g' forces that would be exerted, if the pilot ejected while still wearing his NVG a broken neck seemed almost a certainty. The Nightbird goggles system, however, is unique in having a miniature detonation system fitted to the helmet clip; this in turn is attached to the ejection seat firing mechanism by a 'pigtail' lead from the back of the pilot's flying

Close-up of the 'blindfolded crow' artwork, applied for the early night tests.
Andy Sephton

The GEC Nightbird NVG set. GEC

helmet. In the case of an ejection, a fraction of a second before the seat fires an electrical pulse is generated to blow away the goggles, thus saving the pilot any further injuries. To facilitate this system the normal Martin-Baker ejector seats have been replaced by the Mk.12-2, which combines the new circuitry for NVG wearers. The pilot therefore wears, as standard for night profiles, a Mk.4 helmet fitted with a clear plastic visor clipped to the front to form a protective barrier between his face and the NVG. For ordinary missions they continue to wear the multilayered Mk.10.

With GR.7 soon to be introduced to squadron service, the SAOEU's work continued apace, and during March 1991 Wg Cdr Keith Grumbly took a detachment of three GR.7s to MCAS Yuma to work alongside the Night Attack AV-8Bs, flying over 70 hrs of operations and monitoring the progress made by the US Marine Corps in nocturnal operations. Procedures were developed for night landings using electro-luminescent stripes to mark landing zones, and other important tactics were developed, such as the use of a Tornado GR.1 with its powerful radar to guide a flight of Harriers through bad weather. Trials were undertaken to bring all of the weaponry and defensive systems used by the GR.7 into service, including the use of TIALD with laser-guided munitions. During the course of 1992 four GR.7s were operated by the SAOEU, based both at Boscombe Down and BAe Dunsfold. This work is a

continuing task as the Harrier continues to develop as a weapons system.

The SAOEU also pioneered the GR.7's introduction to carrier operations when Wg Cdr Nick 'Slats' Slater, the then OC of the unit, deployed three GR.7s to RNAS Yeovilton for ski-jump training on 20 June

---

SAOEU Markings

When the unit began work in the 1990s it carried three red-handled white swords on a blue disc on the forward fuselage sides, along with a white disc bearing the red letters 'AWC' on the tailfin. These markings changed in 1995 to reflect the OEU's own logo. They now consist of a yellow outlined triangle with a blue background over which is laid a white silhouette of a Tornado with a red Harrier superimposed over its centre, painted on the forward fuselage sides. On the tailfins may now be found a stylized blue arrowhead with a single white sword with a yellow handle and three feathered wings in the background.

1994. Flt Lt Chris Norton, flying ZG475, had the honour of becoming the first RAF pilot to land a second-generation Harrier on a ship when on 27 June he alighted on HMS *Illustrious*. Sadly on 1 June 1995 Slater was killed when his Harrier GR.7, ZG475, flew into the sea off Wigtown Bay while on an equipment evaluation trial from Boscombe Down. His replacement, Wg Cdr Mark Green, continues the valuable work begun by his predecessor. The GR.7 also made a long deployment aboard HMS *Illustrious* during her visit to Malaysia in 1997, with elements from No.1 Squadron taking up temporary residence.

An SAOEU Harrier GR.7 is prepared for its next trials sortie by its groundcrew; the portable toolkit is being unpacked, while the demineralized water tank is being replenished from the yellow bowser by the crewman atop the aircraft. Author

An SAOEU GR.7 pilot discusses a minor snag discovered after an equipment evaluation sortie. Author

Pegasus 11-61 Test: 'Blue-Bird' ZD402

Based on a demonstrator engine, the XG-15 (X for extra power, 15 for 15 per cent) co-funded by Rolls-Royce and the MoD, the Pegasus 11-61 was the key to a series of improvements for the second generation of Harrier. Derived from the Pegasus 11-21, the 11-61 offered greater thrust, and a series of other developments, including a new front fan, and a full authority digital engine control unit (FADEC). The improvement in thrust increased the engines output from 22,000 to 23,800lb, reduced the maintenance requirements and added a greater flexibility of operation.

For the British part of the 11-61 flight test programme, the new engine was installed in a specially painted Harrier GR.5 – ZD402, which was delivered by

Sqn Ldr Gerry Humphries of No.1(F) Squadron displays the Nightbird set as he settles into the cockpit for a late afternoon into night sortie from Wittering. Author

(Below) **Harrier ZD402 taken during one of its Pegasus 11-61 engine test flights.** BAe

road to Rolls-Royce at Filton in April 1989. The first flight trials of the new engine took place on 9 June 1989, and in all six test pilots flew a total of forty sorties occupying 36 hrs of test flying. The aircraft was fitted with a MODAS system as well as a MARS (Modular Airborne Recording System) for its evaluation flights. Incorporated in the testing cycle were a number of new time-to-height record attempts, all set on 6 June: 36.38 sec to 300m and 81.00 sec to 9,000m were set by Andy Sefton; 55.38 sec to 6000m and 126.63 sec to 1,2000m were set by Heinz Frick. The other four pilots involved in the tests were Chris Roberts from BAe, Flt Lt Dave Mackay from the A&AEE, Capt Glen 'Gremlin' Hoppe of the USMC, and 'Jackie' Jackson from McDonnell Douglas.

ZD402, the thirty-third Harrier GR.5 built was delivered direct to Filton from the Dunsfold paint shop where it had received its smart 'one-off mix' colour scheme of 75 per cent roundel blue, BS.C381C:110, and 25 per cent black with white trimmings. Rolls-Royce and USMC badges were applied above the fuselage roundels, and the Rolls-Royce Flight Test Centre badge was applied forward of the jet nozzles. A large BAe badge was placed on the engine access bay panel on top of the fuselage, and the USMC and Rolls-Royce Flight Test Centre badges were also applied on either side of the tailfin. Late in June a small yellow duck motif was added above the fuselage roundel, and for a few days in July when McDonnell Douglas pilot 'Jackie' Jackson took the helm, the company logos were added to the underfuselage strakes.

During the test programme areas of paint and decal began to peel off, and because of the short duration of the scheme were never repainted. The rudder and right auxiliary door were replaced by standard NATO green components and all but the missile pylons were removed for the record attempting flights.

ZD402 made its final flight on 16 August, following which the engine was removed for transporting to the USA and the aircraft was shipped back to the Dunsfold paint shop on the 22nd for return to its service scheme. It subsequently reappeared with No.1 Squadron coded '04' on 15 January 1990, thereafter being converted to GR.7 standard and working with No.20(R) Squadron, the Harrier OCU, in 1993 at RAF Wittering.

'War Does Not Stop When Darkness Falls': Harrier GR.7, Nocturnal Warrior

As the GR.5 was a quantum leap in technology over the GR.3, so the GR.7 registered great strides over the GR.5. Even though externally the GR.7 is still a GR.5 with a different nose, in terms of capabilities those of the GR.7 are exceptional. The GR.7 has given the RAF the ability to operate its Harrier Force by night and in all but the most foul weather; however, as the Service is at pains to point out, the latest incarnation has its limitations in that not being equipped with a radar means the GR.7 cannot claim the title 'all weather'. The 'night' capability is afforded by the addition of a GEC FLIR fitted on the upper surface of an elongated nose section, which also houses the external antennas for the forward hemisphere Marconi Zeus ECM system on its underside and the 'eye' for the ARBS system. The second element in the night suite is the addition of GEC Nightbird NVG, and these two systems combined have almost doubled the hours available to the Harrier Force for combat duties.

The FLIR is an off-the-shelf GEC unit, mounted ahead of the windshield, in direct line with the pilot's vision, and its image can be overlaid on to the new Smiths Industries wide-angle HUD, which is also able to display the usual flight information to the pilot. The FLIR will also display small 'V' markers that represent its sensing of 'hot spots' such as vehicle engines. The FLIR is, however, limited by thick cloud because of the effects that water vapour has on its image. Below the new HUD, on either side of the main panel and UFC are two MPCDs, which display the colour moving-map data on the left and FLIR imagery on the right. Controlled from the HOTAS throttle quadrant are the means to alter the FLIR's polarity, according to what the pilot feels best suits his mission.

The Nightbird goggles are an excellent complement to the FLIR and are invaluable when the pilot is searching for a target or 'looking into a turn' ahead of the FLIR's view. The cockpit lighting has been suitably reduced to account for the performance of the goggles. Carried over from the GR.5 is the Hughes AN/ASB-19(V) ARBS already mentioned, which although it has no night-time capabilities,

Specification – Harrier GR.7	
ENGINE	One 21,800lb (9,900kg) Rolls-Royce Pegasus 105 turbofan.
WEIGHTS	Empty 13,000lb (5,900kg); loaded 31,000lb (14,000kg).
DIMENSIONS	Span 30ft 4in (9.2m); length 46ft 4in (14m).
PERFORMANCE	Max level speed at sea level: 622kts (1,150km/h); range (typical): 660nm (1,200km); ceiling: 50,000ft (15,500m).
ARMAMENT	2x25mm Aden cannon, bombs, CBUs, LGBs, Sidewinder & AMRAAM AAMs, CRV-7 rockets.

remains an extremely useful piece of equipment in the hours of daylight, with its x 6 magnification TV picture, which may be displayed on either MPCD. The HOTAS controls have also been enlarged to aid the operation of the new systems. The tailcone of the Harrier is designed to accommodate the Plessey radar-jamming semi-active MAWS (a piece of equipment still uncleared for service at the time of writing). The ejection system is the standard Martin-Baker Mk.12 zero-zero unit.

Many of the GR.7s now have GPS fitted, in a fleet-wide modification programme; this is used in conjunction with the GEC Ferranti FIN 1075'G' (for GPS fitted) INS and colour moving-map display and has given the aircraft a highly precise navigational ability to within 30m of the intended 'target', and also serves to aid any dispersed operations in less than ideal weather conditions. GPS-fitted aircraft may be identified by a small, white, circular aerial fitted flush to the spine.

The GEC Marconi ARI 23333 Zeus threat identification and jamming system utilizes a programmable library of known radar threats (and may be quickly updated); once one is detected it activates jamming procedures and will operate chaff and flares accordingly. The threat data are displayed to the pilot by his HUD or MPCDs as well as by the traditional 'howl' in his headset.

These new systems are known colloquially as 'The Magic' by the Harrier fraternity, as Sqn Ldr Gerry Humphries of No.1(F) Squadron explains:

At night targets stand out well because of their thermal significance, and any light shining can be picked up and seen up to 100 miles away (depending on operating level). Also operating nocturnally we are less likely to be seen by the optical defences that threaten us in daylight, such as shoulder-launched SAMs, visually directed AAA or small arms fire.

The GR.7 is able to carry the same variety of weaponry as the GR.5, including the SNEB and the CRV-7 rocket pods, as well as standard iron bombs, LGBs and CBUs. A pair of Sidewinder AAMs are routinely carried. At the time of writing, the Royal Ordi-

Swedish-made BOL system, which cuts and fires chaff from a rear dispenser, the rounded front end containing a propellant gas bottle. In some instances a Philips Matra Phimat pod has been carried on one of the outer wing pylons.

A grey-clad GR.7 from No.20(R) Squadron fires off a volley of CRV-7 rockets. BAe

---

Night Pilots

For a pilot to be declared 'Night combat ready' he must first have been declared 'Day combat ready' on his squadron before starting out on the programme of twenty-five sorties, which covers all aspects of day operations – except they are performed at night. Early sorties include general handling, circuits, night tanking over the North Sea, working in pairs, and operating with other radar-equipped fighters, before embarking on Forward Air Control work with live weapons and simulated attack profiles.

The turning performance of the GR.7 has been enhanced by the fitting of the 100 per cent LERX, which will become standard on all Harriers, rather than the smaller version originally installed on the GR.5/7. The full sized LERX was introduced in 1991 on ZG506, following modifications to the Honeywell AN/ASW-46(V)2 SAAHS; at the same time new engine fire access panels were observed, now shaped like small air-scoops above the LERX, because the 100 per cent type covered up the original 'holes'.

nance 25mm, pneumatically-cocked Aden revolver cannons were still not cleared for service, and the aircraft continue to carry the old but empty 30mm packs to aid VSTOL performance. The Sidewinder launch rails have been refitted with the

Mission planning had always been a headache for the Harrier pilot, having to input way points and co-ordinates direct to the aircraft's computer via the UFC. Just entering service as this book is in preparation, is the EDS Scicon AMPA (Advanced

One of the development GR.7s toting an unusual warload, further evidence on the flexibility of the aircraft. BAe

A Harrier GR.7 fires a salvo of projectiles from underwing SNEB launchers. BAe

Mission Planning Aid) which allows the pilot to pre-plan on the ground by the of reconnaissance photographs, computer-generated graphics and calculations in a similar manner to the MOMS used in the US; all the data are stored in a pod and fed direct to the computer when the pilot inserts the 'brick' into the cockpit interface.

The last thirty-four of the ninety-six single-seat Harrier Mk.IIs built for the RAF were delivered as GR.7s and the remainder were converted by BAe from either existing GR.5s or GR.5As. The GR.5A (which covered airframes ZD430 to ZD438 and ZD461 to ZD470) was so designated as an interim measure, being basically a GR.5 with an empty GR.7 nose, complete with all the wiring for the new systems. These interim airframes almost all went into store at Shawbury, except for ZD433 which went

to Wittering as a maintenance trainer, ZD466 to Rolls-Royce at Filton, and ZD470 to the A&AEE. The first Dunsfold reworked GR.5 ZD380 was delivered to service on 21 December 1990, joining No.4(AC) Squadron at Gütersloh; the first Mk.5A fitted as a full GR.7 arrived for upgrade in September 1990 and also joined No.4(AC) Squadron in April 1991. The first new-build GR.7, ZG471, entered service with No.1(F) Squadron, and ZG472 was the first to arrive at the SAOEU in May 1990. In 1989 ZD318 (DB1), one of the two original Harrier development aircraft, was fitted out with the night systems and new nose section and moved to the A&AEE to continue work on the new equipment, and ZD319 (DB2) was fitted out as a GR.5A. Both retained their original development medium sea grey and dark sea grey colours; ZD318 gained black and white photo-reference markings and was used for airframe assessments including ski-jump trials.

June 1992 No.1(F)'s Harrier GR.5s began to be exchanged for a modified batch of GR.5As, now with full mission fit as GR.7s, the first two being ZD461 and ZD434. The first GR.7 night sortie was made on 2 June 1992 in ZD434, and on the 19th Flt Lt Lance Nichol in ZD437 made the first trip using the FIN 1075G, with which six other aircraft (ZD431/435/437/438/463/464) had also been equipped as a special trial fit. It was not envisaged that the other units should use the night systems until the mid 1990s, but it was prudent to continue the converting of them to the new type; therefore No.

Change programme, both No.3 and No.4 moved from Gütersloh to Laarbruch during the latter part of 1992. It was intended that the complete removal of Harriers from Germany should be accomplished by 1999, when the two units would return to RAF Cottesmore, thus making a 'twin-base' arrangement with nearby Wittering. The Harrier OCU, which by this time had assumed the title of No.20(R) Squadron, began receiving both reworked and new-build aircraft from January 1993.

With the coming of 1994, the last of the GR.5s were 'passing out'. Some losses had

The first deployment of Harrier GR.7s aboard a Royal Navy carrier was made by aircraft from the SAOEU.
Royal Navy

In order to bring the Night Attack Harrier into service with the front-line squadrons, it had originally been intended to establish a specialist flight of six aircraft attached to No.1(F) Squadron at RAF Wittering to act as a training organization. In the event it was decided that the whole Squadron should be night-capable, thereby making it the RAF's first fully operational Night Attack Harrier unit, without standing it down from its NATO commitments. In

4(AC) Squadron, then based at Gütersloh, the only unit not equipped with the GR.5 and the last unit to fly the GR.3 operationally, began converting straight to the GR.7 on 12 September 1990 with the arrival of ZG473. No.3 Squadron also located at Gütersloh traded up its GR.5s for GR.7s on 30 November 1990, receiving its first aircraft ZG479.

As a result of the ending of the Cold War and the adoption of the Options for

occurred in the interim: ZG473, the first new GR.7, was destroyed in May 1991; ZG430, the first conversion, was lost in June 1993; and an electrical failure aboard ZG473 was followed by a similar occurrence in ZD353, which led to the temporary grounding of the Harrier fleet. It was discovered that chafing wires were responsible for the problems; BAe swiftly rectified the matter. The last GR.7 ZG862 was delivered to Gütersloh on 2 June 1992.

MOD-95

For service over Iraq (described elsewhere) many GR.7s had received a 'war-fit' for their part in Operation *Warden* but not a full 'night-fit'; other factors also needed to be addressed. *Warden* aircraft received an overall light grey ARTF paint scheme which soon began to peel and flake, as well as taking wear and tear from technicians and engine staining. Coupled with this was the new operational use of the Harrier at medium level, where the traditional European green scheme was most inappropriate. The RAF therefore established a requirement, under the title 'MOD-95', to give all the Harrier fleet a standard fit and colour scheme. Under this, all the *Warden* aircraft were given the night systems and all the non-*Warden* aircraft were given the *Warden* war-fit (described below). The final eighteen aircraft off the Dunsfold production line were given the new 100 per cent LERX, and all the 65 per cent LERX-fitted aircraft will be so modified in the near future. The eighteen aircraft were initially delivered to No.IV Squadron in Germany. The new camouflage scheme retained the same pattern as the original green but intro-

duced the colours of dark sea grey uppersurfaces and dark camouflage grey lower surfaces. During Operation *Deny Flight* a mix of ARTF and MOD-95 schemed aircraft operated from Gioia de Colle in Italy The aircraft also now feature two-digit 'build numbers' on their tailfins, replacing the old individual squadron codes. Because of the policy of rotating airframes around the squadrons and detachments, it was discovered that the composite materials did not take to having areas removed, repainted only for the paint to be removed again if the aircraft changed unit. Therefore individual unit markings were placed on a suitably removable panel, usually on the intakes and on the top of the tailfin, which needed only to be 'swapped' if a new aircraft arrived. Most of the insignia are now 'stick-on' decals covered with a coat of polyurethane varnish. Mistakes may occur even in this, and No.20(R)'s fighter bars on either side of their insignia suddenly turned much lighter when they received their 'grey' jets – not, as was at first suspected, a bow to low-visibility, but an error by the maker of 'stickers'.

The Harrier GR.7's new greys demonstrated by this factory-fresh example. BAe

Training for the Next Generation: RAF Harrier T.10

Like the US Marine Corps before it, the RAF did not at first appreciate the need for a dedicated two-seat trainer for its Harrier II pilots. The initial thinking was to convert some of the existing T.Mk.4s to T.Mk.6s giving them re-equipped cockpits, fitted with the GR.7's Night Attack avionics, and probably a reshaped nose section to accommodate the FLIR and ECM equipment. It was clear however, that the handling characteristics of the Harrier I (GR.3/T.4) were totally different from those of the Harrier II (GR.7) and would therefore not meet the requirements of the RAF to train future Harrier pilots cost-effectively. Having already viewed the in-service American TAV-8B,

the RAF issued a requirement based on that airframe, but with the avionics, night attack and operational fit of the GR.7 and powered by the trusty Rolls-Royce Pegasus 105 turbofan engine, delivering 21,000lb of static thrust. Parliament was advised of an order for fourteen 'Harrier T.Mk.10's' on 28 February 1990, however this figure was subsequently lowered by one before the finalization of the contract.

The first Harrier T.10, ZH653/TX001, made its maiden flight from Warton Aerodrome on 7 April 1994 and was then passed to BAe Dunsfold for trials, before making its way to the DTEO at Boscombe Down. The last airframe, ZH665 was delivered to No.20(R) Squadron the Harrier OCU at RAF Wittering on 26 October 1995. No.20(R) Squadron is the main user of the T.10, operating seven of the type with the

three operational squadrons each having one on strength. The HOCU first flew its new T.10 on 1 March 1995, and the unit was instrumental in developing the aircraft in order to gain the maximum benefits for the service. The commanding officer of No.20(R) Squadron, Wg Cdr Glenn Edge, explains that the T.10 is 'worth it weight in gold', and is employed 'most productively' in training the student on both the basics and the advanced features of the Harrier. Although slightly heavier than its GR.7 counterpart, it 'flies like a GR.7', is a 'superb piece of machinery' and is 'rock steady at low level'. The front cockpit is laid out exactly the same as in the GR.7, except for a fuel proportion switch which regulates the flow from the aircraft's internal tanks, which, because of the extra cockpit, differ in size from those of the GR.7.

Showing off its clean lines, a No.20(R) Squadron Harrier T.10. BAe

The rear cockpit differs in that it has the two MPCDs, throttle and stick, but the remainder of the displays and controls are for monitoring and emergencies; but both the older T.4 and the BAe Hawk T.1 offer a marginally higher vantage point than the T.10. Instructors have bemoaned the lack of hydraulic gauges in the rear, and the view looking down into the front cockpit is somewhat restricted by the so-called 'dog kennel' effect; however these complaints pose few real problems. Perhaps one of the more unusual, added problems is the lack of any internal steps, the aircraft being reliant on the T.4's access ladders while on base, and off base it is sometimes hard for the crew to board,

nose section that carries the external appendages for the GEC Systems FLIR, the Hughes AN/ASB-19(V) ARBS and the Marconi Zeus ECM, these making it about a yard longer than the GR.7 at 51ft 9in. The cockpits are also NVG-compatible and crews are able to use the GEC Nightbird goggles. The T.10 possesses comparable handling qualities to its single-seat partner, except during vertical work where it does not have the VSTOL performance of the GR.7.

The T.10's arrival with the front-line units now allows instructors to carry out the all important 'check rides', and being NVG-capable they prove extremely useful during the early sorties of individual

tation was imposed because the RAF programme was a limited purchase it was not possible to place an airframe on a stress rig, as was done with the GR.7. Therefore, because of its differing fit from the TAV-8B, all the airframe loading data have to be recovered by structural analysis and flight trials. The principle fear is that the point where the larger cockpit is joined to the fuselage might experience problems under high g loadings, so as a precaution a 4.5 g limit has been imposed.

No.20(R) Squadron's aircraft rarely fly with wing tanks or pylons fitted, resulting in a lightweight aircraft. Although they are cleared to carry a full range of weaponry and fuel, the more usual sight would be

Getting the low down on the T.10? This superb head-on shot shows off all of the trainer's characteristics.
BAe

especially if the canopies have been closed; boarding from the roof of a handy Landrover is not unheard of …

The most noticeable airframe change from its American counterpart is a revised

squadrons' night-flying programmes. The T.10 is fully cleared for nocturnal operations, however it remains at the time of writing g-limited, and has still to receive its grass operations clearance. The g-limi-

the fitting of CBLS and 3kg 'bean tin' training bombs. Take-off weights are quoted as being in the region of 25,000lb, giving a sortie time of 1 hr for basics and 55 min to 1 hr 5 min for SAPS (simulated

Harrier T.10: Disposition at May 1997

ZH653	MoD DTEO Boscombe Down
ZH654	BAe Dunsfold
ZH655	Wittering (damaged)
ZH656	No.3 Squadron
ZH657	No.20(R) Squadron
ZH658	No.20(R) Squadron
ZH659	No.20(R) Squadron
ZH660	No.20(R) Squadron
ZH661	No.1 Squadron
ZH662	No.20(R) Squadron
ZH663	No.20(R) Squadron
ZH664	No.4 Squadron
ZH665	No.20(R) Squadron

T.10-17 ZH654 with photo reference markings.
f4 Aviation Photobank

(Below) **ZH655 in the hangar at Wittering after being damaged.** F4 Aviation Photobank

No.1(F)'s T.10 ZH661/109 sits ready for its next crew, connected to the orange-cabled ground power unit.
Author

attack profiles) work. The lack of external stores is not unusual for the T.10 since in the training regime performance is all-important and the aircraft needs to be as light as possible, the OCU not requiring the 'legs' the extra fuel tanks provide.

A possible future role for the RAF's T.10 could be that of stand-off laser designation for the Harrier force using the TIALD system which proved so effective when fitted to the Jaguar GR.1Bs which operated in conjunction with the Harriers over Bosnia.

The Harrier Training Course

With the introduction of the T.10 at Wittering, the RAF had, for the first time since the T.4/GR.3 partnership, the means to train pilots effectively 'straight through' on the same system. Before 1995 (prior to the T.10) the course designed for the GR.5 and 7 began with the T.4 as its basis. This commenced with the student joining 'B' Flight (the Harrier Long Course is split into two 'Flights', 'B' for 'Basics' and 'A' for 'Advanced') for two weeks ground school and four weeks flying the T.4; this is totally different from the GR.5/7, but did teach

Harrier Pilot

Demonstrating the latest flight kit for the Harrier fast jet flyer, a pilot from No.1(F) Squadron catches a moment in the afternoon sun at Nellis AFB in the USA for the camera. He will have graduated at the top of his course during training, and be one of the 'few' posted to fly the Harrier GR.7. Referring to the glasses, as one Harrier jock once quoted to the author, 'If you're a part of the Harrier community it's never too dark to wear shades!'

'Sorry, could I use your ' phone? I've just ditched a Harrier in one of your fields!'

Returning from APC (armament practice camp) at RAF Akrotiri in Cyprus on a snowy, windy January morning in 1995, Flt Lt Simon Jessett eased his Harrier GR.7 ZG476 into the Wittering circuit.

Suddenly there was a loud 'bang' and the aircraft began to shake, and there I was at 1,000ft doing 220kts with no power. I went for a relight, but the engine stayed in surge, I sat for a few seconds watching an engine running hot and running slow and 'growling' behind me. I thought, 'This is it Jezz, you're over the side son'. It goes against every instinct to bang out but I sat back and pulled the handle – an enormous boom, immediate backpain at the 25 g kick in the pants, the .45sec rocket burn forcing all the air out of my lungs. As I tumbled over I saw the jet flying away straight, it was fairly surreal! The parachute tugged me back and I floated down into the branches of a tree, and sat suspended at about 20ft, muttering more than a few unrepeatable phrases! I felt OK so let go the harness and the PSP and legged it toward a farmhouse. I saw my ejector seat in one of the fields, and saw a pall of smoke in the distance, and was glad that the aircraft had impacted in open countryside. I knocked on the farmhouse door and said, 'Sorry, could I use your phone? I've just ditched a Harrier in one of your fields!'

The board of inquiry reported that a compressor blade had failed, causing the engine to surge, an event that could not be foreseen and Jessett was exonerated of any blame He was back in the air a couple of weeks later, none the worse for his experience.

Flt Lt Simon Jessett of No.1(F) Squadron. Author

the rudiments of V/STOL. Two more weeks of ground school using computerized work packages followed before the students were sent to MCAS Yuma to fly the Marines' simulator. By this time the students have yet to get their hands on a 'live' GR.5/7, but on their return from Yuma they had their first experience – solo. A lot of supervision was needed: an instructor on the pan, one in the tower and another in a second 'Harrier chase plane' (the OCU used some of the old GR.3s as chase aircraft in the GR.5 days before they were retired). Having mastered all that, the student had another ten weeks with 'B' Flight, before joining 'A' Flight for more ground school, now looking at weapons delivery, tactics and avionics. This was followed by more work in the simulator before he set out on more weapons, evasion, SAPs, culminating in deployment to a front-line unit.

With the T.10, the lead-ins are the same, but the course proper now begins with two weeks of T.10/GR.7 ground school, two sorties dual, and then the student goes solo. Wittering now has its own fully operational GR.7 simulator (simulator technicians can 'fly' the Harrier very well, like a video game). The student concentrates on emergencies and procedures, before returning to the T.10/GR.7 for more flying techniques to complete the 'convex' phase, before joining 'A' Flight, a far less complex training regime. The Harrier Long Course is one of the most extensive OCU courses in the RAF at 76 hrs, with ninety-eight sorties in thirty-one weeks.

Camouflage and Markings

Currently all of the RAF's T.10s carry the standard colour scheme of NATO green top surfaces (which extend 2in under the wing root, and 1½in under the tailplane and around the total ring of the intakes) and lichen green undersurfaces. Plans are in hand to repaint the entire fleet in the latest MOD-95 permanent greys, as the aircraft emerge from major overhauls. The inside of the huge Pegasus intake is gloss white. National insignia and caution and warning symbols are full colour and the individual squadron markings are applied in a similar style as on the GR.7s, mostly on removable panels on the tailfin and intakes. Squadron tail letters/numbers are being replaced by the aircraft's build number in a standardization exercise.

GR.5(K): the 'Big Wing' Harrier

Hawker Siddeley had always maintained close links with McDonnell Douglas in the USA, who, like HSA in the late 1960s, were also looking for a successor to their AV-8A programme. The matter under consideration was the joint UK/US study for a much revised AV-8A, the AV-16, designed around a larger Pegasus 15 engine which, no matter how impressive it looked, was, first, considered too much of a major engineering effort, secondly, going to prove far too costly, and, thirdly, would not meet the requirements of the hoped for users: the RAF, the US Navy and the US Marine Corps; it was consequently sidelined. McDonnell Douglas went their own way with independent studies that eventually led to the AV-8B, while Hawker Siddeley began to investigate the possibilities of what might be achieved by modifying the existing Harrier GR.3 airframe.

Their objective was to keep the existing Pegasus engine and most of the airframe but to find a way to increase the aircraft's payload and range, and this it was felt could be achieved by designing a new wing. Although it was contended that it was feasible to bring the new aircraft into production quickly and easily, it was also an effective idea actually to convert all the existing GR.3s as part of their MLU. Therefore the so-called 'Big Wing Harrier' or 'Tin Wing GR.5(K)', as it would have been known, was to have an all-metal and much thicker wing section than the GR.3, increasing the area by 50 sq ft, enlarging the fuel capacity, more than doubling the weapons carrying capability, and featuring wing-tip mounted Sidewinder missile rails. Furthermore, by fitting LERXs, this would improve the Harrier's turning abilities. However, the proposal became less attractive when set against the airframe hours available on the Harrier fleet. Therefore the 'Big Wing' was, like many other projects, cancelled in August 1981, and the American development, the Harrier AV-8B, ordered in its place, an aircraft that would also be designated GR.5.

(Left) **An artist's impression of what the AV-16 might have looked like in service.** McDonnell Douglas

A cutaway of the proposed AV-16. McDonnell Douglas

CHAPTER TEN

Second Generation Sea Harrier

Specification – Sea Harrier F/A.2	
ENGINE	One F402-RR-408 Pegasus turbofan.
WEIGHTS	Empty 13,000lb (5,900kg); loaded 25,600lb (11,600kg).
DIMENSIONS	Span 25ft 3in (7.65m); length 48ft 3in (14.6m).
PERFORMANCE	Max level speed at sea level: 643kts (1,200km/h); range (typical): 300nm (560km); celing: 51,000ft (15,500m).
ARMAMENT	2x30mm Aden cannon, Sidewinder & AMRAAM AAMs, Sea Eagle ASMs, bombs, CBUs, LGBs.

Sea Harrier F/A.2: Upgraded Firepower

One of the many consequences of the Falklands conflict of 1982 was the need to have a better equipped Sea Harrier force. Although its performance in the South Atlantic was outstanding, there were many areas where the FRS.1 fell short. The Blue Fox radar had only a limited look-down facility – having great difficulty detecting low-flying targets over the sea – much to the relief no doubt of the nightly C-130 Hercules flights into Port Stanley. The questions of endurance, limited missile armament and self protection all needed to be addressed. Some shortcomings were corrected by adding twin Sidewinder mounts and larger fuel tanks – the so-called 'Falklands Fit'; but what was needed was a better radar, linked to missiles with a greater kill range.

Plans to accommodate this were to be introduced as part of the Sea Harrier's MLU, and contracts were issued in 1983 for a feasibility study and in 1985 for further studies. In early December 1988 the MoD awarded BAe a contract to update all existing FRS.1s to a new FRS.2 standard, and in March 1990 announced an order for ten new-build FRS.2s.

This new 'standard' incorporated a new radar, the Ferranti Blue Vixen, which is a track- while-scan pulse Doppler set giving an all-weather, look-down, shoot-down ability, together with the capability to engage multiple targets simultaneously. The radar data from the Blue Vixen would be presented on the pilot's right hand MFD, with the left-hand one being used for navigational data. The left-hand MFD can also be used as a 'tactical' display putting a radar 'slice' on to the screen. The radar set offers a 150km (80nm) range in 40km blocks, and tracks can be established at distances reportedly greater than 85km. The Blue Vixen has already proved its ability to meet the stringent requirements to detect and engage sea-skimming missiles and slow-low targets. The pilot can use 'auto designate' or 'specific designate' to fire his missiles, and he gets range and attack cues in his HUD to determine the kill probabilities when they are launched. In the air-to-air mode, as mentioned, the pilot can separate his radar picture on to both MFDs, having a 'God's-eye' view on the right side and a 'side on' view on the left, which shows the separation and gives him greater SA (situational awareness). The radar's central processor has been relocated to the rear of the airframe and the links are established by fibre optic cables. The new radar is housed in a restyled, bulbous nose radome, being larger and more rounded than of the rather 'sharp' FRS.1, and the latter's above mounted pitot tube has been relocated to the leading edge of the tailfin, rather reminiscent of the P.1127 and over three generations earlier. The radar was

first trialled aboard ZF433, a BAC-111 which carried the FRS.2's radar and radome, and two BAe-125s, XW930 and ZF130, with the latter being outfitted with the full FRS.2 avionics suite.

The missile of choice is the Hughes AIM-120B AMRAAM, which, when combined with the Blue Vixen set, made the new Sea Harrier one of the most potent combat aircraft in the world. The AIM-120, successor to the Sparrow, uses its own inertial mid-course guidance, with updates being given in flight from the aircraft by data link, conferring an excellent BVR ability on the Harrier. The original plans had called for four AIM-120s to be fitted on the outboard pylons, complemented by short-range Sidewinders mounted on the wingtips; however, this was abandoned in favour of having two wing-mounted AIM-120s fitted on Frazer Nash Common Rail Launchers, which would also allow the carrying of the AIM-9, and a further two AIM-120s on American LAU-106 launch rails in place of the underfuselage gun packs.

It was also decided to change the designation of the aircraft to reflect its new capabilities, so out went the FRS (Fighter Reconnaissance Strike) and in came the American-sounding F/A – for Fighter Attack – Mk.2, the F/A.2. A new powerplant was also fitted, the Pegasus 106, a 'navalized' 105, and the fuselage was also lengthened by just under 14in to improve stability and provide space for the extra equipment. This was originally to be a 'plug' just behind the engine, but on new and upgraded aircraft a complete new

Hughes AIM-120 AMRAAM			
After protracted development, the AMRAAM entered service in 1992. It is of the same basic layout as the Sparrow III but with increased speed, better guidance, longer range, less smoke and superior ECM capabilities. Guided by a Nortronics INS and a Hughes active radar, it carries a 45lb proximity and impact delay-fused bast/fragmentation warhead.	LENGTH	12ft	
	DIAMETER	7in	
	SPEED	Mach 4	
	WEIGHT	335.2lb	

An F/A.2's radome opened for the ground technician to work on; note the clamp holding the radome in place. Author

(Below)
First development aircraft ZA195 showing the full AMRAAM fit, as well as its nose pitot. BAe

Sea Eagle Missile

Designed from the P.3T in 1976, the Sea Eagle carries the same structural and aerodynamic characteristics as the Martel ASM. The Sea Eagle is powered by a Microturbo TR1 80-1 Model 087 turbojet and armed with a Royal Ordnance 500lb impact delay penetrating blast/frag-

mentation warhead. Launched from Sea Harriers, it has a totally modern guidance system, the host aircraft providing last minute guidance updates before launch. The missile flies at low level to reduce the chance of its being spotted by visual or electronic means.

LENGTH	13.7ft
DIAMETER	1ft 3.75in
WEIGHT	1,325llb
RANGE	Mach 4
SPEED	595kts

BAe Sea Eagle missile drill round fitted to an F/A.2 'below decks' on HMS Invincible**; note the launch rail shape.** BAe

rear fuselage has been fitted. On the wings the leading edge has been slightly altered: another small fence added and one of the vortex generators has been removed, with wing hardpoints being strengthened to carry up to 1,000lb each. The aircraft has retained its internally-mounted F.95 oblique reconnaissance camera and a number of additional air scoops associated with the cooling of the new systems. A Garman 100 GPS has been added as a 'strap-on', mounted on

the left side of the cockpit coaming, its data being input by hand.

A modern 'office' for the pilot has been designed, with a new HUD and two multi-functional displays added – with the radar's presentation being sited mainly on the right MFD. Also fitted are improved HOTAS controls, which allow more 'heads-up flying' than in the FRS.1; HOTAS allows the pilot to select the radar and weapons (whether AMRAAM, AIM-9 or guns) without any 'heads-down' time.

The FRS.1's ARI 18223 RWR has been replaced in the F/A.2 by the Marconi Sky Guardian, and all the F/A.2's avionics are routed through a 1553B digital databus with the addition of a MADGE transponder. Some components, such as the ram air turbine, have been removed to save on weight. The pilots are reasonably happy that the aircraft has retained its smaller 'fighter' wings, and, although it has many impressive new systems, the F/A.2 is still a 'first generation' Harrier in most of its air-

XZ439 showing its photo-reference markings on the nose and tail. Steve Gensler

frame, as shown by the original 'cascade' exhaust nozzles.

ZA195, the first pre-series aircraft converted to the FRS.2 configuration (it flew originally in 1983 as FRS.1 DB1), took to the air in September 1988, followed by XZ439 (first flight as an FRS.1 DB2 in March 1979) in March 1989. BAe began to convert the FRS.1 airframes to FRS.2 standard in the early part of 1991, and the first aircraft completed, ZE695, was handed back to the Royal Navy in April 1993.

Initial sea-going trials were carried out with both ZA195 and XZ439 on board *Ark Royal* in November 1990 after ZA439 had spent most of October at RNAS Yeovilton carrying out seventy-six ski-jumps, eight of them at night. These 'leaps' included about every configuration likely with the new air-

craft including 1,000lb bombs, tanks, Sidewinders and AMRAAM missiles. The shipboard trials covered every aspect of the FRS.2's compatibility with the ship, from deck handling, ski-jumps, recovery techniques, to handling AMRAAMs. XZ439 now also had the near 'production standard' avionics and radar fit. ZA195 still had its photo reference markings visible and also carried a twin Sidewinder fit, as well as underfuselage AMRAAM pylons

To bring the aircraft to squadron service an Operational Evaluation Unit was formed at Boscombe Down on 1 June 1993 as an off-shoot of No.899 Squadron and received its first aircraft, ZE695 and ZD616, in August with the aircraft carrying the 'Winged Fist' tail motif with small white 'OEU' lettering on top of the tailfin.

The OEU will remain an integral part of the Squadron for as long as the F/A.2 remains in service. No.899 Squadron itself took on charge its first FRS.2, ZA176, later in the same month. Anxious to get the aircraft out to one of the carriers for extended sea trials, four newly designated F/A.2s joined HMS *Invincible* on an Adriatic cruise, working with the No.800 Squadron's Sea Harrier FRS.1s; these four were ZD612, ZD615, ZE696 and ZE697, all from No.899 Squadron OEU. This not only gave the aircrew valuable experience in seeing just how their new mounts performed aboard ship but also gave the deck crews an opportunity to work with the aircraft that would soon be with them in squadron strength. Two F/A.2s had been lost in unrelated incidents and both had

ZF130, a BAe 125 fitted with the full F/A.2 radar and avionics fit. Steve Gensler

---

Flying the F/A.2

'As I once said to an interested RAF flyer, it's much better to 'stop' and then 'land', rather than 'land' and then try to 'stop'!'

'To get involved in a "furball"in the FRS.1 and engaging the "enemy" with AIM-9s could be well compared to having a knife fight in a telephone box', explains Lt Cdr David Baddams, Senior Pilot of No.899 Squadron at RNAS Yeovilton, 'with the F/A.2, however, we can now fight BVR, getting in close only if neccessary – we believe we now have the best and most compact air defence aircraft in Europe.' The Sea Harrier pilot community is relatively small, with only fifty in total, just over half actually serving in flying posts; the numbers break down into ten each with Nos. 800 and 801 and fourteen with No.899. 'The SHAR2 is makes us perhaps the "meanest new kids on the block",' continues Baddams, 'and when we come up against aircraft belonging to our allies in DACT sorties, we offer more than a few surprises, and even when pitted against AMRAAM-armed American aircraft, they know what they're going to get in advance. The aircraft is not designed to be a dogfighter; we do not have the low wing loading of an F-16 or F-18, but we can mix it if neccessary. VIFFing gives us some advantages, but

it's really a last ditch effort, as what we might gain in positioning we sacrifice in energy, so we excel at being able to hold people off at a distance without getting close in.'

'On a conventional runway the first thing that anyone new to the F/A.2 always comments on is the massive acceleration. The engine is run to full power, the STO stop set to 50 degrees, brakes off and the 'g' pushes you into the seat. At 120 kts the nozzle lever is snapped smartly back to the STO stop and the Harrier leaps into the air. We then "collect" the aircraft, and make sure the yaw vane is straight, and its nozzles aft, gear up and away. Aboard ship we use the ski jump to allow us a greater take off weight, using a type of "ballistic lob" to aid us to wingborne flight.'

'Despite the fact that the F/A.2 is a tremendously flexible aircraft – in fact, we can undertake any mission once airborne – fighter, bomber or recce – we are basically a day-only bomber, with no night capacity, however. In the past it was always the Sea Harrier's role to be a "stopper", but now we are more the "shooter", and the Royal Navy has in the new seaborne Harrier a terrific asset.'

---

borne the side number '713'. The OEU, understandably, decided that no further aircraft should have this number, so the aircraft following '712', ZE696 was numbered '712 1/2'.

The Royal Navy's first fully operational F/A.2 Squadron was No.801, which received its first two aircraft, ZA176 and XZ455, on 5 October 1994. The unit replaced No.800 Squadron's FRS.1s aboard HMS *Illustrious* off the coast of Italy, where it gave support to Operation *Sharp Guard*, flying a dual role, armed each with a single 1,000lb bomb on the centreline and two AIM-120Bs on the outboard wing stations together with Aden cannons and the internal F.95 camera. On its return to RNAS Yeovilton, No.800 Squadron retired its FRS.1s and the first F/A.2 joined the unit on 17 March 1995. The first totally 'new build' F/A.2 was delivered in October 1995.

(Above) **On the deck of** Invincible **an F/A.2 is 'pushed' into position on the rear of the deck.**
BAe

An unmarked F/A.2 recovers aboard HMS Invincible **during her Adriatic cruise; it carries two AIM-9M Sidewinders and the fixed IFR probe.** HMS *Invincible*

ZD611 from No.801 Squadron banks away, giving a good view of the undersides, with the fuselage extension being visible behind the rear of the wing. BAe

An 899NAS Sea Harrier being serviced on the Yeovilton line; note the FOD bin by the gunpacks and the panel that contains the chaff and flare dispensers to the rear. Author

Camouflage and Markings

The F/A.2s have adopted an all-over grey scheme as did the FRS.1s. This has been in two distinctive colours. Some aircraft received the dark sea grey which, although proved the right choice for the Falklands style of operations, did not really reflect the evolving role of the F/A.2. Lt Henry Mitchell, on an AWI course, wrote a paper

on why the camouflage should change; this view was accepted and a lighter grey adopted instead as a fleetwide scheme. In the DSG garb, all markings, including serial numbers and codes were black with full-colour roundels. In the medium grey scheme, all markings, including serial number and codes, are in white with pale pink/pale blue roundels and pale pink engine access markings. Individual

squadron emblems have varied from light grey, to white and black. ZA195, the first F/A.2 conversion, carried black and white square photo reference markings on its nose and tail for most of 1992/93.

Shark SHAR: BAe's AMRAAM Trials F/A.2

The sea-going Harrier F/A.2 is rather drably adorned for obvious tactical reasons, the all-over coat of medium grey broken only by the occasional addition of either black or white squadron markings. However, one of the development aircraft, XZ439, broke the mould, adding a welcome splash of colour and an aggressive tone to the aircraft.

XZ439 had its first flight in March 1979, having been originally built as an FRS.1. It undertook several live firing trials of Sidewinder AAMs before serving briefly with both Nos. 899 and 809 Squadron during 1992 and then being returned to British Aerospace where it was converted to the originally titled 'FRS.2 Standard' in October 1989; this later became F/A.2 and was the second radar-carrying prototype.

During January 1993 the aircraft was shipped out to the USA on board the *New Atlantic Conveyor* to take part in live firing trials of the Hughes AIM-120 AMRAAM missile, which is the principle in-service armament. It arrived at Norfolk, Virginia and was unpacked, refuelled and dispatched to Eglin AFB where it expended ten missiles against scale MQM-107 and QF-106 target drones during late March 1993.

During this time abroad, the BAe engineers applied the garish, full-colour sharkmouth with staring eyes in order to 'Showboat those Yankees'! In front of the port intake 'mission symbols' are visible in the shape of ten AMRAAM missiles, although the significance of the car is open to conjecture. On both sides of the tail in bright blue is the legend 'British Aerospace Dunsfold'; this was repeated on the intake sides, although by the time of the aircraft's return to the UK these had begun to peel off. On the tailfin RWR fairing (which contains a transponder linked to the trials equipment) is an excellent Dayglo variation on No.899 Squadron's badge, now turned from the 'Winged fist' to the 'Winged finger', the purpose of which may be left to the imagination of the reader. Also on the RWR, again in Dayglo is a

Lt Cdr David Baddams, RN – Sea Harrier Pilot

An ex-Royal Australian Navy Skyhawk pilot, David was on the last cruise of the *Melbourne* before its retirement. Plans to buy HMS *Invincible* for the RAN disappeared after the Falklands and David found himself redundant at the age of 23. He applied to transfer to the Royal Navy in 1984 and was accepted, going on to fly the Sea Harrier FRS.1, and latterly the F/A.2. He was appointed Senior Pilot of No.800 Squadron in 1992

Lt Cdr Baddams climbs aboard one of 899NAS's F/A.2s. Author

before moving to the Standards Squadron in 1993 and is currently Senior Pilot with No.899 Squadron. A keen student of things vintage, David also flies the Hawker Sea Hawk of the Navy's Historic Flight.

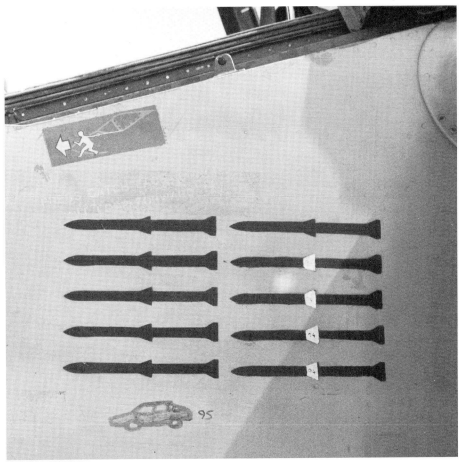

small No.801 Squadron trident, and further down on the rudder are No.809's chequerboards. The crew chiefs' names were also added, but deleted on return to the UK. The Royal Navy wording is in black, with a grey panel at the root and tip of the tailfin and at several points along the fuselage may be found white photo reference stripes. Full two-colour roundels are carried on the sides of the nose and of the upper and lower wings, as are the normal fire, rescue and access markings.

For its trial work the aircraft carried an inert Sidewinder missile tube modified as an instrumentation pod on the starboard outer wing pylon and a converted CBLS pod serves as a centreline camera mount. It is interesting to note that the aircraft has no pitot static tube fitted; the engineers found it difficult to replace the item that was originally housed above the radome

AMRAAM missile 'mission' markings'. Author

(Below) **An overall view of XZ439 on the Boscombe Down ramp.** Author

The now peeling 'Dunsfold' marking, and a view of the photo reference stripes behind the intake doors.
Author

on the FRS.1. Eventually it was refitted on the leading edge of the tailfin, although Development Aircraft ZA195 had a pitot tube fitted to the tip of the rounded radome. Back in the UK, XZ439 now operates between the DTEO site at Boscombe Down and BAe Dunsfold.

Black SHAR: Harrier T.8N, the Fleet Air Arm's Two-seat F/A.2 Trainer

With the introduction into service of the Sea Harrier F/A.2 and the retirement of the Sea Harrier FRS.1, a new method was urgently required to train the next generation of naval pilots on the latest version of the naval Harrier. For many years the T.4.A/N had been used for general han-

dling skills, along with a modified version of the Hunter, the T.8M, for training pilots in the use of the Blue Fox radar. Both of these aircraft types were excellent vehicles for the FRS.1 but wholly unsuited to the 'new' F/A.2.

The Navy's existing Harrier T.4A/Ns were therefore upgraded to a new standard, the T.8N, with some ex-RAF Harrier T.4 trainers with acceptable airframe time remaining being held in storage and earmarked for future conversion. Externally, apart from a new paint scheme, they are unchanged from their former designation; but the internal changes are more significant. It is in the front cockpit where the major upgrades lie, with the FRS.1 style of instrumentation being removed and replaced by the quite different fit of the F/A.2, with the exception of the Blue Vixen radar. Included are a new HUD,

UFC and MFD, along with the same data-bus and INS platform. The rear seat retains its FRS.1 ancestry with just a few changes to the technology that allows the instructor to monitor the student. The lack of an airborne radar-training vehicle is not seen as a disadvantage now since much of the initial radar training is undertaken in a state-of-the-art simulator before the fledgling pilot continues the work in a single-seat F/A.2. Sea Harrier Pilots undergo the longest and costliest training programme in the British services, and around nine pilots a year are so trained. After their T.8N experience the students move to one of the single-seaters, which come in two 'fits': 'Clean' for initial handling and work up, and 'Fighter Trainer', loaded with two wing tanks, two AMRAAM tactical training pods under the fuselage and two captive AIM-9 Sidewinders.

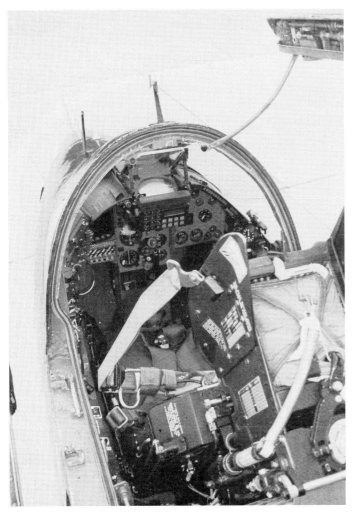

Described by the instructors in No.899 Squadron as 'an extremely valuable tool', the T.8N is especially good in the air-to-ground mode, and can carry an ACMI pod and additional fuel tanks, thereby making it more economical on the bombing ranges; some T.8Ns have been noted carrying a pair of grey-clad cannon pods. Although essentially a 'new variant' the F/A.2 is still described by British Aerospace as the Harrier I because it is derived from the GR1/GR.3/FRS.1/T.4 family, rather than the Harrier II with its GR.5/7/T.10 relations.

No.899 Squadron operate five Harrier T.8Ns from their base at Yeovilton, and took delivery of the first conversion, ZB605 (a former T.4N), from British Aerospace on 1 May 1995, the aircraft making its maiden flight on 27 July 1994.

In line with the thinking of the late 1990s on high-visibility colour schemes for training aircraft, the T.8Ns had received an all-over, high gloss black colour scheme, with white canopy edges, step markings, caution/warning markings and a gloss

(Top left) **The forward nose area showing the hinged canopy and the yaw vanes on the nose and above the cockpit coaming.** Author

(Top right) **The Martin-Baker Mk.12 'bang seat' fitted in the rear cockpit, with straps placed in the ready position by the groundcrew to accept its next instructor.** Author

(Right) **No.899 Squadron's traditional 'mailed fist' emblem, carried in gold by T.8 ZB605/720.** Author

white intake in front of the Pegasus fan. ZB605 arrived sporting a golden outline of No.899's emblem, a 'Winged fist' applied to its tailfin, matched by a white 'Royal Navy' legend beneath it, with its naval ID code of '720' being added sometime later. Serial numbers are in white, as are code letters, with engine access and fire access panels painted red. Noteworthy are the silver-headed access panel screws, found in abundance over the airframe, along with their white alignment stripe.

CHAPTER ELEVEN

Keeping the Peace

Combat Zone # 4: Operation *Warden*

Set up as a direct result of the aftermath of the Gulf War, Operation *Warden* was the British contribution to the United Nations efforts with *Provide Comfort*, under which the UN provided safe and protected 'havens' for the Kurds. These areas were policed by the air forces of the United States, the UK and France, former western partners in *Desert Storm*.

After the war the initial British *Warden* force was provided by RAF Coltishall's Jaguar Wing, whose 18-months aerial policing deployment was passed on to the Harrier GR.7 in April 1993, giving further credence to the aircraft's growing capabilities. Eight Harrier GR.7s, drawn from Nos.3 and 4 Squadrons based at Laarbruch in Germany, made the trip out to Incerlik AFB in Turkey, together with sixteen aircrew and other supporting staff, departing on 2 and 8 April, four aircraft flying out

each day. Their principal tasks were to fly 'armed reconnaissance', providing photographs of a wide variety of targets in the northern 'no-fly' zone sector of Iraq and looking in particular for SAM and radar sites, fuel and ammunition dumps and troop movements and concentrations.

With the introduction of the Harrier II, the traditional reconnaissance role associated with No.4 Squadron was 'lost' with the passing of the GR.3 from squadron service, only to be revived for the *Warden* detach-

En route to Turkey, five GR.7s take on a tank full of 'go-juice' from a No.101 Squadron VC-10 tanker.
Andy Suddards

ment and still continues to play a vital role in Harrier operations. To facilitate the carrying of a pod-mounted reconnaissance system a modification was required to reintroduce the redundant BAe camera pack of GR.3 vintage on to the GR.7. With its fan of F.95 and single F.135 wet film cameras, the pod was successfully mounted on the centreline pylon. Many of the pods were intended mainly for low-level work, and as many of the *Warden* operations were to be from 'medium' altitude the RAF purchased new Vinten VICON 18-603 GP(-1) pods which contained a 91cm LOROP (Long-Range Oblique Photography) camera for use at the new flight level. The Vinten pods offered a movable nose camera as well as horizon-to-horizon coverage from the belly position. Modes available included the vertical, tactical, stand-off and long-range oblique and each aircraft required 650 man-hours for the necessary modifications to enable it to carry the pods. Pilots found the simplest method to track the camera angle was to draw a chinagraph pencil line across the side of their canopies as a rough guide as to where the system was 'looking'.

(Above) **Recovering back to Incerlik after another armed recce sortie.** RAF

Two technicians check out one of the film cassettes from the centreline recce pod. RAF

In order to process the information, a portable RIC was initially borrowed from No.41 Squadron at Coltishall, before equipment that came from the 'original' RICs of GR.3 days was reinstituted, the RICs being able to quickly process and analyse the 550 frame images from the film packs.

As many of the GR.7 pilots were already experienced reconnaissance operators from their GR.3 days, only a short time was necessary for them to hone their skills; others new to the role underwent an intensive work-up period which included all personnel needing to gain their night tanking and night close formation qualifications. The aircraft themselves were brought up to a high maintenance standard, which included the addition of a FIN 1075G navigation system referenced to the GPS, IFF changes, and internal software and hardware upgrades to allow the aircraft to carry US weapons. These changes became universally known as the '*Warden* Standard'.

Jaws GR.7

A set of 'fangs' and a pair of bloodshot 'eyes' briefly adorned the nose of one of the aircraft and ZD408/WK applied for a 'one off' photo-shoot. Reportedly the outrageous size of the molars was to outdo a similar scheme applied to a French aircraft. Suffice it to say that the markings were very short lived.

Nils Mathisrud and Andy Evans

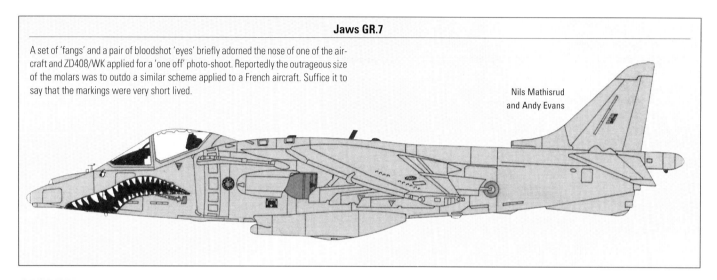

ZG476/T, a No.3 Squadron aircraft on patrol over Iraq; the paintwork soon became discoloured but was well received against the blue sky. Andy Suddards

In all, eighteen Harriers received the 'Warden Standard' fit-out for the detachment, which included an overall wash of a light grey ARTF paint scheme which was designed to make the machines less conspicuous when set against a predominantly blue sky, especially at medium altitude. Markings were non-existent, except for pale pink/pale blue roundels on the wings and intakes, with black (for aircraft from No.4 Squadron) or white (for No.3 Squadron) ID numbers. Tailcodes were in white beginning with 'W' for Warden; from WA to WZ.

Despite being the most war-ready aircraft in the RAF's Harrier fleet, they were not 'night capable', a situation that was rectified under the MOD-95 programme which gave all the Warden aircraft the night fit and the non-Warden ones the war fit. The Warden pool of aircraft were also not selected initially to receive the 100 per cent LERX, retaining their 65 per cent option in the interests of keeping the aircraft to the same standard

The Harriers flew patrols over Iraq fully armed, the principle weaponry being the BL.755 CBU, the US-manufactured CBU-87 CBU, the Canadian built 70mm high velocity CRV-7 rockets housed in a nineteen-round LAU 5003 B/A pod, and the ever comforting AIM-9 Sidewinder AAMs. The gun packs were carried empty as the Aden cannons were still not cleared for use; this aided lift improvement. The standard fit was therefore either two CBUs or two CRV-7 pods and two AIM-9L Sidewinders, self protection was aided by the capable Zeus ECM system, with either a wing-mounted Phimatt chaff dispenser or a Bofors BOL 304 launcher replacing the Sidewinder rail as well as the under-fuselage Tracor AN/ALE-40 flare dispensers. Endurance was enhanced by the addition of 11,800lb of fuel carried in two underwing tanks.

Aircrew were drawn from each of the operational units as well as from No.20(R) Squadron, the Harrier OCU (which participated in 1994). They worked on a two-months rotation basis. Each pilot flew about six 2.5-hrs sorties during his 'working week'. Each sortie into Iraq was treated as a full combat hop, crews being 'sanitized' of

BOL Chaff Launcher

Fitted on to the Sidewinder missile rail BOL dispenser cuts standard bundles of chaff and ejects it from the rear.

The forward portion of the BOL: the black area containing a gas bottle used eject the chaff from the rear and the mechanisms for the Sidewinder AAM. Author

Principle weaponry for the Warden **aircraft; from left to right: AIM-9L Sidewinder, CBU-87 cluster bomb and a Phimat chaff dispenser.** RAF

Nothing like a good washdown to clear the air ... as this GR.7 gets a scrub down at Incerlik; note the protective cover over the ARBS and the cooling cover inside the canopy. RAF

insignia or personal possessions and carrying only survival gear and a pistol. Operating in pairs, using callsigns such as 'Spitfire' and 'Hurricane', the aircraft were assigned from twelve to eighty-one specific targets as well as targets of opportunity which presented themselves. The 'package' that flew in support of the Harriers included USAF F-15 or F-16 fighters, AWACS, EF-111 jammers and SEAD suppressers as necessary.

Only one aircraft was lost during the *Warden* detachment, this being ZD432/WF belonging to No.4 squadron, which suffered an engine surge while refuelling from a VC-10; the pilot ejected near Dahluk and was looked after by local tribesmen following which he was picked up by a USAF CSAR helicopter. The squadron CO, Wg Cdr David Howard, repaid the hospitality by presenting the tribesmen with a gift of pregnant goats!

Combat Zone # 5: Royal Navy SHARs over Bosnia

The Sea Harriers involvement in Bosnia began with the deployment of HMS *Ark Royal* carrying eight 800 Squadron NAS FRS.1s into the war zone on 27 January 1993 for their part in *Deny Flight* operations, being relieved by HMS *Invincible* in July, complete with No.801 Squadron embarked. It was a busy deployment as the aircraft were also operating as part of operation *Sharp Guard* monitoring shipping and any potential 'sanction busters' in the waters around the former Yugoslavia. *Invincible* handed over to *Ark Royal* again in early February 1994, with FRS.1s from No.800 Squadron embarked and were called into action in an abortive mission on 22 February to support a convoy of Swedish soldiers that had come under fire. The

Royal Navy's only combat-related FRS.1 casualty came during a CAS mission on the 16 April 1994, when a pair of Sea Harrier FRS.1s from No.801 Squadron were trying to find their target near Gorazde in bad weather. During a sixth attempt, one of the duo, XZ498/002 became caught in a 'SAM trap' and was hit by a SAM-7 missile. The pilot Lt N. Richardson ejected safely and was rescued by the SAS and a French Puma helicopter. An earlier loss had occurred on 15 December 1993 when XZ493 from No.800 Squadron lost power on its return to HMS *Invincible*, the pilot ejected and was picked out of the sea by a Spanish naval helicopter. *Ark Royal* subsequently returned to the UK, with *Illustrious* taking up the Adriatic station.

The carrier arrived on station in September with four Sea Harrier F/A.2s on board from the SHOEU and six FRS.1s

Having just completed a CAS mission, practising the normal bombing procedures with a French FAC, two Sea Harrier FRS.1s recover to their carrier, tracking high over the mountains to the east of Donji Ribnik. Euan Kelbie via Neil 'Joe' Mercer

(Below) Typical of the view over Bosnia, a shot of the SHOEU's ZE696 over Sarajevo, armed with live weapons; it is easy to appreciate the dilemma of the commanders fighting a war in such areas and needing to minimize 'collateral' damage; the fact that targets were hit with deadly accuracy pays tribute to the excellent systems of the F/A.2. Neil 'Joe' Mercer

from No.800 squadron, making their 'swan song' deployment. Flying CAP and OCA alongside the FRS.1s, the F/A.2s set about proving their worth as part of the carrier's air wing, although not before a pair were targeted by an SA-2 Guideline SAM on 22 November. Happily it was no problem for the crews. The FRS.1s had

depart from HMS *Invincible* on 25 February 1995 for conversion.

The F/A.2s first full 'Adriatic cruise' began in January 1995 with six No.801 Squadron jets aboard HMS *Illustrious*, which continued the policing role until relieved by *Invincible* carrying No.800 Squadron. With them came a notable

action as part of the *Deliberate Force* operations, tasked with bombing a Serb depot, rather than their customary role of fleet defence. It was to be the first time that the latest version of the Sea Harrier was to be used in anger, the acid test. HMS *Invincible* was the carrier on station and four aircraft were quickly 're-roled' from their air-

Two F/A.2s on a 'shake-down' trip before their first deployment aboard ship, a cruise to the Adriatic. BAe

been upgraded for the Adriatic with Mk. X11 Mode 4 IFF, cockpit-mounted GPS, Vinten F-95 camera pods and the latest AIM-9 'Mike' Sidewinders. Following their final operation the six FRS.1s joined the queue of other airframes being remanufactured as F/A.2s on the British Aerospace production line, with ZE968 having the honour of being the last FRS.1 to

addition to the self-defence capability of the SHAR-2 in the form of Texas Instruments' GEN-X Active Expendable Radar Decoys which could be ejected from their standard dispensers.

On the morning of 5 September 1995, seven days after the Serb mortar attack on a marketplace in Sarajevo, the Royal Navy's Sea Harrier F/A.2s were called into

superiority assignments with AIM-9 Sidewinders and AIM-120B AMRAAM missiles to carrying iron bombs. The aircraft were configured with two 1,000lb Mk 13 HE bombs on each outboard wing pylon, together with the standard drop tank fit. Despite its fighter role, the F/A.2 is also a capable bomber, and led by the CO of 800 Squadron in ZD611/123, the aircraft formed up and headed for their target – a military storage site at Visegrad, south of the River Drina. Releasing their bombs from an inverted run-in from 18,000ft the targets were successfully destroyed. Armourers and deck crews added some personal touches to the bombs (until the Captain saw them and had them removed); they included:- 'I'm enjoying this so much I may extend my time with the Squadron', 'No Fear', and 'Roses are Red, Violets are Blue, Big Bombs are Green and this one's for you!!'

Once back on the carrier the F/A.2s were quickly rearmed with their missile fit, ready to continue their patrols. In all, nine missions were flown in support of *Deliberate Force* between 5 and 12 September, working in conjunction with other air assets deployed to the region. One F/A.2 was lost on 23 February 1996 when XZ455 from No.801 crashed on approach to *Illustrious*.

Combat Zone # 6: Operation *Deny Flight* – RAF Harriers over Bosnia

On 30 July 1995 the RAF's Harrier GR.7s were once more called in to help to police another secured airspace, this time a new 'no-fly' zone set up over Bosnia Herzegovina under the aegis of the UN-led Operation *Deny Flight*. As with their previous deployment to Turkey for *Provide Comfort*, the Harriers once more relieved a Coltishall Jaguar Detachment, this time at the Italian Air Base of Gioia del Colle. Twelve Harrier GR.7s from No.4(AC) Squadron, under the leadership of Wg Cdr Chris Morgan, took station at Gioia; the aircraft themselves, although nominally on strength with the unit based in Germany, came from a newly established pool of available airframes being drawn from all the operational units. The pooled aircraft were recognizable by their tailcodes, which were and continue to be non-squadron related but reflect the aircraft's build numbers; thus ZD376 has a white, two-digit tailcode of '24'. The complement was soon reduced to nine as experience dictated the size of the force.

Caught en route to Gioia de Colle, four Harrier GR.7s make the trip to Italy each toting four 'ferry tanks'; three carry the MOD-95 paint scheme and the fourth still wears the Warden **ARTF finish.** via Sgt Rick Brewell

The primary role of the Harrier in *Deny Flight* was directed by the UN Protection Force (UNPROFOR) and their main task was that of providing BAI. Secondary roles included that of CAS, usually operating with a forward operating air controller (FOAC) on the ground and reconnaissance, both vertical and stand-off, all of which the Harrier had proved that it could achieve with considerable success.

The aircraft in the pool were prepared for duty with similar equipment fits to that of the '*Warden Standard*', and reportedly the aircraft had been fitted with an enhanced EW system supplied by BAe at Dunsfold to meet an increased SAM threat, but at the time of writing this has not been confirmed. Initially the camouflage scheme for the aircraft remained that of light grey ARTF, although by now the paintwork was looking very messy. Mixed in with the ARTF aircraft were a couple of examples of the latest MOD-95, two-tone permanent grey scheme, which at that time was beginning to be applied to the entire Harrier fleet. By the end of the detachment the mix had reversed to more MOD-95 than ARTF aircraft.. For the light grey aircraft, markings continued to be at a premium, with pale pink and pale blue roundels, white two-digit tailcodes

Bosnia – a Pilot's View

Flt Lt Simon 'Jezz' Jessett of No.1(F) Squadron undertook two tours in Bosnia:

Our primary roles in theatre were that of CAS and recce; in CAS we operated with TAC-Ps [tactical air control parties] on the ground, the operators coming from a variety of nations (with a variety of dialects) and they would 'talk' us on to a 'target', which was useful training for all concerned, plus it served to keep the Serbs' heads down, hearing our fully-armed aircraft above them. Recce became more important as the job went on, and we used the LOROP pod with great success; this is a single, movable camera mount, and we were looking at the sites that IFOR had designated as gathering areas for the Serbs' heavy weapons, but towards the end we were looking for mass grave sites.

Threats were mainly from small arms fire, SAM-7 and SAM-14 missiles, of which there were an awful lot in theatre. We operated in pairs at 10,000ft, out of their effective range, but if weather drove us lower we would assume a battle formation, with one aircraft recce-ing, the other jinking around, checking the airspace. Generally we left Gioia, headed out talking to Brindisi Military – our callsigns included 'Ice Box' and 'Utah' – checked in with 'Magic' [AWACS], and 'AB triple-C' [ABCCC], if we were CAS or recce we would take on fuel from an RAF Tri-Star and sometimes Spanish Hercules tankers (which was

very entertaining) and begin the 25,000ft transit across the Adriatic.

No.1 Squadron arrived in Gioia before, and after the bombing, so we routinely carried two 1,000lb bombs, two Sidewinders, two wing tanks and a recce pod with us. If we were tasked up toward Mostar we had 40 min on station; down in the Tuzla area this went to 15 min. We were fully sanitized, no ID except a Form 189, as required by the Geneva Convention, DM1,500 for barter, a cold weather kit, and a combat survival waistcoat which had amongst its goodies a Walther PPK pistol with two mags of ammunition, and a vacuum packed Gortex jacket, which was an amazing piece of kit! On CAS we would contact our TAC-P, tell him who were. etc. and he would give us a target, and during this time we would be constantly listening to him because of the stringent ROE. Using a 'wagon wheel' formation we would run in from 5 to 6 miles out, one Harrier riding 'shotgun' while the other tipped in using the velocity vector in the HUD to designate the 'target'.

If we were tasked as recce we would have a pre-planned set of 'targets', from a minimum of eight to a maximum of twenty-two or three, again using tanker support. Because of the number of targets we were assigned, we were very GPS-dependent for positioning, flying down the track-line it gave us; and as a confidence builder we drew a china-graph stripe across the canopy reflecting the camera's view-angle and 'flew' it through the target.

Taking on fuel from a Spanish Hercules tanker during an armed patrol as part of Deny Flight. RAF Wittering

and a much reduced black ID number. Subsequent MOD-95 aircraft rotated through Gioia wore the smart dark sea grey upper surface and dark camouflage grey lower surface scheme, with full-colour red and blue 'D' class roundels on the wings and intakes and a small, swept, red and blue fin flash, white two-digit tailcodes and standard size black ID numbers.

Self-protection was evident again in the shape of Phimatt or BOL chaff launchers, underfuselage AN/ALE-40 flare dispensers, along with two Sidewinder AAMs. Offensive weaponry included the BL.755 CBU, CRV-7 Rocket pods and 1,000lb unguided iron bombs. As the need to make 'surgical' strikes on Serb positions became an increasing possibility, it was decided to bring 454kg

ZD376/24, looking more than a little war-weary and in need of the smart new MOD-95 paint scheme.
Author

Pictured on the day of the Jaguars' return to Gioia to continue their patrols and relieve the Harriers; pictured here an armed GR.7 ZG504/75 in the company of two light-grey Jaguar GR.1s and a dark-grey TIALD-equipped Jaguar GR.1B. RAF

laser-guided bombs into use; stand-off designation was to be provided by two Jaguar GR1.Bs on 48-hrs standby at Coltishall.

Within a month of their arrival, the time for action arrived. After a Bosnian Serb mortar attack on a marketplace in Sarajevo on 28 August killed thirty-seven people, NATO responded with Operation *Deliberate Force* which involved a total of eighty aircraft. The Harriers' first involvement came at 1am BST on the morning of 30 August, under the codename Operation *Vulcan*, when nine GR.7s, each carrying two 454kg LGBs and supported by TIALD-equipped Jaguar GR1.Bs attacked Serb radar installations, and followed this up about two hours later with attacks on an ammunition dump at Lukavica and a factory at Vugosca. Further attacks were carried out on 1 September, followed by a brief respite for the Serbs to comply with the UN resolutions and allow aircraft to examine areas for BDA (battle damage assessment). As there was no such compliance from the Serbs, the air strikes resumed on 5 September, as the Serbs continuined to flout the NATO order to remove their heavy weapons. The Harriers ranged out to Pale attacking military installations, and also undertook strikes at Tuzla, Gorazde and Mostar, before NATO called a halt to the bombing on 14 September. During that time the Harriers had flown a total of 144 BAI, CAS and reconnaissance sorties and by December 1995 the Harrier Force had flown some 758 sorties, 273 of which were for training purposes, consuming over 1,160 flying hours.

The force dropped forty-eight LGBs and thirty-two free-fall 1,000lb bombs, achieving an 85 per cent success rate in either totally destroying or severely damaging its targets – proof positive that the Harriers had the cutting edge.

The complement of nine Harriers fell to six in January 1996, with two aircraft solely employed in the reconnaissance role, and *Deny Flight* became *Decisive Edge* when the peace efforts gathered momentum, and subsequently became *Joint Endeavour* when on 1 January UNPROFOR changed its title to Implementation Force (IFOR). The Harrier detachment was once again relieved by the Jaguar Force on 5 February 1997, with No.3 Squadron being the last to deploy to Gioia.

Jaguar GR1.B: Deliberate Force – Harrier Designators

To minimize 'collateral' damage laser-guided bombs were used by the Harrier force during the 'Deliberate Force' operations. An urgent operational requirement for Jaguars to carry laser designation equipment was pursued in the early 1990s using the British Aerospace TIALD pod, operated with great success by the Tornado during the Gulf War. The system was trialled and released to operations in a short space of time. The aircraft receiving the TIALD fit were designated GR.1B to denote their specialist role and painted in a darker grey finish from their counterparts. A small cadre of pilots was selected to undertake the TIALD tasking.

No.6 Squadron left Gioia del Colle on 31 January 1995, having handed over the manning of *Deny Flight* to the Harrier force; however the Jaguar force continued to maintain two TIALD-equipped aircraft at RAF Coltishall on 48-hrs notice to deploy. No.6 Squadron took over the standby commitment on 24 August 1995, and shortly after this the attack on a Sarajevo marketplace occurred and Operation *Deliberate Force* commenced. The Squadron received notice to deploy its aircraft on the morning of 29 August and as a result Sqn Ldr Alex Muskett left Coltishall in the early evening flying XX725/GU and arrived at Gioia; he was followed by Sqn Ldr Simon Blake in the early morning of 30 August flying XX962/EK. RAF operations began on the afternoon of 30August when a combined force of two Jaguar GR1.Bs and four Harrier GR.7s attacked an ammunition storage depot in the vicinity of Sarajevo.

During the *Deliberate Force* operations, Sqn Ldrs Muskett and Blake flew a total of twenty-five combat sorties, guiding forty-eight LGBs on to target and designating further targets for many 1,000lb free-fall bombs. Some of the targets proved to be quite testing, being less easy to acquire than those attacked in the open terrain of the desert. Nevertheless, the duo achieved an enviable strike rate and fully justified the work undertaken by the DRA and GEC in integrating the TIALD pod and its associated avionics with the Jaguar.

A key piece of equipment of the Jaguar and other combat aircraft in the Bosnia operations area was the decoy flare; shown here launched by XX725/GU.
No.6 Squadron via Alex Muskett

CHAPTER TWELVE

Harriers Today

(Top) **A chirpy looking groundcrewman gets to grips with a little canopy cleaning along a line of No.4 Squadron jets.** RAF

The use of a wide-angle lens seems to elongate the nose, but still shows the purposeful lines of the GR.7 that made more than a little impact at the 'Star'. RAF

Purple Star Harriers: Photofile

During the early part of 1996 elements from all the UK's armed forces took part in a massive deployment to the United States for *Purple Star* 96. For the RAF this meant deploying a number of its Harrier GR.7s to MCAS Cherry Point in South Carolina where they operated alongside the home-based AV-8Bs flying CAS sorties for the 'friendlies'.

'Harriers in Hiding': *Hill Foil* and *Hazel Flute*

Two of the most important exercises in the calendar of the Harrier units are the annually alternating *Hazel Flute* and *Hill Foil* deployments.

During the six days of exercises the Harriers decamp into the 'field', operating as they would in wartime from unprepared strips and woodland hides. However, the 1995 *Hill Foil* and the 1996 *Hazel Flute* exercise saw something of a departure from the customary when the Force put into practice another of their contingency plans by operating from 'bare base' facilities, that is by using a defunct airfield and turning it into an operating centre.

Hill Foil 95 saw the Harriers from 2 Group in Germany taking over the former

Harrier GR.7 sitting on MEXE plank strips inside its hide; the netting does have the desired effect when seen from the air. Author

(Below) **Inside the hide is all the ground support equipment for the aircraft, as seen here.** Author

USAFE base at Bentwaters, which had been vacated some years earlier by the A-10 Warthogs; the Force moved in set up its camp and began operations. 'Hazel Flute 96' was slightly different in that the whole of the Force was involved, and twenty-two aircraft from all the units, including No.20(R), took up residence at RAF Honington. Honington is still an active base, being home to the RAF Regiment, but at present it does not have any resident aircraft so that the infrastructure is still there. However, the Harrier Force treated it like a damaged base, setting up netted hides, operating from tented sites, and using only small stretches of the runways and taxiways to simulate bomb-damaged areas. Besides being a huge logistical operation, the deployment was seen as a resounding success and the pattern was repeated with

Hill Foil 97 when the Force again occupied a former USAFE base, at Sculthorpe in Norfolk.

Wg Cdr Clive Loader, the Detachment Commander for *Hill Foil 97*, commented on the importance of dispersed operations for the Harrier Force:

> It is vital that, as a rapid response force, we stay in tune with the changing face of the global scene. That inevitably must involve our preparedness to move at very short notice, and be able to operate our Harriers quickly and effectively, having not only established ourselves in the aircraft sense, but also have all the command structure, logistics chain, communications and self-defence ingredients in place. To that end exercises such as *Hill Foil* and *Hazel Flute* are vital to our continued training and our flexibility.

Hot Funnel and *Ocean Wave*: UK Harrier Forces' Combined Operations

Early in January 1997 HMS *Illustrious* left the UK along with a twenty-strong Naval Task Group to take part in Exercise *Ocean Wave* 97 off the coast of Malaysia, a deployment designed to show the Navy's ability to assemble a strong, credible and self-sustaining force east of Suez, and give its crews valuable experience working as part of a carrier task group. Before arriving in southern Asia, the embarked Air Group from No.801 Squadron, flying its Sea Harrier F/A.2s were to take part in Operation *Southern Watch*, of which the UK's contribution went under the name of Operation *Jural*, monitoring the forces of Iraq in the UN-imposed southern

Another sortie completed by two Hot Funnel **GR.7s, the pilots exit their aircraft.**

'no-fly zone'. Another aspect of the deployment was the arrival on deck of four RAF Harrier GR.7s, which would join *Illustrious* for a month's embarkation in order that they too might gain valuable carrier-based experience and work with the Sea Harrier units in order to achieve a good working understanding of each other's capabilities.

OCA/DCA (offensive counter air/defensive counter air) aircraft to enter the sector to provide top cover for French, American and British aircraft tasked with reconnaissance over the area. At five miles high, the Blue Vixen radar had an ideal vantage point, watching the reconnaissance jets below ply their trade and being

On 28 February, the four RAF Harrier GR.7s from No.1(F) Squadron joined *Illustrious* off the coast of Oman. Under the title of exercise *Hot Funnel* this was to be the first deployment of a front-line Harrier unit on a naval vessel. This was not, however, the first time that a GR.7 had been on one of the Navy's carriers, as the

Deck crews chain down a GR.7 after recovery, while an F/A.2 arrives in the background. HMS *Illustrious*

Friday, 7 March, saw five F/A.2s, each armed with two AMRAAM missiles, launch from *Illustrious* as she sailed near to Bahrain, on the first of five days policing of the no-fly zone. These fighters had the distinction of being the first British

ready to engage with their AIM-120 missiles should the need arise. The Squadron then provided two aircraft on a daily basis for the operation and for most of the pilots, already blooded over Bosnia, it was yet another valuable lesson to be learned.

way was well paved by a detachment of three Harriers from the SAOEU in June 1994 tasked to work out the aircraft's SOPs (standard operating procedures) for shipboard work. The purpose of the GR.7s' *Hot Funnel* Deployment was to conduct 'mixed fighter force' operations, and also to refine their maritime capabilities, adding more knowledge to their role within the new Joint Rapid Deployment Force strategy. Before the deployment, the four aircraft (ZD400, ZD461, ZD462 and ZD468 all received some maritime modifications. These included the linking of the GPS to the INS, the uprating of the the INS to a FIN1075G, and the adding of an INS software update to prevent the system from 'toppling' during wind up on a moving deck. The water injection system's fill-up point was moved from above the wing to a position inside the undercarriage bay; this was to prevent any unwary RAF crewman who would have to clamber on to the spine of the aircraft to fill the tank running the risk of falling overboard. The final modification was the installation of an I-Band IFF system.

Both day and night carrier landings were undertaken. The GR.7s also flew practice bombing missions and carried out joint training sessions with the F/A.2s flying cover, rediscovering the legendary Falklands double act of the 1980s. RAF technicians worked alongside their naval counterparts, arming the aircraft with a variety of weapons fits, although each Service was responsible for the maintenance and operation of its own jets. The new RAF Harriers and the Sea Harriers forged a formidable working relationship and are now seen as an excellent joint asset in the UK's maritime force.

The Harrier and the New Joint Rapid Deployment Force

As part of the UK's new Joint Rapid Deployment Force, a combination of Sea Harrier F/A.2s providing OCA/DCA and RAF Harrier GR.7s providing CAS would support any Task Force assembled by the military. An example might be an assault by Royal Marine Commandos in which the GR.7s with their night attack abilities would be crucial in the early stages; once a beachhead had been established they would be able to go ashore and operate in their more usual role from a dispersed FOB (Forward Operating Base). The mixed fighter force concept of F/A.2 and GR.7 provides a fully self-contained package, able to supply top cover from the radar- and missile-equipped Sea Harriers, while RAF Harriers sweep in to undertake night or day interdiction sorties.

The carrier air group could therefore be tailored to meet a specific scenario, with say ten F/A- 2s, six GR.7s and a flight of three Sea King AEW helicopters. This force would be more than capable of deploying aboard the UK's carriers and delivering a crushing blow at very short notice with missiles, rockets or bombs.

(Above) **Prepared to go anywhere.** Author

The Harrier's Rivals

Yakovlev Yak-38MP Forger

The Yak-38 is somewhat restricted by its 1960s technology, with only a limited STO capability which restricts its range and payload considerably. With the former Soviet Union's plans to develop a competitive blue-water navy, shipboard fighters were of paramount importance. Powered by two lift turbojets mounted behind the cockpit and a single, two-nozzle vectoring turbo jet in the rear, the aircraft operates from the *Kiev* class ASW carriers. It is lightly armed with 3000lb of stores, usually AA-8 Aphid AAMs, although guns and rocket pods are in its inventory. The Forger 'A' is the single-seat derivative, and the 'B' the two-seat training version. Although underpowered and of limited range, the Forger represents an important milestone for the CIS in carrier operations.

(Above) **Yak-38.** Author

Yakovlev Yak-121

First displayed in the west at the 1992 Farnborough Airshow. It is the first of the current VSTOL types that is capable of supersonic flight. It has a rear-mounted, rotatable, afterburning turbofan, supported by lift engines. Currently still a prototype, it has not as yet been ordered by the CIS, and remains available for purchase or export.

(Below) **Yak-121.** Author

The 'GRIER' System: Special Operations People Pods

The Special Operations Force of the United States face a unique challenge. They must be able to extract personnel or supplies from places that may be 100 miles away, perhaps in a wooded clearing or beside a small road. Enter the Harrier and the 'GRIER' system: GRIER is an acronym for Ground Rescue, Infiltrate, Exfiltrate and Resupply system, in essence two 'people pods' that would fit on to the outer wing pylons and allow the Harrier to fly in or out of crisis or denied areas with small parties of troops. The pods would be able to carry up to four troops and their equipment and would be fitted with a small window to avoid claustrophobia. Although the system sounds like a credible alternative for use by the Harrier, the author feels that it must be one of the most bizarre forms of transport yet devised and, in the words of Anon, 'You'd never get me up in one of those things!'

The Grier system. McDonnell Douglas

A Sea Harrier F/A.2 sweeps towards a golden Atlantic sunset. Royal Navy

APPENDIX 1

Individual Aircraft Profiles

ROYAL AIR FORCE

BuNo.	TYPE	DELIVERY	NOTES
XV738	GR.1/A/3	16.4.68	RAF. Rolls-Royce. Now privately owned by Phoenix Aviation at Bruntingthorpe. Matchcote Trial painted Grey.
XV739	GR.1/A	16.5.68	MOD/A&AEE. Crashed 24.9.73 when with No 1 Sqdn at Episkopi Cyprus/pre-airshow practice.
XV740	GR.1/A/3	22.7.68	Originally to A& AEE. Delivered to the RAF 1.75. Scrapped 1992 at Abingdon.
XV741	GR.1/A/3	5.8.68	Originally to A&AEE. Delivered to the RAF 7.72. Transatlantic Air Race. Passed to SFDO RNAS Culdrose.
XV742	GR. 1/A/3		Hawker Siddeley Demonstrator. Flew for Swiss AF as G-VSTO 11.6.71. Crashed on Holbeach range 28.10.83.
XV743	GR.1		Crashed at Dunsfold 7.1.69 pre-delivery. Was not recovered from spin.
XV744	GR. 1/A/3	9.4.69	When retired the aircraft was passed to the Royal College of Science at Shrivenham to carry the code 9167M.
XV745	GR.1/A/3	18.4.69	No. 233 0CU. Collided with XV754 19.1.76 near Nantwich, Cheshire.
XV746	GR.1/A/3	18.4.69	No. 1 Squadron. Crashed near Bardufoss in Norway 12.3.76.
XV747	GR.1/A/3	7.5.69	Crashed through fence, Wittering. When retired passed to 108.3 ATC at Hucknall with code 8.979M.
XV748	GR.1/A/3	16.5.69	Passed to Cranfield University.
XV749	GR.1	5.5.69	No. 1 Squadron. Crashed in the North Sea 26.4.72 from a bird strike.
XV750	GR.1/A/3	28.5.69	20 Squadron. Crashed Roermond in the Netherlands. 6.8.73.
XV751	GR.1/A/3	2.6.69	Now privately owned at Charlwood.
XV752	GR.1/A/3	27.9.69	Now at No. 2 SoTT Cosford as 9075M.
XV753	GR.1/A/3	15.8.69	Now at SFDO RNAS Culdrose as 9075M.
XV754	GR.1/A/3	13.8.69	223 OCU. Crashed 19.I.76 near Nantwich Cheshire, colliding with XV745.
XV755	GR.1/A/3	18.9.69	Now at SFDO RNAS Culdrose.
XV756	GR.1/A/3	19.9.69	No. 1 Squadron Crashed 8.11.79 Holbeach Range.
XV757	GR.1/A/3	19.9.69	No. 1 Squadron Crashed 21.9.79 Collided with XZ128.
XV758	GR.1/A/3	1.12.69	Now gate guard at Decimonmannu in Sardinia.
XV759	GR.1/A/3	12.3.70	Now on Pendirie Range.
XV760	GR.1/A/3	13.2.70	Now at ETS RNAS Yeovilton.
XV761	GR.1/A/3	25.3.70	No. 4 Squadron. Crashed 28.10.80 when undertaking DACT near Bitburg in Germany with an OV-10A.
XV762	GR.1/A/3	27.2.70	1453 Flight. Crashed 19.11.83 near Lafonia, Falklands.
XV776	GR.1/A/3	3.4.70	No. 1 Squadron. Crashed 9.4.75 near Church Stretton.
XV777	GR.1	1.5.70	No. 1 Squadron. Crashed 1.5.72 at Wittering.
XV778	GR.1/A/3	15.4.70	Scrapped at Valley, 1994 as 9001M.
XV779	GR.1/A/3	29.5.70	Now on display at Wittering as 8931M.
XV780	GR.1/A/3	29.5.70	No.4 Squadron. Crashed 27.6.72 near Wesel, Germany as the result of a bird strike.
XV781	GR.1/N3	29.5.70	No. 3 Squadron. Crashed 12.6.79 Gütersloh, Germany.
XV782	GR.1/A/3	15.7.70	To BDRT at Bruggen as 8982M.
XV783	GR.1/A/3	25.6.70	To AES HMS *Sultan*, Gosport. To SFDO at Cudrose.
XV784	GR.1/A/3	14.8.70	Front fuselage now at DTEO Boscombe Down as 8909M.
XV785	GR.1/A/3	25.9.70	No.4 Squadron. Crashed 26.3.74 Wildenrath, Germany.

XV786	GR.1/A/3	29.9.70	Front Fuselage to Predannack Fire School RNAS Culdrose.
XV787	GR.1/A/3	11.11.70	Har-Det. Crashed 22.7.83 Port Willam Sound, Falklands.
XV788	GR.1/A/3	7.5.70	No.1 Squadron. Crashed Belize 1.12.75 following bird strike.
XV789	GR.1/A/3	27.6.70	To RAF Bruggen for BDRT.
XV790	GR.1/A/3	4.6.70	No.3 Squadron. Crashed 2.11.87 near Otterburn after colliding with XZ136.
XV791	GR.1/A/3	9.6.70	No.20 Squadron. Crashed 9.6.73 in Westphalia, Germany following a bird strike.
XV792	GR.1/A/3	17.6.70	No.3 Squadron. Crashed 14.10.80 near Gütersloh, Germany.
XV793	GR.1/A/3	27.8.70	To RAF Bruggen for BDRT.
XV794	GR.1/A/3	28.7.70	No.4 Squadron. Crashed 4.5.72 near Hulten, Germany following a bird strike.
XV795	GR.1/A/3	15.9.70	No.3 Squadron. Crashed 23.2.83 near Eye, Cambridgeshire after colliding with XW926.
XV796	GR.1	28.8.70	No.1 Squadron. Crashed 6.10.70 near Ouston following engine flame out.
XV797	GR.1/A/3	30.9.70	No.4 Squadron. Crashed 23.1.74 near Vredpeel, Netherlands.
XV798	GR.1(mod)	28.10.70	No.20 Squadron. Crashed 27.4.71 Wildenrath, Germany. To R&EE Foulness for Plenium Burning Chamber trials.
XV799	GR.1	28.10.70	No.233 OCU. Crashed 12.9.72 near Kyle of Lochalsh.
XV800	GR.1/A/3	30.11.70	No.4 Squadron. Damaged beyond repair at Wildenrath in ground accident.
XV801	GR.1/A/3	11.1.71	No.3 Squadron. Crashed 15.12.78 near Eningerloth, Germany.
XV802	GR.1	26.1.71	No.20 Squadron. Crashed 21.3.72 near Stanoldendorf, Germany.
XV803	GR.1	20.7.71	No.1 Squadron. Crashed 3.8.71 near Huntingdon, Cambridgeshire.
XV804	GR./1/A/3	29 1.71	Now at the Defence NBC Centre, Winterbourne Gunner.
XV8O5	GR.1/A/3	22.6.71	No.20 Squadron. Crashed 30.7.73 near Coesfeld, Germany following a bird strike.
XV806	GR.1/A/3	15.6.71	Now at SFDO RNAS Culdrose.
XV807	GR.1/A/3	20.10.71	1417 Flight. Crashed 14.7.81 near Cayo, Belize.
XV808	GR.1/A/3	26.3.71	Now at SFDO RNAS Culdrose as 9076M.
XV809	GR.1/A/3	2.4.71	No.3 Squadron. Crashed 20.5.88 near. Gütersloh, Germany. Matchcote Trial painted Green.
XV810	GR.1/A/3	26.4.71	To St. Athan for BDRT as 9038M.
XW174	T.2		Crashed at Larkhill 4.6.69 on a test flight.
XW175	T.2/A/4/A		HSA Aircraft. Converted to VAAC for DTEO.
XW264	T.2	11.7.70	Crashed 11.7.70 Now at Staverton Aviation Collection, Gloucester.
XW265	T.2/A/4/A	21.5.70	Stored at Shawbury.
XW266	T.2/A/4/A T.4N	25.7.70	Reduced for spares at RNAS Yeovilton 16.11.95.
XW267	T.2/A/4	28.8.70	Currently stored at Boscombe Down.
XW268	T.2/A/4/A. T.4N	7.1.71	No.899 Squadron. Crashed 27.6.94 RNAS Yeovilton. Scrapped 10.96.
XW269	T.2/A/4	1.4.71	Stored Boscombe Down.
XW270	T.2/A/4	10.3.71	In pieces at Cranfield University. Fuselage privately purchased by Phoenix Aviation at Bruntingthorpe.
XW271	T.2/A/4	20.7.71	Now with SFDO RNAS Culdrose.
XW272	T.2/AJ4	10.5.71	No.4 Squadron. Crashed 29.6.82 on the Bergen Hohn Range, Germany. Forward fuselage now with BAe Kingston.
XW630	GR.1/A/3	30.6.71	Passed to RN AES HMS *Sultan*, Gosport.
XW763	GR.1/A/3	5.11.71	Passed to the Imperial War Museum.
XW764	GR.1A/3	5 11.71	Passed to RAF Leeming Fire Section as 8981M.
XW765	GR.1A/3	30.11.71	No.3 Squadron. Crashed 12.3.80 near Lampeter, Wales.
XW766	GR.1A/3	30.11.71	No.3 Squadron. Crashed near Ravensburg, Germany.
XW767	GR.1A/3	1.12.71	No.1 Squadron. Crashed 6.11.82 off Cape Pembroke, Falklands.
XW768	GR.1A/3	24.4.82	Now with No.2 SoTT at Cosford as 9072M.
XW769	GR.1A/3	24.1.72	No.4 Squadron. Crashed 28.6.86 near Cheivers, Belgium.
XW770	GR.1A/3	14.8.72	No.3 Squadron. Crashed 6.7.76 at Borken, Germany.
XW916	GR.1A/3	19.11.71	No.4 Squadron, Crashed 17.6.86 atYeovilton following an electrical failure. Passed to Wittering Fire Section.
XW917	GR.1A/3	20.8.71	On Display at RAF Laarbruch as 8975M.
XW918	GR.1A/3	27.9.71	No.4 Squadron. Crashed 12.1.72 near Tuschenbroich, Germany.
XW919	GR.1A/3	27.9.71	Passed to SFDO RNAS Culdrose.
XW920	GR.1A	21.10.71	No.3 Squadron. Crashed 21.6.72, Sicily.
XW921	GR.1A/3	25.10.71	No 4 Squadron. Crashed 18.8.88 Gütersloh.
XW922	GR.1A/3	30.9.71	RAF Laarbruch for BDRT.
XW923	GR.1A/3	13.10.71	No.1417 Flight. Crashed 26.5.81 on take off from Belize. Front fuselage returned to Wittering, for crash rescue training.
XW924	GR.1A/3	26.10.71	9073M at RAF Laarbruch.
XW925	T.2A/4	1.10.71	Crashed 20.6.89 Gütersloh.

XW926	T.2A/4	11.5.72	Crashed near Eye, Cambridgeshire 23.2.83 after colliding with XV795.
XW927	T.2A/4	28.7.72	RAF Brüggen.
XW933	T.2A/4	22.8.73	No.3 Squadron. Crashed 18.2.85 near Bad Laer, Germany after colliding with MFG2 F-104G.
XW934	T.2A/4	21.12.93	To DRA Farnborough for ground instruction.
XY125	GR.S0/AV-8A	26.9.73	HSA aircraft. Trials on *Jeanne D'Arc* 11.10.73. To USMC as 158969 26.10.73.
XZ128	GR.3	15.3.76	No.1 Squadron. Crashed 12.9.79 atWisbech after colliding with XV757.
XZ129	GR.3	6.4.76	Passed to ETS RNAS Culdrose.
XZ130	GR.3	11.4.76	Passed to No.2 SoTT Cosford as 9079M.
XZ131	GR.3	30.4.76	Forward Fuselage passed to EP & TU at St. Athan 9174M.
XZ132	GR.3	14.5.76	Passed to ATF RAFC Cranwell as 9168M.
XZ133	GR.3	9.7.76	Imperial War Museum.
XZ134	GR.3	31.7.76	No.3 Squadron. Crashed 3.5.83 near Lippstadt, Germany.
XZ135	GR.3	2.11.76	No.3 Squadron. Crashed 30.6.84 Grosstenheim, Germany. Forward fuselage. passed to EP & TU St Athan as 8848M.
XZ136	GR.3	5.11.76	No.3 Squadron. Crashed 2.11.87 Otterburn Range after colliding with XV790. US Exchange pilot killed.
XZ137	GR.3	6.1.77	No. 4 Squadron. Crashed 18.7.79 near Giessen, Germany.
XZl38	GR.3	25.3.77	Forward Fuselage passed to RAF Cranwell as 9040M.
XZ139	GP3	22.3.77	No.3 Squadron. Crashed 25.8.81, west of Ahlorn, Germany.
XZ145	T.4	8.3.76	Stored at RAF Shawbury.
XZ146	T.4		Stored at RAF Shawbury.
XZ147	T.4/A	20.1.77	No.2330 DCU Crashed 25.9.91 near Driffield. UAS Backseater became the first woman to eject from a Harrier.
XZ445	T.4/A	2.5.79	RAF Passed to RN. No.899 Squadron. Crashed 23.2.96 on the Blackdown Hills.
XZ963	GR.3	8.5.80	No. 1 Squadron. Crashed 30.5.82. Hit by small arms fire during Falklands war and ran out of fuel.
XZ964	GR.3	22.4.80	Passed to the Royal Engineers Museum at Chatham.
XZ965	GR.3	28.8.80	Passed to the Old Flying Machine Company at Duxford as 9184M.
XZ966	GR.3	4.9.80	Passed to RAF Cottesmore Fire Section as 9221M.
XZ967	GR.3	3.9.80	Now at Phoenix Aviation, Bruntingthorpe as 9077M.
XZ968	GR.3	10.12.80	Passed to the Muckleborough Collection in Weyborne as 9222M.
XZ969	GR.3	15.12.80	Passed to SFDO at RNAS Culdrose.
XZ970	GR.3	13.1.81	Stored at St Athan.
XZ971	GR.3	4.6.82	RAF Benson on Main Gate as 9219M.
XZ972	GR.3	10.8.81	No.1 Squadron. Crashed 21.5.82 after being hit by a Blowpipe missile in the Falkland Islands.
XZ973	GR.3	27.9.81	No.233 OCU. Crashed 12.2.82 near Corwen, North Wales.
XZ987	GR.3	6.10.81	RAF Stafford Main Gate as 9185M.
XZ988	GR.3	18 12.81	No.1 Squadron. Crashed 27.5.82 after being shot down over Goose Green in the Falkland Islands.
XZ989	GR.3	27.11.81	Crashed 8.6.82 at Port San Carlos in the Falkland Islands, Returned to Gütersloh for ground instruction trainer as 8849M.
XZ990	GR.3	15.12.81	Scrapped at RAF Wittering.
XZ991	GR.3	3.2.82	To St Athan for BDRT as 9162M.
XZ992	GR.3	18.2.82	No. 1453 Flight. Crashed 29.11.84 near Port Stanley in the Falkland Islands following a bird strike.
XZ993	GR.3	18.1.82	St Athan Fire Section.
XZ994	GR.3	4.2.82	To AMS at RAF Brize Norton as 9170M.
XZ995	GR.3	22.2.82	To RAF St. Mawgan Fire Section as 9220M.
XZ996	GR.3	4.2.82	To RN SFDO RNAS Culdrose.
XZ997	GR.3	11.2.82	To RAF Museum, Hendon as 9122M.
XZ998	GR.3	11.5.82	To RAF Bruggen for BDRT as 9161M.
XZ999	GR.3	8.7.32	No.3 Squadron. Crashed 28.3.89 at RAF Laarbruch. Used for ground instruction.
ZA250	T52		G-VTOL HSA Demonstrator Now in Brookands Air Museum, Weybridge.
ZB600	T.4	10.3.83	Stored Dunsfold.
ZB601	T.4	14.4.83	Used for spares at Dunsfold.
ZB602	T.4	18.4.83	Stored at Dunsfold.
ZB603	T.4/T.8	19.8.83	Heavy landing 2.5.95. Repaired and converted to Navy T.8.
ZB604	T.4N/T.8	21.9.83	No.899 Squadron.
ZB605	T.4N/T.8	8.11.83	No.899 Squadron.
ZB606	T.4N	5.1.84	No.899 Squadron. Crashed 7.2.85 north of Yeovilton.
ZD318	GPS/7/DB1	30.4.85	MoD/BAe. Dunsfold.

ZD319	GR.5/7/DB2	31.7.85	MoD/BAe Dunsfold.
ZD320	GR.5/5A	23.9.86	MoD/BAe.
ZD321	GR.5/5A	20.6.88	RAF. Coded 02.
ZD322	GR.5/7	4.10.88	No.1 Squadron.
ZD323	GR.S/7	29.5.87	RAF.
ZD324	GR.S/7	1.7.87	RAF. Coded O5.
ZD325	GR.5		Crashed 22.10.87 in the Atlantic Ocean after test pilot Taylor Scott suffered an involuntary ejection.
ZD326	GR.5/7	6.5.88	RAF.
ZD327	GR.5/7	2.6.88	RAF.
ZD328	GR.5/7	26.7.88	RAF.
ZD329	GR.5/7	22.8.88	RAF.
ZD330	GR.5/7	2.8.88	RAF. Coded 11 for 'Deny Flight' in Mod 95 scheme.
ZD345	GR.5/7	1.9.88	RAF. Coded 12.
ZD346	GR.5/7	18.7.88	RAF.
ZD347	GR.5/7	3.3.89	RAF.
ZD348	GR.5/7	2.9.88	RAF. Coded 15.
ZD349	GR.5	30.8.88	No.20(R) Squadron. Crashed 14.1.94 near Evesham following a bird strike.
ZD350	GR.5	10.11.88	Crashed 7.8.92. Passed to St Athan for BDRT as 9189M.
ZD351	GR.5/7	31.10.88	MoD/BAe.
ZD352	GR.5/7	7.10.88	MoD/BAe.
ZD353	GR.5	11.11.88	Damaged by fire 29.7.91 Fuselage to BAe, Brough.
ZD354	GR.5/7	5.12.88	RAF Coded 21.
ZD355	GR.5	4.11.88	Crashed 17.10.90 on take-off from Alborg Denmark.
ZD375	GR.5/7	27.10.88	RAF. Coded 23.
ZD376	GR.5/7	21.11.88	RAF. Coded 24 for Warden and 'Deny Flight'.
ZD377	GR.5/7	2.12.88	RAF. To St Athan 72.95.
ZD378	GR.5/7	13.12.88	RAF.
ZD379	GR.5/7	12.12.88	RAF. Coded 27.
ZD380	GR.5/7	6.12.88	RAF. Coded 28 for 'Deny Flight'.
ZD400	GR.5/7	12.12.88	RAF. Deployed to Invincible for 'Hot Funnel'.
ZD401	GR.5/7	20.12.88	RAF.
ZD402	GR.5/7	5.12.88	Rolls-Royce Pegasus 11-61 Test Aircraft. To RAF 17.8.93 with No.20(R) Squadron.
ZD403	GR.5/7	22.12.88	RAF. Coded 32.
ZD404	GR.5/7	22.12.88	RAF. Coded 33.
ZD405	GR.5/7	23.12.88	RAF. Coded 34 for 'Deny Flight'.
ZD406	GR.5/7	27.6.89	RAF. Coded 35 for 'Deny Flight'.
ZD407	GR.5/7	27.6.89	RAF.
ZD408	GR.5/7	13.7.89	RAF Coded 'WK' for Warden. Received Sharkmouth.
ZD409	GR.5/7	4.7.89	RAF.
ZD410	GR.S/7	27.7.89	RAF. Coded 39.
ZD411	GR.5/7	19.7.89	RAF.
ZD412	GR.5	5.10.89	No.3 Squadron. Crashed 30.9.91 landing accident. Fuselage to BAe, Brough.
ZD430	GR.5A/7	20.9.91	Crashed 29.6.93 near Heckington in Lincolnshire. First 5A upgrade.
ZD431	GR.5A/7	24.10.89	RAF.
ZD432	GR.5A/7	10.7.89	Har-Det. Crashed 23.11.93 near Dahuk in Northern Iraq following a mechanical failure. Coded WD for Warden.
ZD433	GR.5A/7	5.9.89	To RAF Wittering as Maintenance Trainer 15.9.89.
ZD434	GR.5A/7	2.11.89	RAF. Coded 46 for 'Deny Flight'.
ZD435	GR.5A/7	24.10.89	RAF. Coded 47 for 'Deny Flight'.
ZD436	GR.5A/7	20.10.89	RAF. To FJTS Boscombe Down.
ZD437	GR.5A/7	29.11.89	RAF. First aircraft fitted with GPS. Coded 49.
ZD438	GR.5A/7	17.1.90	RAF.
ZD461	GR.5A/7	16.11.89	RAF. Deployed to Invincible for 'Hot Funnel'.
ZD462	GR.5A/7	22.11.89	RAF. Coded 52. Deployed to Invincible for 'Hot Funnel'.
ZD463	GR.5A/7	7.12.89	RAF.
ZD464	GR.5A/7	21.12.89	RAF. Coded 54.
ZD465	GR.5A/7	18.4.90	RAF. Coded 55.
ZD466	GR.5A/7	24.1.90	RAF Coded 56.
ZD467	GR.5A/7	9.2.90	RAF. Passed to SAOEU 4.6.91. Coded WA for Warden.

ZD468	GR.5A/7	30.3.90	RAF. Deployed to *Invincible* for 'Hot Funnel'.
ZD469	GR.5A/7	19.3.90	RAF. To HMF at Laarbruch. Passed to SAOEU.
ZD470	GR.5A/7	19.6.90	RAF. Coded 11.
ZD667	GP3	16.10.86	To SFDO RNAS Culdrose.
ZD668	GR.3	8.12.86	Privately owned by Phoenix Aviation Bruntingthorpe.
ZD669	GR.3	19.12.86	Now on display at Belize International Airport.
ZD670	GR.3	22.12.86	Privatley owned by Phoenix Aviation, Bruntingthorpe.
ZD990	T.4/A	25.6.87	Stored at St Athan.
ZD991	T.4	23.6.87	Stored at St Athan.
ZD992	T.4/T.8N	24.8.87	No.899 Squadron.
ZD993	T.4/T.8N	2.10.87	No.899 Squadron.
ZG471	GR.7	14.8.90	RAF. Coded 61.
ZG472	GR.7	17.8.90	RAF. Passed to the SAOEU.
ZG473	GR.7	12.9.90	No.4 Squadron. Crashed 29.5.91 south of Gütersloh.
ZG474	GR.7	24.9.80	RAF. Coded 64.
ZG475	GR.7	29.8 90	SAOEU. Crashed 1.6.95 in the Solway Firth, killing the CO of the unit, Wing Commander Nick Slater.
ZG476	GR.7	28.11.90	No.20(R) Squadron. Crashed 19.2.96 near Wittering. Coded WT.
ZG477	GR.7	5.11.90	RAF.
ZG478	GR.7	5.11.90	RAF. Coded 78 for Warden.
ZG479	GR.7	30.11.90	RAF. Coded 69.
ZG480	GR.7	5.12.90	RAF. Warden aircraft. No code.
ZG5OO	GP7	13.12.90	RAF. Coded 71 for 'Deny Flight'.
ZG5O1	GR.7	20.12.90	RAF. To SAOEU.
ZG5O2	GR.7	21.12.90	RAF.
ZG5O3	GR.7	21.12.90	RAF. Coded 74 for 'Deny Flight'.
ZG504	GR.7	26.2.91	RAF. Coded 75 for 'Deny Flight'.
ZG505	GR.7	12.3.91	RAF. Coded 76.
ZG5O6	GR.7	19.6.91	RAF. Coded 81 for Warden and 'Deny Flight' First aircraft to receive 100 per cent LERX.
ZG507	GR.7	4.11.91	RAF. Coded 78.
ZG508	GR.7	4.11.91	RAF. Coded 79 for 'Deny Flight'.
ZG509	GR.7	25.7.91	RAF.
ZG51O	GR.7	7.11.91	RAF.
ZG511	GR.7	4.11.91	RAF.
ZG512	GR.7	8.1.92	RAF. Coded 83.
ZG530	GR.7	10.12.91	RAF.
ZG531	GR.7	28.11.91	RAF. Specially marked for Farnborough 1992.
ZG532	GR.7	12.2.92	RAF. Specially marked for Farnborough 1992. Coded 86.
ZG533	GR.7	10.12.91	RAF.
ZG856	GR.7	22 11.91	RAF. Coded 88 for 'Deny Flight'.
ZG857	GR.7	20.1.92	RAF. Coded 89.
ZG858	GR.7	24.12.91	RAF. Coded 90.
ZG859	GR.7	18.1.92	RAF.
ZG860	GR.7	14.1.92	RAF.
ZG861	GR.7	11.5.92	RAF.
ZG862	GR.7	2.6.92	RAF. Last GR.7 delivered.
ZH654	T10		RAF.
ZH655	T10	27.3.95	RAF. Damaged, now in store at Wittering.
ZH656	T10	30.10.95	RAF. Coded 104.
ZH657	T10	30.1.95	RAF.
ZH658	T10	6.2.95	RAF.
659	T10	17.2.95	RAF.
660	T10	6.3.95	RAF.
661	T10	12.4.95	RAF.
662	T10	25.5.95	RAF.
663	T10	24.8.95	RAF.
664	T10	20.9.95	RAF. Coded 112.
665	T10	26.10.95	RAF.

ROYAL NAVY

BuNo.	TYPE	DELIVERY	NOTES
XZ438	FRS.1	19.4.82	No.809 Squadron. Crashed 17.5.82 at Yeovilton with fuel problem.
XZ439	FRS.1/2/F/A.2	19.4.79	RN MoD. First aircraft to ski-jump at sea.
XZ440	FRS.1	5.9.79	To BAe Brough after fuel system overpressurised 29.10.79.
XZ450	FRS.1	3.8.82	No. 800 Squadron. Crashed 4.5.82 at Goose Green after being hit by AAA fire.
XZ451	FRS.1	18.6.79	Crashed 3.11.89 off Sardinia; two kills in Falklands including Argentine C-130.
XZ452	FRS.1	12.10.79	No.801 Squadron. Crashed 6.5.82 after colliding with XZ453, one kill in Falklands.
XZ453	FRS.1	1.2.80	No.801 Squadron. Crashed 6.5.82 after colliding with XZ452.
XZ454	FRS.1	15.2.80	Crashed 1.12.80 off Lizard Point after colliding with the mast of HMS *Invincible*. Wreck now used by RN divers for practice.
XZ455	FRS.1/F/A.2	18.11.79	Crashed in the Adriatic 30m off Bosnia. Two kills in Falklands.
XZ456	FRS.1	4.1.80	No.801 Squadron. Crashed 1.6.82 after being hit by a Roland SAM at Port Stanley, Falklands.
XZ457	FRS.1/F/A.2	31.1.80	No.899 Squadron. Destroyed by ground fire at Yeovilton, 20.10.95. Two kills in Falklands.
XZ458	FRS.1	22.2.80	No.800 Squadron. Crashed 1.12.84 near Fort William after suffering a bird strike.
XZ459	FRS.1/F/A.2	15.5.80	RN.
XZ460	FRS.1	29.5.80	No.800 Squadron. Crashed 8.5.90 flew into the sea off Sardinia.
XZ491	FRS.1	30.4.82	Crashed 16.4.86 in the. sea off Benbecula when pilot Lt.Cdr Sinclair ran out of fuel.
XZ492	FRS.1/F/A.2	29.12.80	RN. One kill in Falklands.
XZ493	FRS.1	6.1.81	Crashed 15.12.94 – ditched into sea near *Invincible*. Now in Fleet Air Arm Museum, Yeovilton.
XZ494	FRS.1/F/A.2	5.12.80	RN.
XZ495	FRS.1/F/A.2	11.3.81	No.899 Squadron F/A.2OEU. Crashed 5.1.94 in the Bristol Channel following an engine failure.
XZ496	FRS.1	12.2.81	Crashed 16.3.84 in the North Sea off Norway following an engine failure. One kill in Falklands.
XZ497	FRS.1/2/F/A.2	22.4.82	FJTS Boscombe Down.
XZ498	FRS.1	13.5.81	No.801 Squadron. Crashed 16.4.94, near Gorazde, shot down by SAM-7. Pilot ejected safely.
XZ499	FRS.1/F/A.2	18.7.81	RN. Outrigger wheel torn off in accident. One kill in Falklands.
XZ500	FRS.1	5.8.81	Crashed 15.6.83 in the Bay of Biscay after an inverted spin. One kill in Falklands.
ZA174	FRS.1	16.11.81	No.801 Squadron. Crashed 28.5.82 after slipping off the side of *Invincible*.
ZA175	FRS.1/F/A.2	7.12.81	RN. One kill in Falklands.
ZA176	FRS.1/2/F/A.2	16.12.81	Landed on Spanish freighter *Alriago* after NAVHARS failure 7.6.83.
ZA177	FRS.1	6.1.82	No.899 Squadron. Crashed 21.1.83 near Cattistock in Dorset. Two kills in Falklands.
ZA190	FRS.1	7.12.81	No.801 Squadron. Crashed 15.10.87 in the Irish sea following a bird strike. Two kills in Falklands.
ZA191	FRS.1	5.1.82	No.801 Squadron. Crashed 4.10.89 off Lyme Regis after hitting *Ark Royal*'s mast during a fly-past.
ZA192	FRS.1	3.3.82	No.800 Squadron. Crashed 24.5.82 Exploded on take off from *Hermes*.
ZA193	FRS.1	4.2.82	No.800 Squadron. Crashed 28.5.92. off Cyprus after aircraft lost nozzle control and ditched near *Invincible*. One kill in Falklands.
ZA194	FRS.1	28.4.82	No.899 Squadron. Crashed 20.10.83 near West Knighton, Dorchester. One kill in Falklands.
ZA195	FRS.1/2/F/A.2	22.5.84	DB1 built to replace XZ450.
ZD578	FRS.1/F/A.2	27.3.85	RN.
ZD579	FRS.1/F/A.2	30.4.85	RN.
ZD580	FRS.1/F/A.2	10.7.85	RN.
ZD581	FRS.1/F/A.2	29.8.85	RN.
ZD582	FRS.1/2/F/A.2	7.10.85	RN. Coded 718.
ZD607	FRS.1/F/A.2	6.11.85	RN.
ZD608	FRS.1/F/A.2	17.10.85	RN. Coded 128.
ZD609	FRS.1	13.11.85	No.801 Squadron. Made a wheels-up landing at Pensacola Airshow 10.5.86.Crashed 10.5.91 near Chepstow.
ZD61O	FRS.1/F/A.2	11.12.85	RN.Last FRS.1.
ZD611	FRS.1/F/A.2	12.12.85	RN. Led bombing mission into Bosnia 7.9.95. Coded 714.
ZD612	FRS.1/F/A.2	9.1.86	RN.
ZD613	FRS.1/F/A.2	4.11.86	RN. Coded 005.
ZD614	FRS.1/F/A.2	7.4.86	RN.
ZD615	FRS.1/2/F/A.2	19.6.86	RN.
ZE690	FRS.1/F/A.2	13.11.87	RN.
ZE691	FRS.1/F/A.2	23.11.87	RN. Coded 002.
ZE692	FRS.1/F/A.2	8.12.87	RN.
ZE693	FRS.1/F/A.2	5.1.88	RN. Coded 693.
ZE694	FRS.1/F/A.2	8.3.88	RN.

ZE695	FRS.1/2/F/A.2	2.2.88	RN.
ZE696	FRS.1/F/A.2	6.4.88	RN. SHOEU. Coded 712-and a half!
ZE697	FRS.1/F/A.2	13.5.88	RN. Was the last FRS.1 to undertake an operational sortie, on 18.2.95.
ZE698	FRS.1/F/A.2	16.8.88	RN.
ZH796	F/A.2	20.10.95	RN.
ZH797	F/A.2	14.12.95	RN.
ZH798	F/A.2	13.3.96	RN.
ZH799	F/A.2	19.3 96	RN.
ZH800	F/A.2		RN.
ZH801	F/A.2		RN.
ZH802	F/A.2		RN.
ZH803	F/A.2		RN.
ZH804	F/A.2		RN.
ZH805	F/A.2		RN.
ZH806	F/A.2		RN.
ZH807	F/A.2		RN.
ZH808	F/A.2		RN.
ZH809	F/A.2		RN.
ZH810	F/A.2		RN.
ZH811	F/A.2		RN.
ZH812	F/A.2		RN.
ZH813	F/A.2		RN.

UNITED STATES MARINE CORPS

BuNo.	TYPE	DELIVERY	NOTES
158384	AV-8A/AVBC	19.1.71	McDD. Crashed 9.8.80 while in service with the NATC.
158385	AVBA	5.2.71	McDD. Passed to NASA as N716NA.
158386	AVBA	15.3.71	VMA-513. Crashed 18.6.71 at Chesapeake Bay.
158387	AVBA	12.3.71	USN. TPS Patuxtent River.
158388	AV-8A	11.5.71	VMA-513. Crashed 25.3.75 at Beaufort following a bird strike.
158389	AV-8A/C	30.4.71	USMC.
158390	AV-8A/C	30.4.71	USMC.
158391	AV-8A/C	28.5.71	USMC. Stored AMARC.
158392	AV-8A/C	30.7.71	USMC. Stored AMARC.
158393	AV-8A/C	29.11.71	USMC. Stored AMARC.
158394	AV-8A/YAV-8B	31.1.72	USMC. McDonnel Douglas. NASA Ames.
158395	AVBANAVBB˙	21.3.72	USMC. Crashed 15.11.79 at the Lake of Ozarks due to engine failure.
158694	AV-8A/C	4.5.72	USMC.
158695	AV-8A	31.5.72	USMC. Now on display at MCAS Yuma.
158696	AV-8A/C	13.7.72	USMC.
158697	AV-8A/C	10.7.72	USMC. Stored AMARC.
158698	AV-8A	19.9.72	USMC. On display MCAS El-Centro.
158699	AV-8A	22.9.72	VMA-542. Crashed 22.9.83 at MCAS Yuma.
158700	AV-8A/C	6.9.72	USMC. Stored AMARC.
158701	AV-8A/C	3.10.72	USMC. Stored AMARC.
158702	AV-8A/C	11.10.72	USMC. Stored AMARC.
158703	AV-8A	6.10.72	USMC. Crashed 26.6.81 in the Pacific while operating for the NATC from the USS *Tarawa*.
158704	AV-8A/C	11.12.72	USMC. Stored AMARC.
158705	AV-8A/C	26.10.72	USMC. Stored AMARC.
158706	AV-8A/C	7.12.72	USMC. Stored AMARC.
158707	AV-8A/C	29.11.72	USMC.
158708	AV-8A	28.12.72	VMA-231. Crashed 29.11.77 at Kadena, Japan following an engine failure.
158709	AV-8A	28.12.72	VMA-542. Crashed 10.1.76 at NAS Jacksonville.
158710	AV-8A/C	2.1.73	USMC.
158711	AV-8A/C	19.1.72	USMC.
158948	AV-8A/C	2.2.74	VMA-542. Crashed 5.4.74 at Camp Lejeune.
158949	AV-8A/C	22.1.73	USMC. Stored at AMARC.
158950	AV-8A	20.2.73	VMA-231. Crashed 26.6.84 at Cherry Point.

158951	AV-8A	11.3.73	USMC. Stored AMARC.
158952	AV-8A	8.3.73	VMA-542. Crashed 3.2.78 with engine failure.
158953	AV-8A	27.3.73	VMA-542. Crashed 27.7.77.
158954	AV-8A/C	6.4.73	VMA-542. Crashed 3.4.85.
158955	AV-8A	17.4.73	VMA-542. Crashed 1.12.82 east of Yuma.
158956	AV-8A/C	25.5.73	VMA-542 Crashed 4.3.82 at Cherry Point.
158957	AV-8A	9.7.73	VMA-542. Crashed 27.8.76 at Cherry Point following engine failure.
158958	AV-8A/C	28.6.73	USMC.
158959	AV-8A/C	5.7.73	USMC. Stored AMARC.
158960	AV-8A/C	17.7.73	USMC.
158961	AV-8A/C	27.7.73	USMC.
158962	AV-8A/C	31.7.73	VMA-542. Crashed 24.9.82.
158963.	AV-8A	30.8.73	USMC. On display at Cherry Point.
158954	AV-8A/C	7.9.73	USMC. Stored AMARC.
158965	AV-8A/C	30.8.73	USMC.
158966	AV-8A/C	21.9.73	USMC. Stored AMARC.
158967	AV-8A	4.10.73	VMA-542. Crashed 11.2.77.
158968	AV-8A	2.11.73	VMA-513. Crashed 26.1.82.
158969	AV-8A/C	11.10.73	USMC. Stored AMARC. Original HSA trials aircraft.
158970	AV-8A	30.11.73	VMA-51 3. Crashed 6.9.77 near Las Vegas.
158971	AV-8A	9.11.73	VMA-513. Crashed 27.7.74 at MCAS Beaufort.
158972	AV6A/C	28.11.73	USMC. Stored AMARC.
158973	AV-8A/C	7.12.73	USMC. Stored AMARC.
158974	AV-8A	20.12.73	VMA-513. Crashed 30.8.76 at Iwakuni after running out of fuel.
158975	AV-8A/C	22.1.74	USMC. Now on display at the National Museum of Naval Aviation Pensacola.
158976	AV-8A	4.1.74	USMC. On display at Cherry Point.
158977	AV-8A/C	7.2.74	USMC. Stored AMARC.
1 59231	AV-8A/C	25.1.74	VMA-231. Crashed 25.4.75.
159232	AV-8AC	13.2.74	USMC. Now on display at the Air/Sea/Space Museum New York.
159233.	AV-8A/C	5.4.74	USMC. On display FAA Museum Yeovilton.
159234	AV-8A	6.6.74	USMC.
159235	AV-8A	21.6.74	VMA-231. Crashed 13.2.75 near MOAS Cherry Point.
159236	AV-8A	19.6.94	VMA-231. Crashed 4.7.75 at Beaufort following an engine failure.
158237	AV-8A	10.7.74	VMA-231. Crashed 16.7.76 at Mayport following an engine fire.
159238	AV-8A/C	26.6.74	USMC. Stored AMARC.
158239	AV-8A	30.7.74	USMC. NASA Ames for spares recovery programme.
159240	AV-8A/C	23.7.74	USMC. Stored AMARC.
159241	AV-8A	29.8.74	USMC. On display at Pima County Air Museum.
159242	AV-8A/C	15.8.74	USMC.
159243	AV-8A/C	13.9.74	USMC. Stored AMARC.
159244	AV-8A	20.9.74	VMA-231. Crashed 4.7.74 at MCAS Beaufort.
159245	AV-8A	7.8.74	VMA-231. Crashed 9.10.74.
159246	AV-8A	22.8.74	USMC.
159247	AV-8A/C	5.9.74	USMC. Stored AMARC.
159248	AV-8A/C	27.9.74	USMC.
159249	AV-8A/C	4.10.74	USMC.
159250	AV-8A	7.11.74	VMA-231. Crashed 12.7.77 off Cape Hatteras.
159251	AV-8A	7.11.74	VMA-513. Crashed 13.8.80.
159252	AV-8A/C	16.11.74	USMC. Stored AMARC.
159253	AV-8A/C	17.12.74	VMA-513. Crashed 2.2.83 at Cherry Point.
159254	AV-8A/C	23.12.74	USMC. Stored NATTC Memphis.
159255	AV-8A/C	15.1.75	USMC. Stored AMARC.
159256	AV-8A/C	6.1.75	USMC.
159257	AV-8A/C	20.1.75	USMC. Stored AMARC.
159258	AV-8A/C	30.6.76	USMC. Stored AMARC.
159259	AV-8A	3.3.75	USMC. Crashed 27.11.77.
159366	AV-8A/C	20.6.75	USMC. Stored AMARC.
159367	AV-8A/C	20.7.75	USMC. Stored AMARC.
159368	AV-8A	30.6.75	VMAT-203. Crashed 19.1.81.
159369	AV-8A/C	25.7.75	USMC.

159370	AV-8A/C	12.9.75	USMC. Stored AMARC.
159371	AV-8A/C	17.10.75	USMC. Stored AMARC.
159372	AV-8A	28.10.75	VMAT-203. Crashed 6.77.
159373	AV-8A/C	4.8.76	USMC. Stored AMARC.
159374	AV-8A/C	8.10.76	USMC. Stored AMARC.
159375	AV-8A/C	5.1.76	USMC. Stored AMARC.
159376	AV-8A/C	16.5.77	USMC. Stored AMARC.
159377	AV-8A	26.1.76	VMAT-203. Crashed 19.3.77.
159378	TAV-8A	1.10.75	USMC. Stored AMARC.
159379	TAV-8A	16.1.76	USMC. Stored AMARC.
159360	TAVBA	6.2.76	VMAT-203. Crashed 12.8.87 Bayboro, Pimlico County.
159361	TAV-8A	1.24.76	VMAT-203. Crashed 19.4.77. Now at Western Aerospace Museum, Oakland.
159382	TAV-8A	16.9.76	USMC. Stored AMARC.
159383	TAV-8A	28.6.76	USMC. Stored AMARC.
159384	TAV-8A	31.5.77	VMAT-203. Crashed 1.8.80.
159385	TAVBA	13.1.77	USMC. Stored AMARC.
161396	AV-8B	22.4.82	NATC Museum Pensacola.
161397	AV-8B	23.4.82	McDD St Louis.
161398	AV-8B	16.4.82	Preserved at Indian Head.
161399	AV-8B	8.6.82	Preserved at Patuxent River.
161573	AV-8B	14.11.83	VMA-542. Crashed 23.1.91 in Kuwait after failing to recover from steep angle following weapons release.
161574	AV-8B	3.2.84	USMC.
161575	AV-8B	23.2.84	McDD.
161576	AV-8B	16.7.84	USMC.
161577	AV-8B	12.7.84	VMAT-203. Crashed 31.3.85.
161578	AV-8B	26.7.84	NADEP Cherry Point.
161579	AV-8B	24.8.84	McDD.
161580	AV-8B	14.9.84	USMC.CherryPoint.
161581	AV-8B	7.9.84	USMC.
161582	AV-8B	28.11.84	VMAT-203. Crashed 13.7.88 at Cherry Point.
161583	AV-8B	21.12.84	USMC.
161584	AV-8B	3.1.85	USMC. Stored AMARC.
162068	AV-8B	19.1.85	USMC.
162069	AV-8B	1.3.85	USMC.
162070	AV-8B	27.12.84	USMC.
162071	AV-8B	28.12.84	VMA-331. Crashed 11.2.88 at Nellis following an engine flame-out.
162072	AV-8B	18.5.85	USMC. Stored AMARC.
162073	AV-8B	1.5.85	VMA-331. Crashed 5.6.87 at Bamegat Bay following an engine flame-out.
162074	AV-8B	27.3.85	USMC.
162075	AV-8B	6.5.85	USMC.
162076	AV-8B	30.5.85	USMC.
162077	AV-8B	14.6.85	USMC.
162078	AV-8B	26.7.85	VMAT-203. Crashed 4.5.90.
162079	AV-8B	26.6.82	VMA 331. Crashed 27.5.86 at Cherry Point.
162080	AV-8B	30.6.85	USMC.
162081	AV-8B	2.7.85	VMA-231. Crashed 9.2.91 after being shot down by SAM in Kuwait.
162082	AV-8B	22.7.85	USMC.
162083	AV-8B	24.7.85	USMC.
162084	AV-8B	15.8.85	USMC. Stored AMARC.
162085	AV-8B	28.8.85	USMC.
162086	AV-8B	16.9.85	USMC.
162087	AV-8B	9.10.85	USMC.
162088	AV-8B	15.10.85	USMC.
162721	AV-8B	18.10.85	USN VX-9 China Lake.
162722	AV-8B	12.11.85	USMC. Stored AMARC.
162723	AV-8B	7.11.85	USMC.
162724	AV-8B	4.12.85	VMA-231. Crashed 17.1.86 at Yuma following a bird strike.
162725	AV-8B	9.1.86	USMC.
162726	AV-8B	14.1.86	USMC.

162727	AV-8B	14.1.86	VMA-223. Crashed 11.11.91 at Villagarcia de la Torre, Spain.
162728	AV-8B	20.1.86	USMC.
162729	AV-8B	20.2.86	USMC.
162730	AV-8B	27.1.86	USMC.
162731	AV-8B	8.4.86	USMC.
162732	AV-8B	14.4.86	USMC. Stored AMARC.
162733	AV-8B	8.4.86	USMC.
162734	AV-8B	27.3.86	VMAT-203. Crashed 10.2.90.
162735	AV-8B	21.4.86	VMA-331. Crashed 19.6.90 at Cherry Point following an aborted take-off.
162736	AV-8B	9.5.86	VMAT-203. Crashed 18.9.95 after colliding with TAV-8B.
162737	AV-8B	13.6.86	USMC.
162738	AV-8B	17.6.86	USMC.
162739	AV-8B	14.7.86	USMC.
162740	AV-8B	25.7.86	VMA-331. Crashed 27.2.91 after being shot down in Kuwait by a SAM.
162741	AV-8B	25.7.86	USMC.
162742	AV-8B	28.8.86	USMC.
162743	AV-8B	27.10.86	VMA-331. Crashed 20.3.91 in Red Sea.
162744	AV-8B	10.11.86	USMC.
162745	AV-8B	29.10.86	VMA-542. Crashed 4.11.86 after colliding with an F-18.
162746	AV-8B	17.10.86	VMAT-203. Crashed 12.1.87 at Cherry Point.
162747	TAV-8B	9.12.86	McDD.
162942	AV-8B	30.10.86	VMA-542. Crashed 26.1.90 Le Shima Island.
162943	AV-8B	24.10.86	USMC.
162944	AV-8B	7.11.87	USMC.
162945	AV-8B	12.12.86	VMAT-203. Crashed 10.10.95 in Atlantic.
162946	AV-8B	3.12.86	USMC.
162947	AV-8B	31.12.86	USN at China Lake.
162948	AV-8B	16.12.86	USMC. Stored AMARC.
162949	AV-8B	21.1.87	USMC.
162950	AV-8B	27.1.87	USMC.
162951	AV-8B	25.2.87	USMC.
162952	AV-8B	20.2.87	VMA-331. Crashed 8.8.88 near Turkey.
162953	AV-8B	23.2.87	USMC.
162954	AV-8B	23.3.87	VMA-331. Crashed 22.1.91. Crashed on aproach to USS *Nassau*.
162955	AV-8B	1.4.87	VMA-231. Crashed 10.8.93 at Cherry Point.
162956	AV-8B	12.3.87	USMC.
162957	AV-8B	14.4.87	USMC.
162958	AV-8B	27.4.87	USMC.
162959	AV-8B	30.4.87	USMC.
162960	AV-8B	14.5.87	USMC.
162961	AV-8B	8.5.87	VMA-542. Crashed 9.10.87 at Twentynine Palms.
162962	AV-8B	29.5.87	USMC.
162963	AV-8B	24.7.87	USMC.
162964	AV-8B	10.6.87	USMC.
162965	AV-8B	10.6.87	USMC.
162966	AV-8B	26.6.87	NAWS. Crashed 27.9.94 near China Lake.
162967	AV-8B	30.6.87	USMC.
162968	AV-8B	2.7.87	USMC.
162969	AV-8B	21.7.87	USMC.
162970	AV-8B	24.8.87	VMA-513. Crashed 8.8.90.
162971	AV-8B	3.10.87	USMC.
162972	AV-8B	24.8.87	USMC.
162973	AV-8B	25.9.87	USMC.
163176	AV-8B	29.10.87	USMC.
163177	AV-8B	31.10.87	VMA-223. Crashed 21.6.94 at Cherry Point following an engine failure.
163178	AV-8B	6.11.87	USMC.
163179	AV-8B	30.11.87	USMC.
163180	AV-8B	11.11.87	USMC.
163181	AV-8B	19.12.87	VMA-214. Crashed 9.12.92 at MCAS Yuma.
163182	AV-8B	12.12.87	VMA-542. Crashed 1.3.88 at the Piney Island range.

163183	AV-8B	22.12.87	USMC.
163184	AV-8B	17.12.87	VMA-542. Crashed 5.11.88 at Maxwell AFB.
163185	AV-8B	29.12.87	VMA-542. Crashed 3.5.89 at Parris Island.
163186	AV-8B	15.3.88	USMC.
163187	AV-8B	17.1.88	VMA-223. Crashed 12.2.90 at Twentynine Palms.
163188	AV-8B	15.1.88	USMC.
163189	AV-8B	1.3.88	USMC.
163190	AV-8B	7.3.88	VMA-542. Crashed 25.2.91 after being shot down by a SAM over Al Jaber airfield.
163191	AV-8B	1.4.88	USMC.
163192	AV-8B	7.3.88	USMC.
163193	AV-8B	29.3.88	USMC.
163194	AVBB	16.3.88	USMC.
163195	AV-8B	31.3.88	VMA-231. Crashed 16.2.96 at Cherry Point.
163196	AV-8B	2.7.88	USMC.
163197	AV-8B	4.5.88	USMC.
163198	AV-8B	2.5.88	USMC.
163199	AV-8B	8.6.88	USMC.
163200	AV-8B	22.5.88	USMC.
163201	AV-8B	26.5.88	USMC.
163202	AV-8B	15.9.88	VMAT-203. Crashed 28.8.89 at Cherry Point.
163203	AV-8B	4.6.88	USMC.
163204	AV-8B	16.6.88	USMC.
163205	AV-8B	15.7.88	USMC.
163206	AV-8B	7.7.88	USMC.
163207	AV-8B	12.12.88	USMC.
163419	AV-8B	22.6.88	USMC.
163420	AV-8B	1.7.88	VMA-513. Crashed 15.5.91 off Cox's Bazaar, Bangladesh.
163421	AV-8B	14.7.88	VMA-513. Crashed 15.10.93 off the USS *Raleigh* following a bird strike.
163422	AV-8B	30.8.88	VMA-542. Crashed 18.2.95.
163423	AV-8B	4.8.88	USMC.
163424	AV-8B	23.8.88	USMC.
163425	AV-8B	26.8.88	VMA-231. Crashed 22.9.93 Camp Lejeune.
163426	AV-8B	10.8.88	USMC.
163515	AV-8B	16.9.88	USMC.
163516	AV-8B	16.9.88	VMA-542. Crashed 1.9.95 in South China Sea.
163517	AV-8B	29.9.88	USMC.
163518	AV-8B	30.9.88	VMA-311. Crashed 24.1.91, shot down in southern Kuwait by SAM.
163519	AV-8B	5.10.88	USMC.
163659	AV-8B	2.11.88	USMC.
163660	AV-8B	2.11.88	USMC.
163661	AV-8B	11.11.88	USMC.
163662	AV-8B	17.11.88	USMC.
163663	AV-8B	21.11.88	USMC.
163664	AV-8B	21.11.88	USMC.
163665	AV-8B	29.11.88	USMC.
163666	AV-8B	29.11.88	VMA-311 Crashed 31.10.89 at Twentynine Palms following an engine fire.
163667	AV-8B	6.12.88	Crashed 16.12.89.
163668	AV-8B	23.3.89	USMC.
163669	AV-8B	13.12.88	USMC.
163670	AV-8B	1.5.89	USMC.
163671	AV-8B	18.4.89	VMA-311. Crashed 2.2.90 on the Chocolate Mountains Range.
163672	AV-8B	24.4.89	USMC.
163673	AV-8B	25.5.89	USMC.
163674	AV-8B	23.5.89	USMC.
163675	AV-8B	26.4.89	USMC.
163676	AV-8B	20.5.89	USMC.
163677	AV-8B	4.5.89	USMC.
163678	AV-8B	28.4.89	USMC.
163679	AV-8B	28.4.89	VMA-542. Crashed 25.2.94 in Pimlico Sound.
163680	AV-8B	22.5.89	USMC.

163681	AV-8B	6.6.89	VMA-311. Crashed 17.8.84.
163682	AV-8B	15.6.89	USMC.
163683	AV-8B	6.7.89	USMC.
163684	AV-8B	13.7.89	VMA-311. Crashed 13.7.92 MCAS Yuma.
163685	AV-8B	31.7.89	VMA-311. Crashed 21.2.90 off San Diego.
163686	AV-8B	16.8.89	USMC.
163687	AV-8B	14.8.89	USMC.
163688	AV-8B	21.8.89	USMC.
163689	AV-8B	31.8.89	USMC.
163690	AV-8B	20.9.89	USMC.
163852	AV-8B	30.9.89	USMC.
163853	AV-8B	15.9.89	USMC.
163854	AV-8B	10.10.89	USMC.
163855	AV-8B	2.11.89	USMC.
163856	TAV-8B	1.2.89	VMAT-203. Crashed 21.4.90 following a bird strike.
163857	TAV-8B	12.4.89	USMC.
163858	TAV-8B	6.5.89	USMC.
163859	TAV-8B	25.7.89	USMC.
163860	TAV-8B	18.9.89	USMC.
163861	TAV-8B	10.10.89	USMC.
163862	AV-8B	20.11.89	USMC.
163863	AV-8B	14.11.89	USMC.
163864	AV-8B	29.11.89	USMC.
163865	AV-8B	18.12.89	USMC.
163866	AV-8B	18.12.89	USMC.
163867	AV-8B	18.12.89	USMC.
163868	AV-8B	19.12.89	VMA-311. Crashed 2.2.90 at the Chocolate Mountains Range.
163869	AV-8B	14.2.90	USMC.
163870	AV-8B	31.1.90	USMC.
263871	AV-8B	23.3.90	USMC.
163872	AV-8B	1.3.90	USMC.
163873	AV-8B	6.3.90	VMA-214. Crashed 4.2.91, Twentynine Palms.
163874	AV-8B	20.3.90	USMC.
163875	AV-8B	5.4.90	VMA-214. Crashed 29.6.92 Davenport, Iowa.
163876	AV-8B	1.5.90	USMC.
163877	AV-8B	1.5.90	USMC.
163878	AV-8B	31.5.90	VMA-211. Crashed 6.11.90.
163879	AV-8B	12.6.90	USMC.
163880	AV-8B	27.6.90	USMC.
163881	AV-8B	29.6.90	USMC.
163882	AV-8B	16.7.90	VMA-214. Crashed 6.3.92 at Pasir Gudang, Johore, Malaysia.
162883	AV-8B	30.8.90	USMC.
164113	TAV-8B	1.14.90	USMC.
164114	TAV-8B	1.5.90	USMC.
164115	AV-8B	26.9.90	USMC.
164116	AV-8B	29.10.90	USMC.
164117	AV-8B	9.11.90	USMC.
164118	AV-8B	10.12.90	VMA-211. Crashed 19.8.92. Flew into sea.
164119	AV-8B	10.12.90	USMC.
164120	AV-8B	17.12.90	VMA-211. Crashed 13.4.92 on the Barry Goldwater Range after colliding with another AV-8B.
164121	AV-8B	2.2.90	USMC.
164122	TAV-8B	2.9.90	USMC.
164123	AV-8B	13.6.91	USMC.
164124	AV-8B	5.7.92	USMC.
164125	AV-8B	26.7.91	VMA-211. Crashed 12.5.93 at MCAS Yuma following an engine failure.
164126	AV-8B	7.8.91	USMC.
164127	AV-8B	2.8.91	USMC.
164128	AV-8B	29.8.91	USMC.
164129	AV-8B	25.9.92	USN. China Lake. Used as radar integration aircraft.
164130	AV-8B	4.9.91	USMC.

164131	AV-8B	27.3.91	USMC.
164132	AV-8B	2.74.92	USMC.
164133	AVBB	18.3.92	VMA-211. Crashed 13.4.92 after colliding with another AV-8B.
164134	AV-8B	9.4.92	USMC.
164135	AV-8B	27.4.92	USMC.
164136	AV-8B	2.8.91	USMC.
164137	AV-8B	21.5.92	USMC.
164138	TAV-8B	21.5.92	USMC.
164139	AV-8B	11.6.92	USMC.
164140	AV-8B	28.7.92	USMC.
164141	AV-8B	14.10.92	USMC.
164142	AV-8B	16.9.92	USMC.
164143	AV-8B	15.9.92	USMC.
164144	AV-8B	1.10.92	USMC.
164145	AV-8B	8.12.92	USMC.
164146	AV-8B	9.2.93	USMC.
164147	AV-8B	29.1.93	USMC.
164148	AV-8B	21.12.92	USMC.
164149	AV-8B	30.4.93	USMC.
164150	AV-8B	22.6.93	USMC.
164151	AV-8B	10.8.93	USMC.
164152	AV-8B	3.12.93	USMC.
164153	AV-8B	10.8.93	USMC.
164154	AV-8B	28.10.93	USMC.
164540	TAV-8B	20.1.92	USMC.
164541	TAV-8B	25.5.92	VMAT-203. Crashed 14.1.95 at Rocky Mountain.
164542	AV-8B	18.7.92	USMC.
164543	AV-8B	2.2.93	USMC.
164544	AV-8B	7.4.93	USMC.
164545	AV-8B	13.5.93	USMC.
164546	AV-8B	15.7.93	USMC.
164547	AV-8B-Plus	9.12.93	VMA-211. Crashed 30.1.95 in the Red Sea while operating from the USS *Essex*.
164548	AV-8B-Plus	16.4.93	NAWS China Lake.
164549	AV-8B-Plus	7.5.93	VX-9 China Lake.
164550	AV-8B-Plus	10.6.93	USMC.
164551	AV-8B-Plus	30.6.93	USMC.
164552	AV-8B-Plus	28.7.93	USMC.
164553	AV-8B-Plus	29.7.93	USMC.
164554	AV-8B-Plus	31.8.93	USMC.
164555	AV-8B-Plus	1.10.93	USMC.
164556	AVBB-Plus	6.10.93	USMC.
164557	AV-8B-Plus	21.12.93	USMC.
164558	AV-8B-Plus	24.2.94	USMC.
164559	AV-8B-Plus	8.4.94	USMC.
164560	AV-8B-Plus	23.5.94	USMC.
164561	AVBB-Plus	23.6.94	USMC.
164562	AV-8B-Plus	31.1.94	USMC.
164566	AV-8B-Plus	29.7.94	USMC.
164567	AV-8B-Plus	16.8.94	USMC.
164568	AV-8B-Plus	6.10.94	USMC.
164569	AV-8B-Plus	21.8.94	USMC.
164570	AV-8B-Plus	19.10.94	USMC.
164571	AV-8B-Plus	10.11.94	USMC.
165001	AV-8B-Plus	28.2.95	USMC.
165002	AV-8B-Plus	30.3.95	USMC.
165003	AV-8B-Plus	19.4.95	USMC.
165004	AV-0D-Plus	26.5.95	USMC.
165005	AV-8B-Plus	14.8.95	USMC.
164006	AV-8B-Plus	22.11.95	USMC.
164007	AV-8B-Plus	18.12.97	USMC.
165306	AV-8B-Plus	12.5.96	USMC.

Allocated AV-8B airframes to be re-manufactured as Harrier II Plus

AV-8B-Plus	USMC.
AV-8B-Plus	USMC.
AV-8B-Plus	USMC.
AV-8B-Plus	USMC.
AV-8B-Plus	USMC.
AV-8B-Plus	USMC.
AV-8B-Plus	USMC.
AV-8B-Plus	USMC.
AV-8B-Plus	USMC.
AV-8B-Plus	USMC.
AV-8B-Plus	USMC.
AV-8B-Plus	USMC.
AV-8B-Plus	USMC.
AV-8B-Plus	USMC.
AV-8B-Plus	USMC.
AV-8B-Plus	USMC.

INDIAN NAVY SEA HARRIERS

IN601	FRS.51	5.10.84	Indian Navy 300 Squadron.
IN602	FRS.51	12.7.84	Indian Navy 300 Squadron.
IN603	FRS.51	13.12.83	Indian Navy 300 Squadron.
IN604	FRS.51	13.12.83	Indian Navy 300 Squadron.
IN605	FRS.51	13.12.83	Indian Navy 300 Squadron.
IN606	FRS.51	12.7.84	Indian Navy 300 Squadron.
IN607	FRS.51	24.7.90	Indian Navy 300 Squadron.
IN608	FRS.51	14.12.90	Indian Navy 300 Squadron.
IN609	FRS.51	10.4.90	Indian Navy 300 Squadron.
IN610	FRS.51	14.12.90	Indian Navy 300 Squadron.
IN611	FRS.51	14.12.90	Indian Navy 300 Squadron.
IN612	FRS.51	10.4.90	Indian Navy 300 Squadron.
IN613	FRS.51	24.7.90	Indian Navy 300 Squadron.
IN614	FRS.51	24.7.90	Indian Navy 300 Squadron.
IN615	FRS.51	23.4.91	Indian Navy 300 Squadron.
IN616	FRS.51	17.9.91	Indian Navy 300 Squadron.
IN617	FRS.51	17.9.91	Indian Navy 300 Squadron.
IN618	FRS.51	23.4.91	Indian Navy 300 Squadron.
IN619	FRS.51	23.4.91	Indian Navy 300 Squadron.
IN620	FRS.51	17.9.91	Indian Navy 300 Squadron.
IN621	FRS.51	17.9.91	Indian Navy 300 Squadron.
IN622	FRS.51	14.1.92	Indian Navy 300 Squadron.
IN623	FRS.51	7.4.92	Indian Navy 300 Squadron.
IN652	T.60	16.4.85	Indian Navy 300 Squadron.
IN653	T.60	10.4.90	Indian Navy 300 Squadron.
IN654	T.60	14.1.92	Indian Navy 300 Squadron.

ITALIAN NAVY HARRIERS

MM7199	AV-8B-Plus	17.6.95	Italian Navy.
MM7200	AV-8B-Plus	16.1.95	Italian Navy.
MM7201	AV-8B-Plus	16.1 95	Italian Navy
MM7212	AV-8B-Plus	11.11.95	Italian Navy.
MM7123	AV-8B-Plus	16.12.95	Italian Navy.
MM7124	AV-8B-Plus	7.3.96	Italian Navy.
MM7125	AV-8B-Plus	15.5.96	Italian Navy.
MM7126	AV-8B-Plus	23.7.96	Italian Navy.
MMT127	AV-8B-Plus	25.9.96	Italian Navy.
MM7128	AV-8B-Plus	10.11.96	Italian Navy.

MM7129	AV-8B-Plus	5.1.97	Italian Navy.
MM7220	AV-8B-Plus	21.3.97	Italian Navy.
MM722I	AV-8B-Plus	30.5.97	Italian Navy.
MM7222	AV-8B-Plus	9.7.97	Italian Navy.
MM7233	AV-8B-Plus	due 9.97	Italian Navy.
MM7244	AV-8B-Plus	due 11.97	Italian Navy.
MM55032	TAV-8B	18.1.95	Italian Navy.
MM55033	TAV-8B	16.1.95	Italian Navy.

SPANISH NAVY HARRIERS AV-8B/PLUS

VA2-1	EAV-8B	6.10.87	Spanish Navy.
VA2-2	EAV-8B	6.10.87	Spanish Navy.
VA2-3	EAV-8B	6.10.87	Spanish Navy.
VA2-4	EAV-8B	10.12.87	Spanish Navy.
VA2-5	EAV-8B	10.12.87	Spanish Navy.
VA2-6	EAV-8B	10.12.87	Spanish Navy.
VA2-7	EAV-8B	17.5.88	Spanish Navy.
VA2-8	EAV-8B	17.5.88	Spanish Navy.
VA2-9	EAV-8B	17.5.88	Spanish Navy.
VA2-10	EAV-8B	10.9.88	Spanish Navy.
VA2-11	EAV-8B	10.9.88	Spanish Navy.
VA2-12	EAV-8B	10.9.88	Spanish Navy.
VA2-13	EAV-8B	10.9.88	Spanish Navy.
VA2-14	EAV-8B-Plus	15.1.96	Spanish Navy.
VA2-15	EAV-8B-Plus	29.3.96	Spanish Navy.
VA2-16	EAV-8B-Plus	16.5.96	Spanish Navy.
VA2-17	EAV-8B-Plus	21.7.96	Spanish Navy.
VA2-18	EAV-8B-Plus	18.10.96	Spanish Navy.
VA2-19	EAV-8B-Plus	12.1.97	Spanish Navy.
VA2-20	EAV-8B-Plus	25.4.97	Spanish Navy.
VA2-21	EAV-8B-Plus	28.7.97	Spanish Navy.

AV-8S

VA1-1	AV-8S	1.5.76	Spanish Navy.
VA1-2	AV-8S	29.6.76	Spanish Navy.
VA1-3	AV-8S	7.6.76	Spanish Navy.
VA1-4	AV-8S	9.3.76	Spanish Navy.
VA1-5	AV-8S	25.3.76	Spanish Navy.
VA1-5/6	AV-8S	22.4.76	Spanish Navy.
VA1-6	AV-8S	27.6.80	Spanish Navy.
VA1-7	AV-8S	24.7.80	Spanish Navy.
VA1-8	AV-8S	31.10.80	Spanish Navy.
VA1-9	AV-8S	31.10.80	Spanish Navy.
VA1-1O	AV-8S	19.12.80	Spanish Navy.
VAE1-1	TAV-8S	24.3.76	Spanish Navy.
VAE1-2	TAV-8S	11.6.76	Spanish Navy.

Glossary

A&AEE	Aeroplane & Armament Experimental Establishment	CIS	Commonwealth of Independent States	INS	inertial navigation system
AAA	anti-aircraft artillery	CWIS	Close In Weapons System	IP	initial point
AAM	air-to-air missile	DACT	dissimilar air combat training	JPT	jetpipe temperature
ABCCC	airborne battlefield command and control centre	DB	development batch	KAAAB	King Abdul Aziz Air Base
		DCA	defensive counter air	LAU	LAuncher Unit
ACMI	air combat manoeuvring instrumentation	DDI	digital display indicator	LERX	leading edge root extension (BAe)
ADF	automatic direction finding	DECS	digital engine control system	LGB	laser-guided bomb
AEW	airborne early warning	DMT	dual mode tracker	LHA	Landing Helicopter Assault
AFB	Air Force Base (US)	DRA	Defence Research Agency (UK)	LID	lift-improvement device
AMPA	Advanced Mission Planning Aid			LOROP	LOng Range Oblique Photography
AMRAAM	Advanced Medium-Range Air-to-Air Missile (Hughes/Raytheon)	DSU	data storage unit	LOX	liquid oxygen
		DTEO	Defence Test and Evaluation Organisation	LPD	Landing Platform Dock
				LPH	Landing Platform Helicopter
AOA	angle of attack	ECM	electronic countermeasures	LRMTS	laser-ranging and marked target seeker
APC	armament practice camp (RAF)	EDSG	extra dark sea grey		
		EW	early warning	MADGE	microwave aircraft digital guidance equipment
ARBS	Angle-Rate Bombing System (Hughes)	FAC	forward air controller		
		FADEC	full authority digital engine/electronic control	MARS	Modular Airborne Recording System
ARTF	alkaline removable temporary finish	FARP	Forward Area Rearm/Refuel Point	MAWS	Missile Approach Warning System
ASM	air-to-surface missile	FAST-FAC	Fast Forward Air Controller	MCAS	Marine Corps Air Station
ASRAAM	Advanced Short-Range Air-to-Air Missile (BAe)			MEB	Marine Expeditionary Brigade
ASW	anti-submarine warfare	FDO	flight deck officer	MER	multiple ejection rack
ATHS	Automatic Target Hand-off System	FLIR	forward looking infra-red	MFD	multi-function display
		FOAC	forward operating air controller	MIRLS	Miniature Infra-Red Linescan
ATO	air tasking order	FOB	Forward Operating Base	MLU	mid-life update
AWACS	Airborne Warning And Control System	FOD	foreign object damage	MMI	Marina Militare Italiano
		FSD	full-scale development	MoD	Ministry of Defence (UK)
AWC	Air Warfare Centre (RAF)	GPS	Global Positioning System	MOMS	Maintenance Operator and Mapping Station
AWI	Air Warfare Instructor	HAS	hardened aircraft shelter		
BAI	battlefield air interdiction	HOTAS	hands-on-throttle-and-stick	MoU	Memorandum of Understanding
BDA	battle damage assessment	HTPS	Harrier Tactical Paint Scheme		
BuNo	Bureau of Aeronautics Number			MPCD	
		HUD	Head-Up Display	NADEP	Naval Aviation Depot, MCAS Cherry Point
BVR	beyond visual range	ID	identification		
CAP	combat air patrol	IFF	identification, friend or foe	NAVHARS	Navigation Heading and Altitude Reference Systems
CAS	close air support	IFOR	Implementation Force (former Yugoslavia)		
CBLS	carrier, bomb, light store (RAF)			NBC	nuclear, biological and chemical (warfare/weapons)
		IFR	in-flight refuelling		
CBU	cluster bomb unit	IFTU	Intensive Flying Trials Unit (UK)	NDC	navigational display computer
CCIP	continuously-computed impact point				
		ILS	instrument landing system	NVG	night-vision goggles
CD	compact disc	IMS	inertial measuring system	OBOGS	on-board oxygen generation system
CILOP	Conversion In Lieu Of Procurement	INAS	Integrated Nav/Attack System		
				OCA	offensive counter air

OCU	Operational Conversion Unit	RWR	radar-warning receiver	STOVL	short take off/vertical landing
OEU	Operational Evaluation Unit	SA	situational awareness	TACAN	TACtical Aid to Navigation
OTR	operational turn round	SAAHS	Stability Augmentation and Attitude Hold System	TEZ	Total Exclusion Zone
PSP	pierced steel planking	SACEUR	Supreme Allied Commander Europe (NATO)	TIALD	Thermal Imaging Airborne Laser Designator (Bae)
PWR	passive warning radar			TOGW	take-off gross weight
RAN	Royal Australian Navy	SAM	surface-to-air missile	UFC	Up Front Controller
RAT	ram air turbine	SAOEU	Strike Attack Operational Evaluation Unit	UNPROFOR	UN Protection Force (former Yugoslavia)
RCS	radar cross-section				
RHWS	Radar Homing and Warning System	SAPS	simulated attack profiles	USAFE	US Air Forces in Europe
		SARH	Semi Automatic Radar Homing	USMC	United States Marine Corps
RIC	reconnaissance interpretation centre	SEAD	suppression of enemy air devices	VSTOL	vertical or short take-off and landing
RNAS	Royal Naval Air Station (UK)	SHOFTU	Sea Harrier Operational Flying Training Unit	VIFF	vectoring in forward flight (BAe)
ROE	Rules of Engagement	SOAH	School of Aircraft Handling	VTOL	vertical take-off and landing
RP	rocket projectile (UK)	SOP	standard operating procedure	WAC	weapon-aiming computer
RVTO	rolling vertical take-off				

Index